The Scorsese Psyche on Screen

The Scorsese Psyche on Screen

Roots of Themes and Characters in the Films

Maria T. Miliora

McFarland & Company, Inc., Publishers
Jefferson, North Carolina, and London

Frontispiece: Martin Scorsese (Photofest).

Library of Congress Cataloguing-in-Publication Data

Miliora, Maria T., 1938–
The Scorsese psyche on screen : roots of themes
and characters in the films / Maria T. Miliora.
p.   cm.
Includes filmography.
Includes bibliographical references and index.

ISBN-13: 978-0-7864-1763-6
(softcover : 50# alkaline paper) ∞

1. Scorsese, Martin—Criticism and interpretation.   I. Title.
PN1998.3.S39M55   2004   791.4302'33'092—dc22   2004001526
British Library cataloguing data are available

©2004 Maria T. Miliora. All rights reserved

*No part of this book may be reproduced or transmitted in any form
or by any means, electronic or mechanical, including photocopying
or recording, or by any information storage and retrieval system,
without permission in writing from the publisher.*

Cover photograph: Martin Scorsese with Robert DeNiro (left)
in the role of Travis Bickle, on the set of *Taxi Driver*. (Photofest)

Manufactured in the United States of America

*McFarland & Company, Inc., Publishers
Box 611, Jefferson, North Carolina 28640
www.mcfarlandpub.com*

To the memory of my immigrant parents,
Andrea (Andrew) and Maria Civita Migliorini,
and to all the Italians who left the safety of their
homes and came to and labored in America

Acknowledgments

I am indebted to a number of people who have contributed their time and energy during this writing project: Richard B. Ulman for his ideas as well as for his unswerving support; the staff of the Mildred Sawyer Library of Suffolk University for locating materials that I needed and, especially, to Kathi Maio, assistant library director, author of film criticism, and researcher extraordinaire; friends Martin Anderson and James Costa for their generous sharing of information about Scorsese; and my literary agent, James Schiavone, for sharing my travails.

Contents

Acknowledgments	vii
Preface	1
Introduction	5
1. Roots and Career	11
2. *Gangs of New York* as a Return to Roots	21
3. Plot Summaries, Characters, and Themes	33
4. Narcissism and Male Sexuality	69
5. Rageful Warriors and Batterers	75
6. Demigods	97
7. Boys in Men's Clothing	121
8. Self-Image, Rage, and Violence	139
9. The Good Guys	149
10. Women and Relationships	159
11. *The Last Temptation of Christ* as Template	177
12. Conclusion	189
Filmography	193
Notes	197
Bibliography	203
Index	207

Preface

Martin Scorsese is perhaps the most esteemed of living American filmmakers. The idea for delving into his life and work evolved from my conversations with my colleague and writing collaborator, Richard B. Ulman, a fellow psychoanalyst and film buff.

For a number of years I have been interested in the lives of artists whose respective works reflect their personal experiences. Having written psychologically-based biographies of two American dramatists, Eugene O'Neill and Tennessee Williams, I was curious to discover if and how film directors, like artists in other media, expressed their personalities in their work. Martin Scorsese, whose work derives explicitly from his roots, was the obvious choice.

I was drawn to exploring the life and work of Scorsese also because his early background and mine have much in common. Both of us were brought up within Italian-American-Catholic working-class families and communities during the same era, the 1940s and early 1950s. Because of this commonality, I felt that I would be able to bring a special insight into understanding this kind of cultural milieu as well as how Scorsese's early experiences in this milieu later affected his films.

I was raised by parents who had emigrated from Italy, as had Scorsese's grandparents, and who had retained many of the traditions and values, including the Catholic religion, of their old country, as had his parents. However, there are important differences in our respective experiences. Scorsese's community of Little Italy was an insular one situated within New York City; mine was a more diverse community located only a few miles from Boston. In addition, there is an obvious gender difference between Scorsese and me. Because of this particular difference, my sense is that he and I reacted quite differently to macho milieus that tended to restrict women to stereotypical roles and supported the prevalent cultural perspective that limited and denigrated women. My sensitivity to the sexist issues that I find in Scorsese's films is apparent in the book.

This book links the personal Scorsese, his roots and his ethical and religious attitudes with his films more explicitly than has been done previously. It shows that his 1988 film, *The Last Temptation of Christ*, and his 2002 release, *Gangs of New York*, both of which have engaged Scorsese's passions for decades, can serve as templates with regard to the thematic underpinnings of essentially all of Scorsese's feature films.[1] Moreover, these two movies indicate that Scorsese's world view, which includes his attitudes about masculinity and femininity as well as his values, has been present in all of his major films.

I also show that Scorsese's film characters represent parts of him—his experiences, feelings, values, fantasies. Thus, in viewing and appreciating the psychology of his characters, we can better understand Scorsese the man. Conversely, in understanding Martin Scorsese's early life and how internalized aspects of his experiences (his mental "map") appear in his characterizations, we can appreciate his characters and his films more profoundly.

A few words about methodology and the format of the book. Scorsese has given countless interviews, and most of these are available in published form. I have relied on this interview material as well as Scorsese's autobiography, *Scorsese on Scorsese*, to determine the director's opinions, attitudes, and values. Except as noted in chapter 3, the films surveyed in the book were each viewed a number of times in VHS format. The dialogues that are quoted throughout the book were taken from the words spoken by characters in their respective films or videos.

Chapter 1 presents Scorsese's biography and includes my opinions about how his early experiences in an Italian-American-Catholic milieu affected him.

Chapter 2 discusses Scorsese's most recent film, *Gangs of New York*, and explicates the link between this film and the director's history.

Chapter 3 contains detailed information about all of Scorsese's films, including those he made while he was a student at New York University.

Chapter 4 explains the psychological or psychoanalytic basis for the behavior of the narcissistic characters in Scorsese's films. The clinically-based analyses in this chapter as well as those in Chapter 8 help to establish a chain of causality and thus explain, to some extent, the reasons why a number of these characters engage in violence. Readers who have no interest in these clinically-based conclusions can omit these two chapters without affecting the understanding or enjoyment of the book as a whole.

Chapters 5, 6, and 7 focus on psychological analyses of those male characters in Scorsese's films who show prominent and disturbed narcissistic characteristics. These analyses are presented *in the context of the respective film stories*.

Chapter 9 presents those male characters who show no disturbance with regard to narcissism.

Chapter 10 discusses all of the female characters who play important roles in Scorsese's films.

Chapter 11 discusses *The Last Temptation of Christ*. It is shown to contain a number of Scorsese's major themes that are contained in his other feature films.

Chapter 12 is a conclusion.

Introduction

During the last thirty-five years, film director Martin Scorsese has given American cinema an impressive opus of more than twenty feature films, which span a wide range of genres, as well as a number of documentaries.[1] Scorsese is one of the innovative filmmakers who emerged during the 1960s in the wake of the decline of Hollywood's Golden Age. His work has been influenced by the neorealism of the post–World War II Italian films, the French New Wave, as well as American films that were made during the earlier era.

Scorsese has commented on his place in the world of moviemaking:

> I get stuck in between the European films of the forties, fifties, and early sixties and the American films. And I don't know. I don't know if I belong anywhere. I just try what appeals to me.[2]

The focus and inspiration for *The Scorsese Psyche on Screen* were derived from Scorsese's self-description of his work: "All my films are personal. I put myself on the screen."[3] He also often stated that if we want to know him, we should watch his films.[4] The book examines the director's life or roots, his films, and the characterizations portrayed in his fictional films, and it searches for personal meaning. One feature of the book is the inclusion of psychological analyses, using general psychoanalytic concepts, of each of the major characters who appear in Scorsese's fictional films made since 1968.[5] The book uses these characterizations as well as the thematic underpinnings of Scorsese's films to suggest linkages between his history, his personal psychology, and his cinematic work.

Scorsese's films have included personal expressions of his roots, which are grounded in family, street, and church and the values and beliefs derived from them. His films reveal various aspects of his experiences as a boy and adolescent within an Italian-American-Catholic family who lived in Manhattan's Little Italy. The community of Little Italy included a criminal element (underworld) and, because of the community's proximity to the Bowery, an underclass of the homeless poor and derelicts. Moreover, the heavily Catholic milieu, which was insulated from the mainstream society, tended to stereotype women and their roles in the world as well as to demean people who were homosexual or black. Scorsese's films have reflected all of these aspects of his roots in some way.

The connections between Scorsese's roots and his films made or suggested in this book are not necessarily literal or parallel to his actual life experiences. In a number of instances, the linkages derive from the impressions of a sensitive boy who had a powerful, imagistic mind. As a matter of fact, it may be assumed that some of Scorsese's early experiences may have been fantasies. In other words, whatever the reality was that Scorsese experienced when he was a boy, this reality was filtered through his personal lens. This lens was conditioned by his psychology, other experiences that he had had, and contributions from his unconscious. Thus, some of the connections suggested or speculated about in this book derive from a psychoanalytic understanding of his early life and what Scorsese has said about it as well as knowledge about and familiarity with his films and the psychology of his characters.

Now more than sixty years of age, the mature Scorsese shows that he remains passionate about his roots. His two recent releases make this conclusion evident.

One of these, *Il Mio Viaggio in Italia* (2001), is a documentary about post–World War II Italian films. During his narration in the documentary, Scorsese recounts that when he was a child, he watched these neorealistic films with his family on their old black-and-white, sixteen-inch television set. These Italian films enabled the young Scorsese to idealize the Italian people as willing to sacrifice their lives for the sake of freedom, and they contributed to his feeling inspired to make films himself. We can appreciate how the young boy living in Manhattan, watching these films with his parents, came to feel a sense of connection to his roots and to establish a chain of continuity involving him and his parents in Little Italy, his immigrant Sicilian grandparents, and the people of Sicily and Italy.

The second of Scorsese's recent films, *Gangs of New York* (2002), although fictional, is based on historical events that occurred in lower Manhattan during the middle of the nineteenth century. This film has personal meaning for Scorsese as well. The setting of the film, the former and notorious Five Points, is proximate to that area of lower Manhattan that became Little Italy. Moreover, the gang violence, the xenophobia, and the struggle of immigrants to make a life for themselves in America, all of which are themes in *Gangs*, are experiences that connect directly to Scorsese's roots. The gangs in the film are considered predecessors to the gangsterism that was rampant in Little Italy when Scorsese was growing up, and the struggles of daily life in a new place hearken back to the experiences of Scorsese's parents and grandparents as newcomers to America. Moreover, as explained in Chapter 2, Scorsese's consuming interest in making *Gangs* derives, at least in part, from his having had a special relationship with his father when he was a boy, a relationship that was strengthened by their watching movies together.

Scorsese has had extensive influence on and control over the work he has produced. Accordingly, as a film director and filmmaker, he may be classified as falling within the theory of auteurism.[6] He has authored or participated in the writing of the screenplays for a number of his films. Moreover, in those cases where the story line of a film originated from a source written by others, Scorsese is a director who "re-creates the script into something else—the film itself, which is more than the script."[7] Applying the label of auteurism helps to underscore that Scorsese is a filmmaker who is able to choose the extent to which his creative products reflect him, his passions, and his values. Having formed his own production company, Cappa, in recent years, at this stage of his career Scorsese is also intimately involved in the *business* of the films he creates.

An example of Scorsese's control over the product that eventually appears on the screen applies to the release of *Gangs of New York*. According to sources, the release was delayed, at least in part, because of the conflict between Scorsese, who insisted that the film satisfy his artistic demands, and an executive of Miramax, Harvey Weinstein, who was concerned that the film be commercially viable.[8]

Although he has walked a fine line between creating artistic products that have personal meaning and satisfying the demand for box-office success, Scorsese has succeeded in producing a body of films, a number of which give expression to his experiences, values, and world view which have depth, extraordinary coherence, and psychological acuity. He has received a number of prestigious awards including the American Film Institute Life Achievement Award in 1997, the Outstanding Achievement in Directing Award at the Sixth Annual Hollywood Film Festival in 2002, and a Golden Globe for his direction of *Gangs of New York* in 2003.

Scorsese's cinematic world is peopled primarily by men; that is, male characters are the foci around which almost all of Scorsese's film stories are based. This determination is entirely consistent with Scorsese's description of his work as "pictures of worlds where men predominate."[9] Therefore, of necessity, the personality analyses offered in this book focus on Scorsese's male characters or "men." In his early films, Scorsese drew his characters from what he knew about himself and other men he had observed in his immediate environment (social milieu) of Little Italy. Viewing his opus in its entirety, this book suggests that Scorsese's film characterizations express different aspects of himself, including his ambition, his insecurities, his rage, and his pride. Moreover, the characterizations reveal a number of aspects of Scorsese's world view including the relative place of women in that world.

A prominent theme in Scorsese's films is the question of what it means to be a (heterosexual) man within a social milieu either as a loner (for example, as characterized through Travis Bickle in *Taxi Driver*, Rupert Pupkin in *The King of Comedy*, Frank Pierce in *Bringing Out the Dead*, and Paul Hackett in *After Hours*) or as a member of a group (for example, J.R. in *Who's That Knocking at My Door?*, Johnny Boy and Charlie in *Mean Streets*, the gangsters in *GoodFellas*, Newland Archer in *The Age of Innocence*, Amsterdam Vallon, and Bill Cutting in *Gangs of New York*). Scorsese explores the effects on these men of cultural pressures including issues relating to power, performance, success, and sexuality. Moreover, he examines the quality of their relationship to other men as well as to women. In a number of films, Scorsese's characters are aggressive, violent, and brutal; criminality, drug abuse, misogyny, and racism abound. In these films, he includes dialogue that permits an exposition of the psychological roots of narcissistic rage and violence. In effect, Scorsese's film characterizations elucidate a number of the key dynamics that are known from clinical practice to relate to violence. As depicted on the screen with remarkable psychological acuity, these dynamics include narcissism, aggression, and a man's insecurities about his sexual potency.

Although Scorsese's films do not lack for action, the director's special skill lies in the area of character development. In this context, Scorsese was asked in an interview about the role of films in making socially relevant statements, and he responded: "You have to start by understanding individual characters. You begin by going into a microcosm.... I always start with a person, not a statement."[10] Because of his experience of how his roots—family, street, church—affected him, Scorsese is keenly aware that a character's personality derives from and is dependent on that character's social environment in the broadest sense of the terms "time" and "place." Indeed, given his background and apparent insight, it is not surprising that Scorsese makes films whose characters and their sense of place and dramatic action form a cohesive whole.

Scorsese plumbs the psychological makeup of his focal characters with genuine acuity and empathy. They are presented on the screen with prominent personality features that are clearly articulated. Because of this clarity, the motivational bases of their behavior and of their relationship issues are illumined. In short, Scorsese's characters can be appreciated as if they are real people. This realistic presentation of personalities derives from Scorsese's keen psychological insight that enables him to link a character's personal psychology with behavior. A special feature of Scorsese's characterizations is his demonstration that even the most brutal and perverse behaviors and self-destructive acts derive inevitably from a person's character or personality, which, in turn, is affected by a sense of self in relation to place. In this context, "place" is broadly defined as the social milieu in which characters are embedded and from which they derive values and beliefs as well as the fantasies they create about themselves in relation to this milieu. In short, a character's sense of place contributes to his (or her) sense of self.

One example of a Scorsese film character who has a clearly defined sense of place is Newland Archer in *The Age of Innocence*. This character is a member of the social elite in New York during the early 1870s. His class and the social and economic opportunities they provide enable Archer to live a fashionable life with little necessity for earning money but considerable time for books and the theater. Archer develops a sense of himself as superior to other men largely because he can locate himself as belonging within this milieu of a high-class family that lives on a fashionable street of New York City.

Another Scorsese film character who is a product of his time and place is Amsterdam Vallon in *Gangs of New York*, set during the middle of the nineteenth century. Growing up in drastically different social circumstances from those of Archer, Vallon is one of the slum poor, and he witnesses horrific violence and human suffering even as a child. As a member of the underclass, Vallon knows nothing about literature and the theater; his world is one where he must fight and perhaps kill to survive.

In a number of Scorsese's films, the "place" in which a male character is embedded is a "church"—something in which he believes fervently and about which he obsesses. As examples of this application of terms, playing pool is the "church" of Eddie Felson in *The Color of Money*; the world of television celebrity functions as a church of sorts for Rupert Pupkin in *The King of Comedy*, while the boxing ring is Jake LaMotta's "church" in *Raging Bull*. Scorsese adroitly utilizes church symbols, including music, not only to affect the viewer's mood but also to underscore the experience of the characters. At the opening of *Casino*, for example, ecclesiastical music helps to emphasize Nicky Santoro's feeling that The Tangiers, a gambling casino and hotel, represents paradise on earth or, in effect, his church. Similarly, the music accompanying Eddie Felson's entrance into an auditorium filled with pool tables underscores the sanctity of his experience and identifies this world as his church.

Utilizing this context of people and place, we can better appreciate the characters' motivations for their actions, the outpouring of rage and violence, issues of belonging and alienation, relative states of disturbed behavior, and their frequent misogynous attitudes shown toward women as well as the director's sense of sin and redemption. In turn, since these characters inevitably represent aspects of Scorsese's experience, an analysis of people and place enables an appreciation of Scorsese in relation to *his* sense of place and world view.

This analysis does not suggest that Scorsese's films are simply displaced autobiographies. Rather, in evolving a movie, Scorsese is affected by multiple influences including his early history, his professional training, his extensive knowledge of techniques that have been applied in other films, the input of others who are involved with the production of a particular film, marketing considerations, and the constraints imposed by the industry. Within all of these limits, however, Scorsese's choice of material; the nuances of the characterizations, dialogue, lighting, and music; and other details about filmmaking that are within his control are affected by his mental image of the world and his values, both of which have been influenced by his roots.

Scorsese, the film director who once wanted to be a Catholic priest, imbues his films with "life lessons" about the evils of pride and greed and, conversely, the blessings of family as well as the struggles men encounter by living in a materialistic society whose temptations include money, power, sex, and drugs. The spiritual or mystical quality of life—usually but not exclusively focused on the redemptive quality of suffering—is present in almost all of his films, a feature that is a trademark of the director who grew up feeling a strong connection to the teachings of Jesus Christ. Moreover, in a number of his films, Scorsese includes quasi-religious rituals and symbols that he internalized from his early years of having had a strong involvement with the Catholic Church.

1

Roots and Career

Martin Scorsese was born on November 17, 1942, in Corona, Queens, New York, to Catherine and Luciano Charles Scorsese, both of whom were children of Sicilian immigrants. Martin's brother, Frank, is six years older than Martin. The Scorsese parents both worked in the garment industry, he as a presser and she as a stitcher and seamstress. Neither parent had gone to high school. In Queens the family lived near Martin's aunts and uncles in a two-family house that had a backyard and trees.[1]

Scorsese has suffered from asthma since early in his life, this affliction having become more serious when he was three years old. At four, he had a tonsillectomy, which, because of what Scorsese termed "complications," may have caused the young boy physical and emotional distress.

Scorsese was raised in a tightly knit, extended-family circle. His 1974 documentary film, *Italianamerican*, features his parents talking about their history, their respective families, and the neighborhood in Little Italy. As can be deduced from the words of his parents, the most powerful value for the Scorseses was family cohesiveness, and this value was held in higher esteem than material or professional success. The young director's attitude toward and interactions with his parents in this film, as well as the fact that he included his parents playing small parts in a number of his movies, show his love and respect for and his attachment to them.

In an interview, Scorsese commented that his parents, who were integral to his sense of roots, had been involved intimately in his developing passion for movies and in his evolution as a filmmaker. Therefore, it seemed appropriate to him to continue this chain of their involvement in his films as long as they were alive.[2] In another interview, Scorsese recounted memories of going to see movies with his father when he was a young child and said that these shared experiences provided him with important avenues of communication with his father.[3]

Charles and Catherine Scorsese (the director's parents) in their home in a scene from Scorsese's documentary, *Italianamerican* (Photofest).

In 1949 the family left Queens and moved back to Elizabeth Street in Manhattan's Little Italy, where his parents had lived before relocating to Queens. Scorsese has said that this move occurred because "my father had some problems with the landlord. I've never found out what it was all about, exactly, but basically, we couldn't afford to live in Corona anymore."[4] The family's four-room tenement apartment on Elizabeth Street in Little Italy was only a few doors away from that of Scorsese's grandmother. A number of scenes of Scorsese's 1969 film, *Who's That Knocking at My Door?*, which he scripted, were shot in the family's apartment.

> [M]y little bedroom—the bedroom I lived in with my brother until he got married and moved out—goes to the living room, through the kitchen, and winds up in my mother's bedroom ... all the religious artifacts were as they were in the film ... especially the crucifixes over the beds.[5]

Scorsese lived in the limiting cultural milieu of Little Italy until 1966, when he was twenty-four years old. The neighborhood was within walking distance of the Village, the Bowery, and New York University, and although situated within the vast metropolitan city, it seemed to be cut off from the rest of the world. The insular nature of the area was characterized as such by Scorsese as not having the "influx of other cultures."[6] There were also gangsters in the area, and Scorsese perceived them as members of a threatening and powerful elite. He captured this sense of gangsters as an elite group in his portrayal of the "wiseguys" in *GoodFellas* (1990). Moreover, reminiscent of the young Martin's perception of these gangsters, Scorsese cogently characterized the young Henry Hill in *GoodFellas* as idealizing the gangsters in his neighborhood. Scorsese has described his old neighborhood in an interview:

> I lived only half a block away from the Bowery. We saw the dregs, the poor vagrants and the alcoholics. Most mornings on the way to grammar school, I'd see two bums fighting each other with broken bottles—and I'm just eight years old.[7]

Given these early experiences of young Martin, we can appreciate the visual memories that were available to Scorsese in creating the street scenes of derelicts and addicts that occur in *Taxi Driver* (1976) and *Bringing Out the Dead* (1999) as well as his conflicted and confused feelings of fear, repulsion, and compassion toward these outcasts from society.[8]

Scorsese describes his "uprooting" from Queens to the tenement in Little Italy as a "traumatic experience," a shock to him as a young boy of about eight.[9] Two obvious and noteworthy changes occurred that affected the young boy's sense of place: He left a public school in Queens, where he presumably had some friends, and entered St. Patrick's Old Catholic School, where he encountered a new peer group and had nuns as teachers for the first time. Second, he now found himself in a tough and rough neighborhood, and the boys were expected to behave as such if they were to fit in. Martin probably found it difficult to feel accepted in this new milieu.

Not understanding why he was in this neighborhood that challenged and frightened him, Scorsese has said that he needed "some sort of security."[10] Around the corner from his home was St. Patrick's Cathedral, on Mott Street, a place that offered the boy the sense of safety that he needed. "I needed to be accepted somewhere," Scorsese has explained,

> I couldn't do in the streets—the kids were really rough. I had asthma, so I couldn't play as strongly as the other kids.... I made some friends there, but it was a tough area, so I guess the acceptance I went for was in the church.[11]

Because of his frail health and small physique, Scorsese was not able to be as physical as the other boys, play sports as they did, or fight and compete successfully with them. Scorsese said in this context:

> [O]n my block, people took games seriously.... If a kid dropped the ball, they could get very mad. I wasn't good at sports; they became anathema to me.[12]

It seems evident that it was difficult for this sensitive boy to fit in and feel a sense of belonging in this harsh street environment.

In an interview, Martin's brother, Frank, described the neighborhood:

> [It was] very violent with gangs and frequent fights. It could break out instantly. In the middle of the night, you could hear all kinds of fights and violence.... My brother [Martin] was a sickly boy—he had to go for shots for his asthma ... [he] had a tough childhood.... He was six years younger, so I'd look out for him.[13]

Martin's peer group was tough and exclusionary with its code of aggressive and violent behavior that the boys had to adhere to in order to be accepted. Years later, in making the film *Mean Streets* (1973), Scorsese gave artistic expression to this time and place of his childhood. Scorsese responded to the question of whether he wanted to be like the wiseguys in his neighborhood in this way:

> I *couldn't* do it personally, but as a boy of thirteen or fourteen, I had to harden my heart against the suffering. I had to take it. My friends go to beat up somebody, I went with them. I didn't jump in, but I watched or set it up.[14]

In recounting events during his formative years in this milieu, Scorsese also related his experience of feeling lonely:

> I realize that all my life I've been an outsider and, above all, being lonely ... remembering how lonely I was as a kid. My parents worked, and I came home from school at three o'clock and sat at the kitchen table making up stories on my drawing board or watching television or escaping to the movies.[15]

Scorsese's loneliness as a child and his experience of feeling like an outsider in a world that felt inimicable to him have enabled the director to apply a special empathy in presenting characters—like Travis Bickle in *Taxi Driver*, Alice Hyatt in *Alice Doesn't Live Here Anymore*, Rupert Pupkin in *The King of Comedy*, and Frank Pierce in *Bringing Out the Dead*—who are similarly afflicted.

The Catholic Church, which the young Scorsese idealized, provided escape from the streets and a sense of security, and it engaged the boy's passion. Indeed, Martin was more religious than his parents, becoming an altar boy at St. Patrick's, and when he was a teenager, he thought that he had a religious vocation. As an altar boy he was specially trained to assist at the Saturday funerals called the Mass for the Dead. Because of Martin's frail health and fears about his own demise, his frequent attendance at sermons that tended to focus on sin and death and the fires of hell, and his witnessing of violent behavior on the streets, as a young boy he developed an awareness of death and a sensitivity about living a good life to avoid eternal damnation.

Growing up in this neighborhood exposed the young Scorsese to two different, indeed opposite, kinds of role models—that is, men who had power—with which he could identify and strive to emulate: the petty criminals and gangsters, on the one hand, and the priests, on the other. Since he "grew up in a house without books," higher education was not seen as an end in itself.[16] In this context, Scorsese has said that his parents "wanted me to continue [school] because they understood one thing: you go to school, you make a little more money."[17] Although obviously loving and respecting his father, apparently Martin did not idealize him in the sense of wanting to emulate his father's limited educational and blue-collar work history. However, Martin did identify with his father's love of movies.

Essentially, the young adolescent Scorsese felt that the church, especially if he became a priest, would provide him with a better chance of living a life that revolved around love and compassion as compared to living a secular life on the streets. In addition, by being a priest, Martin presumed that he had a better chance of attaining salvation and ultimate happiness. We can imagine that Martin internalized the rituals, images, smells, and sounds of the church, these becoming a part of his identity, and a number of which he incorporated into *Mean Streets* (1973), which he coscripted with Mardik Martin.

In addition to the church, movies and television provided avenues of escape from the limited world in which Scorsese was embedded, and these engaged his interest and artistic talent. Martin had a powerful and pictorial imagination, and he liked to draw. His parents began taking him to movies when he was perhaps three years old, and they apparently did so often because they had no other means for entertaining the boy. Martin was enchanted with films, and he drew little pictures to reproduce what he had seen on the big screen and mimicked the actor-heroes he admired by fantasizing in front of a mirror. According to his mother, Scorsese "painted two eyes on the wall in his bedroom."[18] The close-ups of eyes that appear in a number of his films indicate that Scorsese is an intensely visual person. Moreover, these images of eyes suggest his desire to penetrate deeply beneath the surface into the very soul of his characters.

In his presentation of his *Personal Journey with Martin Scorsese through American Movies* (2000), Scorsese describes the impact films had on him when he saw them as a child, the visual and emotional impressions playing into his imagination and dreams. He says of himself that he was "fanatical about westerns." Given his idealization of film heroes like John Wayne, which is apparent from J.R.'s idealization of Wayne in *Who's That Knocking at My Door?*, the films of the 1940s and 1950s probably contributed to Scorsese having taken in (or internalized) a macho image of masculinity wherein a man proves his worth by virtue of his aggressiveness and, dominates and perceives women as objects.[19] Scorsese watched a number of these films from the 1940s and 1950s with his father and, indeed, has stated that movies provided important avenues of communication with his father. It would have been natural for the young Scorsese to look to his father in forming his own sense of masculine identity. Since his relationship with his father was mediated by these movies, it is likely that Scorsese gained a perception that real men were of the type that he saw in the movies.

In addition to the impact American films had on him as a child, Scorsese was influenced by the post–World War II Italian films that he watched with his parents on their small television set. In *Il Mio Viaggio in Italia*, a documentary Scorsese released in 2001, he explains that these films helped him to feel connected to his Italian-Sicilian roots and that they contributed to his feeling inspired to become a filmmaker.

A sense of Scorsese's creativity as well as his loneliness as a child appear to have been captured in the opening scenes of *Alice Doesn't Live Here Anymore*. The young Alice, who dreams of becoming a famous singer, is seen walking alone holding her doll, and she is set apart from her mother and brother, who are in the kitchen of the farmhouse, as well as from her father, who is working on the farm. Undoubtedly, the young Scorsese, similar to his characterization of Alice, dreamed and fantasized about becoming a famous artist of some sort. Moreover, perhaps he, like Alice, did not feel entirely understood or affirmed by his social milieu.

When Martin was thirteen, he went to a preparatory seminary on 86th Street. However, according to Scorsese, by the time he was fourteen, he was dismissed from the school because of failing grades and his newly-discovered interest in the opposite sex.

Scorsese has recounted a number of memories from his childhood and adolescence that are associated with the church. While in grammar school he loved to draw pictures of Jesus on the cross, and stories about Jesus's suffering drew Scorsese to the idealized Christ-figure. In an interview, Scorsese related the story of an Irish nun who would admonish him if he were shaking his leg because, in her mind, this behavior had sexual implications.[20] A retreat he attended while in high school evolved into a frightening experience. Triggered by his feeling guilty about something and a "fire and brimstone" sermon on the evils of sex and its punishment, the adolescent had disturbing visual and auditory hallucinations.[21]

Scorsese relates that he idealized a particular young priest—Martin was eleven or twelve at the time—and he wanted to emulate this man and become like him. The priest liked movies, and this mutual interest in films provided Scorsese with an even greater sense of connection to him. Scorsese recounted:

> [I] went through four or five years with him. And then he threw me out because I would show up late—for the seven o'clock Mass, yet. I mean give me a break.[22]

In addition to this experience, which the adolescent Martin undoubtedly experienced as a betrayal and abandonment by the priest, Scorsese became disenchanted with the church because its views on sex were not consistent with his experience. A sensitive boy and adolescent, the "fire and brimstone" sermons affected him profoundly; he developed a belief that there was a conflict between the material and spiritual worlds, much as his stand-in Charlie in *Mean Streets* feels. Indeed, Scorsese has said that the "conflicts within Charlie were within me, my own feelings."[23]

After the failed seminary year, Scorsese attended another school, Cardinal Hayes High School in the Bronx, and he tried to improve his grade average so he could get into college. After he was rejected by Fordham University, Scorsese decided to go to New York University (NYU) in spite of his parents' concerns that the secular university was "too liberal ... Communist."[24] He entered the university with the idea of majoring in English and becoming a teacher, but Scorsese gravitated toward film studies. He received his bachelor's degree in 1964, took masters courses for two or three years, and served on the faculty during 1969.[25] While he was at NYU, he made *What's a Nice Girl Like You Doing in a Place Like This?* (1963) and two award-winning films, *The Big Shave* (1964) and *It's Not Just You Murray* (1967). Scorsese also coedited *Woodstock* (1970), an epic film that recorded the historic rock festival.

At NYU, Scorsese was influenced by a teacher, Haig Manoogian, who encouraged him to put his feelings into films. What that meant for Scorsese was "acting out whatever good I would be doing with a vocation ... through films." Until about 1960 Scorsese thought that he would become a priest, but eventually he realized "that the Catholic vocation was, in a sense, through the screen for me."[26]

Although he was totally disenchanted with the church by 1965, Scorsese retained his passion for the figure of Jesus Christ and the story and message of his ministry, his bleeding and suffering, his death, and resurrection. Scorsese eventually was able to give expression to this passion by making the film *The Last Temptation of Christ* in 1988. In describing his problems with the church, Scorsese has mentioned its unnecessary doctrine and rules as well as its prejudicing people's minds by its "intolerance toward other groups," including Protestants and Jews.[27]

The church affected the young men of Little Italy with regard to homophobia and misogyny as well, as we can see in the characterizations of the men in *Who's That Knocking at My Door?* and *Mean Streets*. Scorsese has acknowledged that the Sicilian-American-Catholic culture encouraged the "madonna-whore dichotomy" as well as fear and distrust of women. According to Scorsese, "[women] didn't seem like real human beings," and this culturally-based perception made it difficult for men in that milieu, including Scorsese, to relate effectively to women.[28] Moreover, as alluded to previously, the films Scorsese saw as a youngster may have contributed to his having a stereotypical view of women that included a sense of their powerlessness and their submissive role in relationships. For example, in *The Red Shoes*, a film Scorsese saw and loved as a young child, the heroine is forced to choose between a career as a ballet dancer and her love for a young composer. This conflict reflects the limited options available to women in that era; women could not be married *and* have a career.[29]

The young Scorsese was angry with, perhaps even enraged by, the church. In addition, he may have been angry because of the limited and threatening milieu of his youth, one that was antagonistic to his sensitive, curious, and creative nature. Apparently, Scorsese was also angry about women. In a 1993 interview, he was asked whether he had ever felt angry at women. Scorsese responded:

> Oh, I think in my early times ... [Y]ou can see it in *Taxi Driver* and *Raging Bull* ... [Paul] Schrader's script for *Taxi Driver* was about being angry at women and many other things. I felt very strongly about it, and part of that was not being able to communicate or not being able to have that kind of relationship you thought you would want to have with a quote-unquote idealized woman. And so the jealousy and the anger were very real. It was crippling for many years.[30]

Given Martin Scorsese's experience in a tough and secular culture with its stringent definition of what it meant to be a man as well as his experience in a patriarchal church whose doctrinal teachings did not resonate with his values, Scorsese emerged from his university education ready to begin a career in filmmaking with a number of experiences, perceptions, and issues that would influence his films.

First, Martin's small size, frail health, and emotional sensitivity had prevented him from engaging in physical activities, including sports, with the other boys and adolescents in his milieu on an equal footing. In addition, he had some difficulty in relating to women effectively. As a result, Scorsese probably had some uncertainties, questions at least, about his masculinity. His perceptions of masculinity and femininity were affected by the macho Italian-American-Catholic culture of his community. As described earlier, these perceptions were also affected by the stereotypical presentations of men and women in the movies that he saw when he was a youngster.

Second, the insular and constraining milieu of Little Italy, in effect, gave him the message that this was all that was available to him and that he could not go beyond it. In one sense Scorsese was a part of this milieu, an insider, and yet he did not feel a deep and abiding sense of belonging to it except for his connection to his family. When he set out to become a filmmaker and thereby extend himself and his sense of place far beyond this cultural domain, Scorsese understandably was determined to succeed, showing as he did in the film *The King of Comedy* that one could be so determined to become a somebody that he will strive to succeed regardless of the cost. In effect, Scorsese wanted to become an insider in the film industry and to belong to a world that was considerably beyond the confines of Little Italy. However, having grown up in this milieu gave Scorsese an awareness of the effect of roots on himself and others.

Third, Scorsese felt disenchanted with the church, which he had earlier embraced, but his passion for the Christ-figure and Jesus's message of love, compassion, and forgiveness remained an integral aspect of Scorsese's personality. Scorsese's challenge, his life work, albeit in the secular world, became one centered on a religious-like vocation to explore and examine the fundamental question of how one lives a good or spiritual life while remaining in the real world where one has to contend with ambition, sex, greed, and pride, issues that he has considered in his film characterizations. As Scorsese expressed in *Mean Streets* through his alter-ego, Charlie: "You don't attain salvation by living in a church or monastery." Later, Scorsese added,

> You gotta live amongst the people and change life that way or help people reach salvation in the street ... [which] could mean Hollywood.... It's like a religious vocation.... Mine was harder. I had to do it in the street, I had to do it in Hollywood.[31]

Scorsese struggled to find the money, only about $75,000, to finance his first commercial film released in 1969, *Who's That Knocking at My Door*?[32] The film was shown at the 1967 Chicago Film Festival. He moved to Los Angeles in 1970 to enter into the mainstream film industry. In Los Angeles he met Roger Corman, who offered him the opportunity to make *Boxcar Bertha* (1972), an exploitation film. Returning to using his personal experience in his movies, Scorsese arrived on the filmmaking "map" with *Mean Streets* (1973). His next films—*Alice Doesn't Live Here Anymore* (1974), *Taxi Driver* (1976), and *Raging Bull* (1980)—received critical acclaim and helped to establish his reputation as a talented director with whom the Hollywood establishment would have to contend.

It appears that Scorsese's success with these films early in his career inflated his ego in a way that contributed to his abusing his body. He succumbed to temptations from the "high" life in Hollywood by abusing drugs (as did his character Henry Hill in *GoodFellas*), during the middle to the late 1970s.[33] His next two films, *New York, New York* (1977) and *The King of Comedy* (1982), were not successful at the box office. Scorsese has related that during the filming of *New York, New York*, he did not know if his own relationship with his wife at the time was going to work and that this doubt is reflected in the film story. By the end of 1978, his marriage had come to an end, and he was in poor health.[34] (Scorsese married his first wife, Larraine Marie Brennan, in 1964. He married for the second time in 1975 to Julia Cameron, a screenwriter. Scorsese married Isabella Rossellini in 1979, and the couple divorced in 1983. Scorsese's fourth marriage was to Barbara DeFina, a film producer, in February 1985. They separated in 1991 and divorced sometime later [date not known]. Scorsese married Helen S. Morris in July 1999, and their daughter, Francesca, was born in November 1999.[35])

The lack of success of *New York, New York* and *The King of Comedy* caused Scorsese emotional distress and self-doubt. He had to decide whether he wanted to continue making films.

During this period of his career, Scorsese made extensive efforts to obtain studio financing for *The Last Temptation of Christ*. As explained in Chapter 11, this story of the humanity of Jesus was important to Scorsese, and he suffered years of setbacks and frustration before he succeeded in obtaining the financing that he needed to make the controversial film.

Scorsese recovered his equilibrium and his determination to continue his career. He left Los Angeles and moved back to New York in 1979. He made *After Hours* (1985) to show that he could make a low-budget film in a short period of time, and he made the relatively nonpersonal Hollywood film *The Color of Money* (1986), working with two established stars, Paul Newman and Tom Cruise. Both of these movies were successful by Hollywood standards.

Scorsese made a number of successful and critically-acclaimed films during the 1990s including *GoodFellas* (1990), *Cape Fear* (1991), *The Age of Innocence* (1993), and *Casino* (1995). In 1995, his documentary *A Century of Cinema: A Personal Journey with Martin Scorsese through American Movies* contributed to his reputation as an outstanding film historian and teacher. Scorsese's most recent films are *Kundun* (1998), *Bringing Out the Dead* (1999), *Il Mio Viaggio in Italia* (2001), and *Gangs of New York* (2002).

Scorsese has also filmed a number of other documentaries, shorts, and commercials, and he has taken a leading role in film restoration and preservation. Indeed, Scorsese has been instrumental in organizing an international campaign against the manufacture and use of color-fading film. In addition to these accomplishments, Scorsese has produced and acted in a number of films. He had a role in the film *Guilty by Suspicion*. His appearances in his own films include the gunman at the end of *Mean Streets* and the enraged passenger in *Taxi Driver* who is planning to kill his wife. He produced or coproduced *Mad Dog and Glory*, *Search and Destroy*, *The Grifters*, and *You Can Count on Me*, among others.

The enormous career success that Scorsese has enjoyed is in contrast to his apparent problems in maintaining intimate relationships. His four failed marriages suggest, as he expressed via the character of Jimmy Doyle in *New York, New York*, that his visual "music" or "art" has consumed more of his attention than have his intimate relationships. Commenting on Rupert Pupkin's (*The King of Comedy*) compulsive drive for success and celebrity, Scorsese said that he could identify with Pupkin's ambition. Scorsese stated that "*at the time* ... if I had to make a choice between work and a relationship, the personal would go by the wayside."[36]

The next chapter discusses *Gangs of New York*, another very personal film and a representation of Scorsese's roots, including his special relationship with his father. Moreover, it expresses his passion for the place of his old neighborhood in the history of New York City and that of urban America.

2

Gangs of New York as a Return to Roots

Martin Scorsese's highly anticipated *Gangs of New York* opened in theaters around the country in late December of 2002. The unveiling of the new film was delayed for over a year because of the 9/11 tragedy as well as problems that developed between Scorsese and Harvey Weinstein, the executive who represented the interests of Miramax. According to reports, these problems stemmed from Scorsese's insistence on controlling the finalization of the film until it met his artistic demands and the studio's interest in a product that would guarantee a good box office draw.[1]

With *Gangs*, the epic drama that Scorsese had been wanting to make for three decades, Scorsese returns to familiar territory with regard to his personal as well as his cinematic history. Scorsese's work is grounded in his roots and its triune of family, street, and church, and he has made a number of films that portray his roots explicitly. *Italianamerican* (1974), a documentary, features his parents talking about the history of the family as well as that of their neighborhood in Manhattan's Little Italy. In *Who's That Knocking at My Door?* (1969), Scorsese used his parents' apartment on Elizabeth Street for the indoor scenes. Casting Harvey Keitel as his alter ego, Scorsese depicted a young man, an Italian-American-Catholic, who is in conflict about religion and his sexuality. The character's conflict regarding the madonna-whore complex was Scorsese's at the time.

In his acclaimed *Mean Streets* (1973), Scorsese depicted the day-to-day activities of a group of young men of Little Italy, apparently representing Scorsese and his friends, their conflicts, and their struggles as they try to learn what it means to be a man in their community. In this film, Scorsese also showed that violence was only a heartbeat away from the usual activities of these young men.

In *GoodFellas* (1990), Scorsese depicted the gangsterism in his former community, and in *The Last Temptation of Christ* (1988), Scorsese gave expression to his religious roots and his almost lifelong passion for the Christ-figure.

More recently, Scorsese's four-hour documentary, *Il Mio Viaggio in Italia* (2001), revealed the influence of post–World War II Italian films on his cinematic roots. These films provided inspiration to him as a boy when he watched them with his family. Since his parents, particularly his father, had taken him to movies from the time he was a little boy, watching these Italian films enabled Scorsese to establish a chain of connection among his Sicilian grandparents, his parents, and himself in Little Italy. This connection provides the linkage between Scorsese's cultural history and his early cinematic roots.

Gangs of New York, with its themes of street violence, immigrant struggle for survival and recognition, and its depiction of the despicable living conditions of the slum poor, represents Scorsese's revisiting his cultural roots as a child and adolescent growing up in the "mean" streets of lower Manhattan. Scorsese grew up in a community that included immigrants and the children of immigrants who struggled against ethnic, class, and religious bigotry that derived from different groups vying for opportunities to achieve a share of the American dream. The more recent immigrants felt dispossessed by those perceived as insiders, who, because of their status as longer-term "Americans" saw themselves as more resonate with the mainstream American culture. Moreover, Scorsese's social milieu included a criminal underworld whose gangsters—bent on obtaining control and power—were capable of unexpected and explosive violence. In addition, the area of Little Italy where Scorsese grew up is proximate to the Bowery. Thus, as a boy, Scorsese came into contact with the slum poor who lived in abject poverty as well as with the derelicts and addicts of skid row. In an interview Scorsese gave in 2001 in conjunction with the then-expected release of *Gangs*, he described his old neighborhood where he grew up:

> The two negative things about it were the underworld and skid row. Those were part of my world, and they were also part of the old Five Points.[2]

Gangs is set during the middle of the nineteenth century in the former Five Points area of lower Manhattan, which was south of the community that became Little Italy and north of the present financial district. Scorsese has recounted that the church he attended in his youth, St. Patrick's Cathedral on Mott Street, had a brick wall around it and that a battle between rival gangs had been fought at that wall.[3] One reason that he wanted to make *Gangs* was that Scorsese felt that his old neighborhood had played a part in the history of old New York.

In January of 1970 Scorsese came across a copy of the book *The Gangs of New York* by Herbert Asbury, written in 1928. He was intrigued by this relatively obscure account of nineteenth-century history that involved immigrant struggle and street violence, experiences that he knew well, that had taken place in his beloved Manhattan. The story of the gangs of New York remained in his mind for decades as something he wanted to put on film. Indeed, Paul Schrader, who has written several screenplays for Scorsese's movies, recounted that when he met Scorsese in 1972, Scorsese told him that there were two books he wanted to make into movies: *The Last Temptation of Christ* and *Gangs of New York*.[4]

The screenplay of *Gangs*, which uses the Asbury book only to provide a general framework, depicts the slum conditions of the dispossessed immigrants, political corruption, and religious and class bigotry. There are personal stories as well, one focusing on a young man's struggle to discover himself and become a man and others of two father-son relationships. In addition, a man's conflicted feelings of love, honor, and revenge are portrayed.

Synopsis

Gangs depicts the violence that took place between immigrant and nativist gangs in the years 1846–1863. This era coincided with the American Civil War. The gang of the so-called Nativists, led by Bill "the Butcher" Cutting (Daniel Day-Lewis), resent what they perceive as the intrusion into their country by the newly arrived Irish immigrants. One tribe of Irish immigrants—known as the Dead Rabbits—is led by Priest Vallon (acted by Liam Neeson). The immigrants hate the Nativists by whom they feel oppressed and demeaned. In 1846 there is a ferocious battle involving a number of tribes of Irish-Catholic immigrants, including the Dead Rabbits led by Vallon, fighting in hand-to-hand combat with knives, cleavers, axes, and the like against the Nativists, led by Cutting. Vallon is killed by Cutting. The Dead Rabbits are disbanded and outlawed, and Cutting assumes complete control of the Five Points. Vallon's young son, Amsterdam, witnesses the killing of his father. He tries to escape but is caught by the law and forced to spend the next sixteen years in a reform prison, the Hellgate House of Reform. When he is released, Amsterdam returns to the Five Points, presumably bent on revenge against Cutting. Vallon recovers the knife that killed his father and his medal of St. Michael, to whom he and his father prayed on that fateful morning, from the hole in the earth where he had hidden them years earlier.

When he first appears in the Five Points area essentially incognito, Amsterdam (Leonardo DiCaprio) is recognized as Priest Vallon's son by another young man, Johnny (acted by Henry Thomas). They join together in working for Bill Cutting by stealing and plundering and then turning over their spoils to Bill.

Front row, center left Amsterdam Vallon (Leonardo DiCaprio), (*right*) local gang boss Bill "the Butcher" Cutting (Daniel Day-Lewis), and (*back center*) Johnny (Henry Thomas) with other residents of the slum area known as Five Points in a scene from *Gangs of New York* (Photofest).

Cutting takes notice of Amsterdam because of his skill and courage and grows to like him. Johnny is jealous of the special relationship that develops between the two men. Concurrently, Jenny Everdeane (Cameron Diaz), an accomplished pickpocket, enters the picture. As she reveals later, when she was a young teenager, she had been impregnated by Bill, but the act was not against her will. Her baby had been "cut out of her," and she retains scars on her stomach from the cutting. Because she is marked, Bill no longer wants her as a lover, but they remain friends.

Once Amsterdam is persuaded that Jenny does not have a sexual interest in Bill and that she does not represent "the 'Butcher's' leavings," Amsterdam develops a sexual relationship with Jenny. Johnny, who had wanted Jenny for himself, is jealous of this relationship as well.

The bond between Amsterdam and Cutting continues to grow, and Bill begins to see Amsterdam as the son he never had. For his part, Amsterdam admires Bill and is conflicted about his need to avenge his father's death by killing Bill, on the one hand, and his developing respect and affection for Bill, on the other hand.

Interwoven through the relational themes are the political corruption and machinations of William Tweed (Jim Broadbent) of Tammany Hall, who has forged an alliance with Cutting to exert control of the immigrants, and the fact that the American Civil War is raging.

Because of the war, federal agents move among the Irish immigrants and the slum poor looking for men who will agree or who can be tricked or coerced to join the Union army. The poor, white people, who are struggling to merely survive and cannot relate to the war at all, blame the blacks for the war.

Johnny betrays Amsterdam and reveals his identity as Vallon's son to Bill. At the sixteenth anniversary celebration of the great battle of 1846 held at the Chinese Pagoda on Mott Street, Bill participates in an exceptional knife-throwing exhibition using Jenny, his former assistant in such exhibitions, as his on-stage target. It is apparent that Bill is enraged with Amsterdam for having deceived him, and he is waiting for the opportunity to avenge himself. Bill knows that Jenny and Amsterdam are lovers and he uses the exhibition to frighten them with his expertise and to show Amsterdam that he is a fearsome adversary.

Amsterdam resolves his emotional conflict about Bill and when he believes that he has the opportunity for surprise, he hurls a knife at him. However, Bill is not only prepared for such a move, but he is more skilled at knife-throwing than Amsterdam is. Bill hurls a knife at Amsterdam and wounds him. This occurs in full view of the public. Amsterdam is grabbed by other men, and upon Bill's order, he is placed on a butchering table where he lies helpless and at Bill's mercy. Bill humiliates Amsterdam, calling him a "sneak thief" and a "base defiler" for having hidden his true identity and intentions. Cutting calls out to the crowd and asks them what he should do with the scoundrel. The crowd yells out a number of suggestions that include cutting out his heart.

Bill responds that the "boy has no heart" and that "he ain't earned death at my hand." He spares Amsterdam's life but decrees that this sparing is a "mark of shame." Getting on top of the table and straddling Amsterdam's prone body, Bill proceeds to butt Amsterdam in his head and face until he is bloody. Then he applies a red-hot knife blade to Amsterdam's cheek, marking him with his "brand" as if he were an animal that Bill had captured and was keeping in subjugation.

Jenny nurses Amsterdam back to health and pleads with him to leave the Five Points with her and travel to San Francisco. Amsterdam talks with Walter "Monk" McGinn (Brendan Gleason), a former ally of his father. He is reminded that his father loved his people and that all he wanted was to carve out a part of Five Points for his tribe. Moreover, McGinn gives Amsterdam a small case that contains his father's razor. Amsterdam remembers that as part of his ritual in preparing for battle, his father had cut a slit in his face with the razor and had admonished his young son to leave the blood on the blade. Holding the razor and seeing his father's dried blood on the blade, Amsterdam now realizes clearly what his mission is: He must unite his people and reunite the Dead Rabbits.

Amsterdam, who has now become a man who walks in his father's shoes, realizes the potential power of the progressively growing number of Irish immigrants who arrive on the shores of New York. He says in this context, "15,000 Irish are arriving each week," this is "not just a gang, but an army."

Amsterdam kills "Uncle Jack," a crooked cop who has been cruel and malevolent to the Irish. He places the skin of a dead rabbit on a metal gatepost in the public square, a sign that the Dead Rabbits are back in business. Amsterdam and those who support him begin wearing shirts that have been stained red with blood.

Johnny comes to regret his betrayal of Amsterdam but learns that neither side respects or wants him. Amsterdam discovers Johnny's dying body impaled by the same metal post on which Amsterdam had placed the dead rabbit. Johnny's horrible death is a signal that Bill Cutting is responding to Amsterdam's challenge. With Amsterdam clearly in the leadership role with the Irish immigrants, Tweed now turns to him to deliver votes for Tammany Hall candidates.

As these events are unfolding, the National Conscription Act goes into effect, and men from the Five Points are due to be drafted into the Union army. The law allows men who can pay $300 to escape the draft. Since the slum poor have no money, they feel that the law discriminates against them, and they are enraged.

In return for delivering the Irish votes to Tammany Hall, Amsterdam demands that Tweed back an Irish candidate for sheriff, and McGinn is elected sheriff. Cutting perceives this election of an Irishman as an affront to his power, and he kills McGinn with a knife when McGinn's back is turned. This act is the final spark that ignites the Irish to organize and do battle. Cutting Bill is unmoved by protestations that he has killed an elected official, and he is ready to fight Amsterdam and the Irish in return, saying in this context, "I took the father [Priest Vallon], now I will take the son."

The funeral procession carrying McGinn's body winds through the streets of Five Points. When it approaches Bill Cutting, who is standing outside his shop, Amsterdam walks up to Bill and issues a challenge to battle. Bill accepts the challenge. The leaders of the various tribes and the Nativists assemble a council. Amsterdam decrees that the battle will be waged the following morning at daybreak. Weapons are decided: Knives, axes, and the like are deemed acceptable; pistols are not.

In preparing for the battle, Amsterdam carries the bloodstained knife that killed his father. He cuts a slit in his face with his father's razor. His blood comingles with that of his father, a symbol of the son having becoming one with his father. As Amsterdam prepares for battle, Jenny is preparing to leave him and the Five Points, convinced that everything and everyone will be destroyed in the coming battle. As a way of responding to Jenny's pleas that he leave as well, Amsterdam says: "What would you have me do? I [must be] about my father's business."

At about the time that the battle between the gangs begins, the draft riots—which lasted four days and nights—reach Five Points. Scorsese intertwines the bloodshed and death of the draft riots with that of the battle between Amsterdam and Cutting and their respective gangs.

Because the mobs involved in the draft riots are totally out of control, wreaking havoc throughout Manhattan, federal troops are called in to quell the rioters with gunfire. In their gang battle, Amsterdam and Bill literally cannot see because the ash from the gunfire and cannonballs fills the air. In one scene, both men are thrown to the ground by the force of the cannons, and both are covered with ash. In the end, Amsterdam fatally wounds Cutter, who holds Amsterdam's hand as he dies.

The final scene shows the graves of former gang members and those who died from the gunfire of the federal troops. Amsterdam remarks that fifty or a hundred years from now, no one will remember what happened there. A modern skyline of New York City emerges in the distance across the river. The skyline includes the former twin towers of the World Trade Center.

Themes

Gangs contains a number of themes that have been present in other Scorsese movies. First, there is the theme of a man's identity, psychology, and behavior having been conditioned by his roots or sense of place. Scorsese places Amsterdam Vallon as a boy and a young man within a social milieu that is defined by abject poverty, oppression, and barbaric violence. Given this experience of having been raised in a particularly cruel street culture, how does this man live a life of meaning and purpose? Scorsese first asked this question in *Mean Streets*. Ultimately, Amsterdam strives to unite the social underdogs, the Irish immigrants, into an army to fight the Nativists, who are their most immediate oppressors. As depicted and as he implies to Jenny, Amsterdam has no choice but to engage in violence because to do otherwise would be to succumb to utter hopelessness and death.

Amsterdam's goal is no less inspired or spiritual than that of Bill Shelly (in *Boxcar Bertha*, 1972). Shelly strove to unite the oppressed railroad workers, the social underdogs of his time and place, into a union to fight their oppressors, the wealthy railroad owner, Sartoris.

Moreover, given Amsterdam's roots and experience, if he is to demonstrate his manhood, he has no choice but to avenge his father's killing and thereby provoke great violence. Similarly, Travis Bickle (in *Taxi Driver*) feels he has no choice but to undertake a mission of sorts, as a warrior, to clean up the streets of his New York and to save Iris from a life of prostitution. In undertaking his mission, Bickle also provokes violence and death.

In *Gangs* we see that out of the terrible violence that occurs in Five Points emerges rebirth, new life, and regeneration. This rebirth is thematic in *Mean Streets,* where after the violence that befalls Charlie, Teresa, and Johnny Boy, a child, Christopher, is born: Similarly, rebirth occurs in *Raging Bull* and in *The Last Temptation of Christ.*

Another theme that is present in *Gangs* as well as in other Scorsese films is that of people who are insiders and those who are outsiders, the experience of belonging, and feelings of alienation. In *Gangs* there is a scene of the poor and the underclass looking out from the alley that leads outward, away from the misery of their existence and toward a better life. The idea of outsiders wanting to get in appears cogently in *The King of Comedy* in the scene when Masha's hands appear on the car window, representing her wish to get inside into Jerry Langford's world. Similarly, in *GoodFellas*, Henry Hill strives to get into the life of the mob family.

Gangs underscores the importance of group membership to people's sense of who they are. The individual gangs wear costumes of a sort to identify themselves as belonging to a specific tribe or group. Scorsese has said of this tendency,

> A lot of people couldn't read so to be understood or heard, you had to go on a street corner, make noise, have a parade ... we're dressed in this way, so you'll know who we are.[5]

Similarly, in *Mean Streets,* there is a religious festival that winds its way through the streets of Little Italy. Participating in this type of religious "parade" was one of the ways the people of that area identified themselves as belonging to their particular group.

The final scene of *Gangs* suggests that Scorsese meant to convey the message regarding the terrible futility of violence and warfare. The shooting of the film was finished months before 9/11 and the collapse of the towers of the World Trade Center. Placing the events of 9/11 within the context of the film, it is clear that Scorsese's message about the terrible price wrought by and the futility of violence is ever more powerful. It is an extraordinary coincidence that in the film, Amsterdam and Cutting are covered with ash from the firestorm of the Union troops and in the 9/11 tragedy that occurred in New York City, ash covered much of the area and the people who were near the World Trade Center.

Personal Meaning

Gangs has considerable personal meaning to Scorsese. The struggle of the immigrant poor to get a slice of the American dream connects directly with the experience of Scorsese's grandparents, who were immigrants from Sicily. The film's depiction about bigotry and conflict due to class and religion is the stuff of urban strife, and it was as true when Scorsese was growing up as it was in the 1850s and remains today. Moreover, the gangs portrayed in the film are considered predecessors to the gangs that were rampant in Little Italy during the years that Scorsese lived there.

Giving expression to Scorsese's religious predilections, there are a number of religious or spiritual allusions in the film. *Priest* Vallon, who wears a ministerial collar around his neck, appears to be a religious figure. In preparation for the film's opening battle, Priest and the young Amsterdam pray to "St. Michael, the archangel who cast Satan out of Paradise." This sequence establishes Cutting as representing Satan and Vallon as a Godlike figure, who represents good. As elaborated in Chapter 9, Vallon is also reminiscent of Moses. As he marches through the tunnel under the slums, holding a metal cross in his hand as if it were a beacon, large numbers of the slum poor, who live in "hell," follow him up to the daylight of Paradise Square. In these scenes, Vallon resembles Moses, holding a staff, who leads his people out of oppression and darkness and into the promised land. However, in *Gangs*, Priest Vallon, the father, fails in his mission. Years later, his son, representing a Christlike figure, succeeds in accomplishing the mission to cast the evil Cutting from Five Points and Paradise Square. Amsterdam represents a new beginning or rebirth and redemption. Essentially, the message seems to be that out of death, suffering, and bloodshed, there is hope for new life and redemption.

Blood has had special meaning for Scorsese throughout his cinematic history. Blood has signified a cleansing to Scorsese or the idea that redemption can follow suffering and bloodshed. From this perspective, the extraordinary amount of blood shown in the film as well as Amsterdam's Dead Rabbits wearing bloodstained shirts point to Christ's suffering on the cross and his death which, according to Christianity, enabled mankind to be redeemed and saved.

In addition, the Holy Trinity of Christianity is seemingly represented in the film. This occurs by virtue of Priest Vallon's identification as the *father*, Amsterdam, as the *son*, and Amsterdam's praying to God to put the steel of the "*Holy Spirit*" in his spine. Even the traitor of Jesus, Judas, is represented in the film by virtue of the character of Johnny. Another allusion to Christ is Amsterdam's speaking about his needing to be about his father's business. Words similar to these are attributed to the biblical Jesus.

With regard to the personal story in *Gangs*, Scorsese has said:

> In the case of Amsterdam taking Bill down, ... it's about the transition from boy to man. It has a lot to do with personal issues of my father dying nine years ago and now I'm becoming a father again, with a 3-year-old. I'm struggling to make that transition. The personal story of the film reflects that, I guess.[6]

These comments by Scorsese suggest that Amsterdam's developing into a man in his own right relates to Scorsese's coming to grips with the loss of his father and his replacing his father by becoming the patriarch of the family just as Amsterdam replaces his father as the patriarch of his tribe.

Moreover, Amsterdam undergoes a development from a narcissistic boy, who is only interested in the pursuit of his own goals and needs, to a man who has a larger and unselfish vision. As depicted, he has the opportunity to leave Five Points and have an easier and presumably more pleasurable life with Jenny in San Francisco. Amsterdam refuses to leave because he realizes that he has a mission: to be a leader, a father figure to his people. Mixing his blood with that of his father has the symbolic meaning of his becoming one with the father.

In another recent interview, Scorsese reflected on the personal meaning of the film and, specifically, how the story relates to his relationship with his father, with whom the young Martin developed his love for movies. Scorsese stated:

> My father had this mythological sense of the old New York, and he used to tell me stories about these old gangs, particularly the Forty Thieves in the Fourth Ward, even in the 1930s, even though the neighborhood had become Italian by then.[7]

There is additional meaning in the film that connects to Scorsese's early life. Scorsese has acknowledged that it was primarily his father who took him to movies when he was a young boy. The boy fantasized about the films he had seen on the screen, some of which must have seemed to him to have been dreams. In the opening scenes of *Gangs*, a young boy watches his father, Priest Vallon, ritualistically shave and cut his face with his razor and don a metal collar. During these early scenes, the voice of Leonardo DiCaprio, as an older Amsterdam Vallon, relates that some of his memories of those events that occurred in 1846 seem like a dream. These tender scenes of father and son are probably reminiscent of Scorsese's memories of being with his father, some of these having a dreamlike quality.

After the boy and his father pray to St. Michael, Amsterdam accompanies his father through the tunnel of the slums with the Irish immigrants following behind, forming a veritable religious parade. When they reach Paradise Square, Priest Vallon prepares to wage battle with Bill Cutting while the boy watches the battle from the sidelines *as if he were watching figures on a screen*.

In these early scenes of a father and his young son, moreover, there are no allusions to the existence of a Mrs. Vallon or of any woman who is the mother of the boy. The exclusive father-son relationship depicted in these scenes may be a reenactment of Scorsese's memories and perceptions of his early relationship with his father, a relationship that was focused on their watching movies together. These memories or fantasies have emerged from the shadows of Scorsese's roots. Scorsese's including no mother-figure with regard to Amsterdam probably relates to the absence of Scorsese's mother in his memories of his special relationship with his father. In other words,

Scorsese's memories of this aspect of his relationship with his father do not include his mother. We can speculate that Scorsese's consuming passion about making *Gangs* had more to do with his father, with whom he had an obviously special relationship, having told him stories about the old gangs than any other factor.

There is yet another issue involving Scorsese and his father that seems to relate to the father-son relationship in the movie. In *Gangs*, Amsterdam avenges the death (or failure) of his actual father, and he defeats his surrogate-father. In light of Scorsese's family history, it is possible that in his gaining international celebrity status, Scorsese more than compensated for whatever limits and failures, in a materialistic sense, his father had suffered. In attaining his success, it can be said, metaphorically, that Scorsese "avenged" his father's "failure" by defeating or overcoming the forces that had kept his father down in a limited working-class social structure. Without question, *Gangs* reveals more about Scorsese's relationship with his father than has been known previously.[8]

3

Plot Summaries, Characters, and Themes

The works cited in this chapter constitute a complete filmography of Scorsese's full-length and short films, and student shorts from 1963 through 2002.[1]

One television episode is included. The documentaries listed are those that provide insights into Scorsese's roots and interests. While he was still a student at New York University, Scorsese made *What's a Nice Girl Like You Doing in a Place Like This?*, *It's Not Just You, Murray!*, and *The Big Shave*.

What's a Nice Girl Like You Doing in a Place Like This? (1963)

MAJOR CHARACTERS:
    Harry—Zeph Michaelis
    Wife—Mimi Stark
    Analyst—Sarah Braveman

Scorsese's first film is a nine-minute short featuring the travails of a writer named Algernon whose friends call him Harry. Harry is suffering from writer's block seemingly because of his obsessions. A major preoccupation of Harry's involves a photograph of a man in a boat on a river or lake. His obsessiveness about the photograph has become so severe that Harry cannot eat or sleep. Then Harry throws a party at his place and meets a woman that he really likes. They eventually marry. Having this wonderful woman in his life distracts Harry from the photograph, and now he can eat and sleep as well as write. His wife is an artist who likes to paint nature scenes. Eventually, she paints a picture of the ocean, and Harry becomes obsessed with the scene. Harry meets with his analyst, and she recommends that he help himself and "stare it down." The film ends with Harry trapped inside this photograph, that is, he is literally at the ocean.

The theme of a man trapped inside his mind would appear in a number of Scorsese's later films, including *Taxi Driver* and "Mirror, Mirror." In this early short, Scorsese included a close-up of a man's eyes; this type of camera shot, focusing intensely on a pair of eyes, appears in his later films, including *Taxi Driver*, *Cape Fear*, and *Bringing Out the Dead*.

It's Not Just You, Murray! (1964)

MAJOR CHARACTERS:
   Murray—Ira Rubin
   Joe—Sam De Fazio
   Wife—Andrea Martin
   Mother—Catherine Scorsese

Scorsese's second film is a fifteen-minute satire on the life of a gangster of the type that Scorsese had witnessed in Little Italy. Murray peers into the camera and tells the price of his clothing and car. He introduces himself to the viewers, saying that he is very rich and influential and has many friends. He says that he owes this sweet life to one man, his friend Joe, who appears and says hello. Murray says that the only advice he ever got from his mother was to eat first. Joe, on the other hand, set up Murray in business. We see that the "business" is an illegal gin distillery. As Murray talks to the camera, he really goes places, including to prison. His mother visits him in prison, and, true to form, brings him spaghetti to eat. After he is released, Murray continues to have a number of adventures with criminals and their hit men, and one of these encounters results in his being beaten and going to a hospital. Murray does not seem to have minded the injuries that he has suffered, because while he is hospitalized he meets his wife, a nurse. As before, his mother visits him in the hospital and brings him food.

Murray talks about the wonderful life he has enjoyed as a gangster—going places and doing things such as going to Broadway shows. Unbeknownst to Murray, Joe and Murray's wife begin having an affair. Nevertheless, Murray continues to extol his involvement in "one of the greatest financial syndicates in America" that has affected all people and things, including "motel chains, undertaking services, politics, television, sports, grants, foreign aid," etcetera.

The film shows that, eventually, Murray is forced to appear at a congressional hearing, where he takes the Fifth Amendment to avoid giving information about his friends. In spite of the problems he has had within the criminal underworld, Murray believes that his "empire of wealth and security" has been built from nothing but the love and friendship of Joe. Murray says that he and Joe have done everything together and that Joe is a "second father" to his children.

Murray explains that once there was a misunderstanding between him and Joe, alluding to the affair Joe has been having with Murray's wife. However, Joe manages to assuage Murray's hurt feelings about the affair by giving him a gift of a new car. Murray celebrates his good fortune with his friends. The film ends with a freeze frame showing Murray and Joe standing in front of the new car.

Scorsese satirizes the gangster's way of measuring who he is and what his life represents in terms of his possessions and money. The film depicts the lure of the "good life" and the greed that accompanies it. He also shows that there is no honor among thieves, as is evident in Joe's having an affair with Murray's wife and impregnating her. Scorsese captures these themes more cogently in his later gangster films, *GoodFellas* and *Casino*. Scorsese's mother, Catherine, makes the first of her many appearances in her son's films.

The Big Shave (1967)

CHARACTER:

Young Man—Peter Bernuth

The Big Shave shows a young man shaving while standing in front of the sink and mirror in his bathroom. He places shaving cream on his face and applies a razor. When he repeats this process a second time, blood appears on his face as if he had produced a cut. He continues shaving and draws more and more blood until the white sink is blood-red.

According to Sangster, the working title for this short was *Viet '67*.[2] It represents Scorsese's cryptic comment about the Vietnam War.

Who's That Knocking at My Door? (1968)

MAJOR CHARACTERS:

J.R.—Harvey Keitel
the Girl—Zina Bethune
Joey—Lennard Kuras
Sally GaGa—Michael Scala
a Gangster—Martin Scorsese

Starring Harvey Keitel as "J.R.," *Who's That Knocking at My Door?* portrays young Italian-American men struggling to determine what it means to be a man and gain a sense of belonging within the community of Sicilian-American-Catholic men with which they are familiar and wish to identify. The focus of the action is J.R.'s relationship with a blonde, well-educated woman who is named "the Girl." Seemingly representing Everywoman, the Girl and her history (she had been date-raped) evokes in J.R. his madonna-whore complex. According to the mind of a man who thinks in terms of the madonna-whore complex, if a woman is not a virgin, she is not pure, indeed, she is a whore. Moreover, if a woman is not a virgin, this means that she has been possessed and despoiled by another man. As he is depicted, J.R., who is competitive with other men with regard to attracting women, cannot marry a woman who, in his mind, has been cast off by a competitor. He fails utterly to resolve his inner demons and he loses the Girl.

Scorsese's first feature film that was intended for a commercial audience was *Who's That Knocking at My Door?* (1968), in effect a prelude to *Mean Streets*. Written by Scorsese and shot on the streets of Little Italy and Manhattan familiar to him, he incorporated in the film those aspects of the Italian-American-Catholic street culture with which he was familiar: the Catholic religion, young men seeking to belong within their social milieu, and small-time gangsters. The indoor scenes were shot in the apartment of Scorsese's parents in Little Italy, the apartment in which Scorsese had spent his early and adolescent years. The apartment and the movie are rampant with religious icons and symbolism.

In addition to showing Scorsese's consuming interest in religion, this is the first feature film in which he presents the male lead, in this case, J.R., as a narcissistic man. J.R. is preoccupied with himself, and he has insecurities about his manhood. This type of phallic-narcissistic man, who appears as a major character in a number of Scorsese films, is discussed in detail in chapters 4 and 7.

J.R. is Scorsese's alter ego and the character undoubtedly gives expression to Scorsese's conflict about women.

Boxcar Bertha (1972)

MAJOR CHARACTERS:

Boxcar Bertha—Barbara Hershey
Bill Shelly—David Carradine
Von Morton—Bernie Casey
Rake Brown—Barry Primus
Sartoris—John Carradine

A Roger Corman, low-budget movie, *Boxcar Bertha* was derived from the autobiography of Box-car Bertha.[3] The cover of the book describes it as a "story of a wandering woman of the underworld" with "intimate facts of a woman hobo's methods and habits."

The story is set in the South during the Depression. Bertha, having lost both of her parents, is alone in the world She meets and falls in love with Bill Shelly, a good man, who is trying to help the exploited poor by organizing a union for the railroad workers. Bertha and Bill and their friends, Von Morton and Rake Brown, join together and become a gang of train robbers. Bill and the other men are caught and imprisoned in a chain gang. Alone and struggling to survive, Bertha joins a house of prostitution. Later, she helps Bill and the other men escape from the chain gang. Eventually, Bill is caught by the thugs who work for Sartoris, the owner of the railroad. As punishment for his acts against the powerful Sartoris, Bill is nailed to a boxcar. The film ends with Bertha running after the moving train to which Bill has been crucified.

Aspects of this film are similar to Scorsese's later film *The Last Temptation of Christ*. Bill Shelly is depicted as a good man who fights against the powerful and rich elite who exploit the disenfranchised workers. Bill dedicates himself to helping the poor by trying to organize the workers into a union so they can gain some power. Ultimately, he dies by crucifixion. Bill Shelly is seemingly representative of Jesus.

As the prostitute who changes her ways and follows her lover to his death on the cross, Bertha typifies the character of Mary Magdalene in *The Last Temptation of Christ*, which Scorsese made years later. Interestingly, Barbara Hershey, who played the role of Bertha in this early film and later, Mary Magdalene in *The Last Temptation of Christ* (1988), gave Scorsese a copy of the controversial book by Nikos Kazantzakis during the filming of *Boxcar Bertha*.

According to Sangster, the crucifixion scene in *Boxcar Bertha* was not created by Scorsese, it was in the script given to him.[4] Nevertheless, the scenes of nails entering the man's flesh were reenacted later in *The Last Temptation of Christ*, with Scorsese applying the same or similar camera shots that he had used in *Boxcar Bertha* when he made the Christ film a number of years later.

Scorsese has stated that after he completed *Boxcar Bertha*, he was advised by John Cassavetes not to do that kind of film again.[5] As he relates the story, Scorsese was told that he had spent a year making the film, but a low-budget, exploitation film would not advance his career.

Mean Streets (1973)

MAJOR CHARACTERS:
    Charlie—Harvey Keitel
    Johnny Boy—Robert De Niro
    Tony—David Proval
    Teresa—Amy Robinson

Michael—Richard Romanus
Giovanni—Cesare Danova
Joey Catucci—George Memmoli
Gunman—Martin Scorsese

Scorsese returned to the art of using his explicitly personal experience in his films with *Mean Streets*. The story focuses on the activities of a group of men: Charlie, Tony, Michael, and Johnny Boy. An older man, Giovanni, is Charlie's uncle and the boss of the neighborhood gangsters. Charlie works for Giovanni as a collector and numbers runner; Tony runs a bar; Michael has his own criminal operation that includes loan sharking. Johnny Boy has no job and owes money to men in the neighborhood, including Michael. The young men spend their time drinking in noisy bars, rough-housing and fighting, gambling, playing pool, and whoring. These young Italian-American men are racist, anti–Semitic, and sexist.

There is a rigid code of honor in this milieu that dictates how honorable men should behave. One inflexible rule is that an honorable man should pay his debts. Johnny Boy not only ignores this rule, but he is dismissive of his obligation to pay back the money he has borrowed. Indeed, acting much like an adolescent, he lies and schemes to avoid his creditors while he continues to spend money on gambling, clothes, and booze. His insulting and dismissive attitude toward the "rules of the game," so to speak, eventually leads to violence.

One night, Michael confronts Johnny Boy at the neighborhood bar and demands his money. Johnny Boy whips out a gun (unloaded), humiliates Michael verbally, and chases him out of the bar. Michael sets out to avenge the insult he has suffered at the hands of Johnny. Although Charlie tries to help Johnny Boy escape the inevitable retribution he knows Michael has planned, Michael and his hired gunman (played by Scorsese) hunt down the car with Charlie, Johnny Boy, and Johnny's cousin Teresa in it. Shots are fired and Johnny Boy gets hit in the neck. Charlie is less seriously injured.

Again using Harvey Keitel (in the role of Charlie) as his alter ego, Scorsese presents a finely honed story of young men on the streets of Little Italy who are trying to find their way within the community of men. As was the case in *Who's That Knocking at My Door?*, these young men, perhaps subconsciously, are struggling with the issue of what it means to be a man. Within this tough and harsh milieu of Little Italy, violence can explode at any moment.

Scorsese has commented on the biographical links in the film.[6] Not only was Scorsese, as a boy and adolescent, exposed to the kind of neighborhood gangsterism depicted in the film, but the character of Johnny Boy was drawn to resemble a relative of his. Scorsese alludes to a brother of his father as the "black sheep" of the family. Presumably, this man desecrated some aspect of the neighborhood code of honor and, according to Scorsese, this disrespect was considered a very serious matter.

3. Plot Summaries, Characters, and Themes 39

Martin Scorsese (*center*) giving directorial advice to (*left*) Robert De Niro in his role as Johnny Boy and (*right*) Harvey Keitel, as Charlie, during the filming of *Mean Streets* (Photofest).

Mean Streets is the first movie that Scorsese made with Robert De Niro. The collaboration between Scorsese and De Niro extended to seven other films. It seems apparent that Scorsese and De Niro had a special connection that included mutual understanding and empathy, and the two men understood very well the personalities of the characters played by De Niro.[7] Without exception, the eight characters played by De Niro are arrogant, selfish, and demanding men. Moreover, these characters represent men who are narcissistic and some of them are violent (see chapters 4 and 8). If, indeed, De Niro, and Keital before him, represent Scorsese's alter ego, it is interesting to speculate that these characterizations by Keitel and De Niro may have given expression to Scorsese's fantasies of how virile, strong, powerful, men should act. The genesis of these fantasies may have been Scorsese's observing and perhaps admiring the powerful men in his neighborhood, some of whom were outright criminals. This linking of the fictional with the personal Scorsese is discussed at greater length in chapters 1 and 5 as well as in the conclusion.

Italianamerican (1974)

The documentary *Italianamerican* features Scorsese's parents, Catherine and Charles. They are shown in their apartment talking about their Sicilian roots, the history of the neighborhood, and their families. The recipe for Mrs. Scorsese's tomato sauce is included.

Alice Doesn't Live Here Anymore (1974)

MAJOR CHARACTERS:
- Alice Graham Hyatt—Ellen Burstyn
- David—Kris Kristofferson
- Ben Eberhardt—Harvey Keitel
- Tommy Hyatt—Alfred Lutter
- Donald Hyatt—Billy Green Bush
- Flo—Diane Ladd
- Audrey—Jodie Foster
- Mel—Vic Tayback

After his success with *Mean Streets*, Scorsese was offered the opportunity to do *Alice* and encouraged to do so in order to show the film industry that he could direct women. The film chronicles the journey of a thirty-five-year-old woman, Alice, whose husband has died, and her efforts to make a new life for herself and her twelve-year son, Tommy.

The movie opens with a fantasy or memory of Alice as a child skipping along a path on her farm in Monterey, California. She is alone with her doll, and she dreams of being a singer in the mold of Alice Faye. Indeed, young Alice believes that she can be a better singer than her idol. Singing "You'll Never Know," she seemingly expresses a need to love and be loved. From the nearby farmhouse, her mother calls her to dinner saying, "Come in here before I beat the living daylights out of you." Alice's private and defiant response is a determined, "I'll show them, you wait and see." Included in the scene is a shadowy male figure, who probably represents her father, working in the front yard. Seen in silhouette at the kitchen table in the house is an older male, presumably her brother, as their mother is serving him food. Young Alice, who dreams of a show business career, seems to be set apart and different from the rest of the family. Monterey remains, in memory and in fantasy, the place where Alice was happy because she was at home and able to sing.

The adult, thirty-five-year-old Alice is left virtually penniless after the accidental death of her husband, Donald. Alice and her son, Tommy, leave New Mexico and begin a long drive to Monterey, California, where she hopes she can resume her singing career. During her years of marriage to her emotionally distant husband, Alice had put away her former dream of becoming a singer and had assumed the duties of a 1970s housewife and mother.

Alice and Tommy stop at Phoenix, Arizona, and Alice tries to get a job singing at a club. At the bar she is approached by a good-looking man, Ben Eberhardt. Reluctant at first to get involved with Ben because he is twenty-seven, she eventually relents and has a sexual fling with him.

A few days later, Ben's wife, Rita, comes to call on Alice and asks her to end her involvement with her husband. Alice, who had not known that Ben was married, agrees to stop seeing Ben. As the two women are talking with each other, Ben breaks into Alice's apartment by using his fist to break through the glass partition of her door, and he chases after his wife with a knife. He threatens Rita as well as Alice.

After Ben leaves, Alice and Tommy quickly pack and drive away from Phoenix in a rush.

Alice and Tommy stop next at Tucson, where Alice gets a job as a waitress in Mel's Diner. In Tucson Alice meets David, a divorced man who is a rancher. Eventually, David and Alice begin a relationship. David is willing to leave his ranch if she wants to pursue her singing career. The movie ends

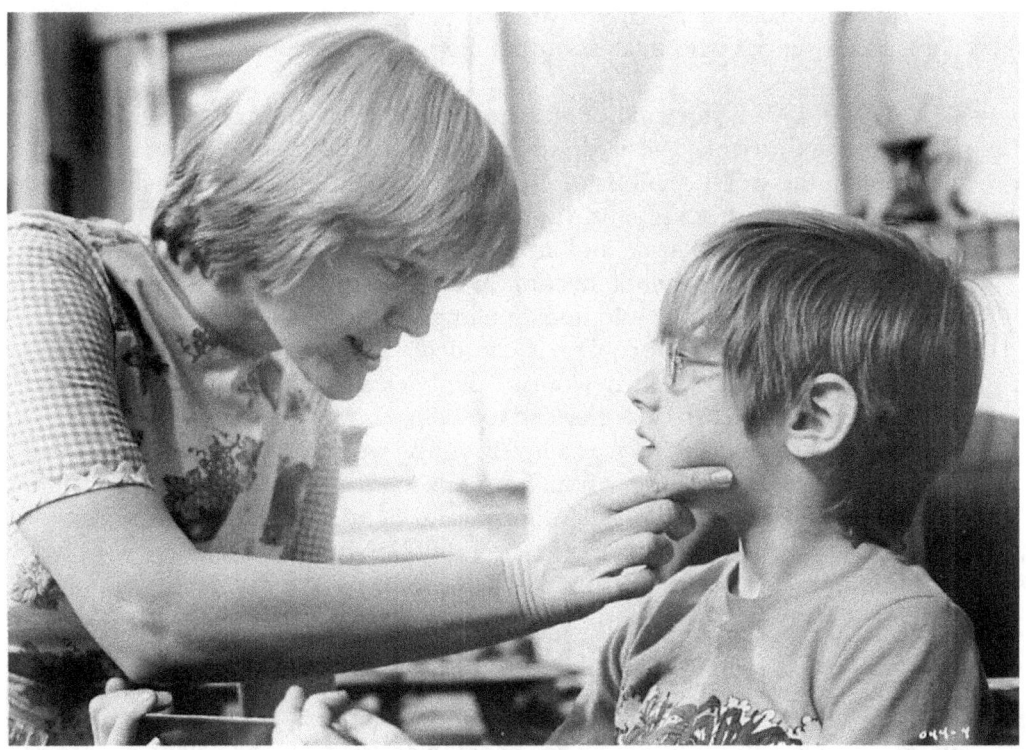

Alice (Ellen Burstyn) with her son, Tommy (Alfred Lutter), in a tender scene from *Alice Doesn't Live Here Anymore* (Photofest).

with Alice and Tommy deciding to remain in Tucson because she wants to live with David, and she reasons that she can pursue her career in Tucson just as well as in Monterey.

Burstyn's portrayal of Alice won her the Academy Award as best actress for 1974. Both Burstyn and Diane Ladd received Golden Globe nominations for best actress and supporting actress, respectively. For a discussion of Alice's character, see Chapter 10.

Taxi Driver (1976)

MAJOR CHARACTERS:
   Travis Bickle—Robert De Niro
   Iris—Jodie Foster
   Betsy—Cybill Shepherd
   Sport/Matthew, Iris's pimp—Harvey Keitel
   Charles Palantine—Leonard Harris
   Andy, the Gun salesman—Steven Prince
   Wizard—Peter Boyle
   Tom. the bartender—Albert Brooks
   Cab passenger who talks about killing his wife—Martin Scorsese

Taxi Driver is a story about an emotionally troubled man, Travis Bickle, who is the taxi driver. Travis drives his cab long hours, including at night, and often in the worst sections of New York City. In this milieu he is witness to the drunks, prostitutes, and junkies that inhabit the streets. Travis is a loner, a consummate diarist, and an obsessive about what he calls the "dirt" on the streets. One day while driving in an area where prostitutes ply their trade, a young, twelve-year-old hooker named Iris jumps into his cab and asks him to take her away. Before Travis can drive away, however, another man, presumably her pimp, pulls her out of the back seat. Travis does not forget Iris and what he perceives as her cry for help.

On another day, Travis sees a lovely young woman walking on the street, blonde and dressed in white, whom he likens to an angel. Betsy is a campaign worker for Senator Charles Palantine, a presidential candidate. Travis succeeds in making contact with her at the campaign headquarters and asks her out for coffee. She agrees. He then asks her for a second date, this time to go to a movie with him.

When Travis takes Betsy to a porno movie, she departs, feeling repulsed and disgusted, and rejects all of his attempts to make contact with her. Betsy's stunning rejection causes Travis to fragment or fall apart and he becomes enraged. In his mind, Betsy now has become entirely bad, like all of the other dirt on the streets. Travis plans a retaliation. First, he tries to get a shot at Palantine, but Travis is foiled by secret service agents. Travis changes course

3. Plot Summaries, Characters, and Themes

and seeks out the pimp, Matthew, who has turned Iris into a whore. Travis enters the house where Iris works and turns his guns on Matthew and the other men who are in the place. After the bloodbath, Travis seemingly wants to shoot himself, but he is out of bullets. Instead of facing criminal charges, Travis becomes a hero in the media because he saved a young woman from prostitution.

After he is released from the hospital and receives extensive and public acknowledgments of his heroic efforts to save Iris, Travis returns to his cab. One day, Betsy enters his taxi. She tries to make contact with him, but he remains emotionally detached and seemingly disinterested in her.

In *Taxi Driver* the madonna-whore complex is enacted more implicitly than in Scorsese's earlier films. At issue are Travis's perceptions of Betsy and Iris. In Travis's initial encounters with Betsy, he sees her as angelic, a virgin. However, after she rejects Travis, he perceives her as dirty, in effect, a whore. In counterpoint, Iris is the whore, whom Travis wants to save so she will become virgin-like.

Martin Scorsese with (*left*) Robert De Niro, in the role of Travis Bickle, on the set of *Taxi Driver* (Photofest).

Another theme in this film is the depiction of how the media and culture create heroes. Travis commits murder and mayhem and yet is hailed as a hero.

It is worth noting that Scorsese, who appeared in *Mean Streets* as Michael's gunman who shoots Johnny Boy, also appears in *Taxi Driver* as a passenger in Travis's taxi carrying a gun and revealing that he plans to kill his wife because she is being unfaithful to him. We may speculate that in playing these roles, Scorsese may have been venting his anger.

Scorsese was awarded the Palme d'Or at the Cannes Film Festival for *Taxi Driver*. De Niro received a Golden Globe nomination for his acting as did Paul Schrader for his screenplay.

New York, New York (1977)

MAJOR CHARACTERS:
> Francine Evans—Liza Minnelli
> Jimmy Doyle—Robert De Niro
> Tony Harwell—Lionel Stander
> Paul Wilson—Barry Primus
> Bernice—Mary Kay Place
> Frankie Harte—Georgie Auld
> Nicky—George Memmoli
> Record producer—Steven Prince

New York, New York is made in the style of a 1950s Hollywood musical extravaganza. The film was not successful at the box office, but it contains some of the most poignant relationship scenes and cogent depictions of a narcissistic personality found in the Scorsese opus. (See Chapter 4 for a discussion of narcissism.)

The story of *New York, New York* revolves around the relationship that develops between a talented saxophonist Jimmy Doyle and Francine Exans, a songstress. They meet during a mammoth party celebrating the end of World War II. Both are eager to resume their respective careers. The film follows the twists and turns of their relationship and careers. Francine and Jimmy eventually get married and work in the same band for a time. Their relationship suffers a dramatic turn when Francine becomes pregnant and decides to leave the traveling band and wait for the baby's arrival in New York. As explained in a detailed analysis of Jimmy's personality in Chapter 7, Francine's leaving Jimmy and the band has a psychological impact on Jimmy, and it contributes to his losing the leadership of the band.

As Francine and Jimmy wait together for the baby's arrival, Jimmy has liasons with other women, and the two quarrel. Adding to their anxieties, Francine and Jimmy are insecure about the fate of their careers.

Immediately after their child is born, (literally, while she is still in the hospital recovering from childbirth), Jimmy leaves Francine. Presumably, they eventually get a divorce. The film concludes years later, showing that both Francine and Jimmy have been successful in their careers.

The film illustrates that two creative individuals may have difficulties in evolving a successful marriage; Scorsese has indicated that this kind of conflict between career and family occurred in his life.[8] It is interesting to note that Scorsese ended a four-year relationship soon after the film was completed. Because this relational breakup was happening in his personal life, Scorsese may have seen himself as the character of Jimmy Doyle, who destroys a meaningful relationship because of his consummate need for attaining success and applause. Scorsese is currently in his fifth marriage, the other four having ended in divorce. It may be that like Jimmy, Scorsese was unable or unwilling to compromise his desire for success to expend the emotional energy needed to maintain an intimate relationship.

The character of Jimmy Doyle is an extraordinarily selfish and narcissistic man who cannot tolerate rejection in any form, including the success enjoyed by his wife. Thematically, the film shows how one can create a church of sorts by devotion to something in which one believes fervently. Jimmy's "church" is the world of jazz music.

New York, New York received a Golden Globe nomination for best picture (musical or comedy) and another for best original song. Both De Niro and Minnelli were nominated for their acting.

The Last Waltz (1978)

The documentary, *The Last Waltz*, presents the Band's—Rick Danko, Levon Helm, Garth Hudson, Richard Manuel, Robbie Robertson—final and all-star concert at the Winterland in San Francisco in 1976. Guest artists who appear at the concert include Eric Clapton, Bob Dylan, Neil Young, Ringo Starr, Neil Diamond, Joni Mitchell, and Muddy Waters. The movie, which commemorates the passing of a particular brand of music, includes footage from the band's first concert at the Winterland as well as interviews with musicians telling their story. The Band plays twelve of their best-known songs.

Scorsese grew up with a love for popular music, and in making this documentary he demonstrates his love for the rock music played by the Band. Scorsese has used music knowledgeably and extensively in his films.[9] Mark Jacobson has commented that Scorsese and Robertson have been friends for years and, indeed, that they were "bachelor coke fiends" in Los Angeles.[10]

Raging Bull (1980)

MAJOR CHARACTERS:

> Jake LaMotta (at various adult ages)—Robert De Niro
> Vickie LaMotta—Cathy Moriarty
> Joey LaMotta—Joe Pesci
> Salvy—Frank Vincent
> Tommy Como—Nicholas Colasanto
> Lenore LaMotta, Joey's wife—Theresa Saldana
> Mario—Mario Gallo
> Patsy—Frank Adonis
> Irma—Lori Anne Flax

Scorsese's highly acclaimed film was adapted from Jake LaMotta's autobiography of the same title. The film focuses on the adult life and boxing career of the former middleweight champion. With Robert De Niro in the title role, the film chronicles LaMotta's career from 1941, when he was an up-and-coming young fighter, to his becoming champion in 1949 and then losing the title to Sugar Ray Robinson in the 1950s. The story concludes with LaMotta's later years in retirement in Miami doing comedy acts in nightclubs.

LaMotta is depicted as a man who is determined that he will never suffer a knock-out. In his personal life, Jake is imperial and abusive with his first wife, Irma, as well as with his second, Vickie. He is also violent and self-destructive. Some parts of fourteen LaMotta fights are depicted in the movie, and because of the film's historical accuracy with regard to LaMotta's boxing career, it has the flavor of a documentary.

Scorsese has explained that De Niro brought the idea of this film to him and that he wanted to play the role of

Robert De Niro as prizefighter Jake LaMotta felling an opponent played by Kevin Mahon in the film (Photofest).

LaMotta. In the same interview, Scorsese reminds us that he never played sports when he was a child because he had asthma and, thus, had known nothing about boxing. He recounts having been taken to Madison Square Garden to watch his first fight as a prelude to making the film.[11] In *Raging Bull*, Scorsese focused the camera inside the ring to bring attention to the punches the fighters threw and absorbed. In other words, in watching the fight sequences, one is aware of what the fighters saw while they were boxing as well as the pain endured by them.

De Niro's portrayal of Jake LaMotta won him the Academy Award for best actor in 1980. Joe Pesci was nominated for supporting actor, and Scorsese received his first Academy Award nomination for film direction. *Raging Bull* also received seven Golden Globe nominations; De Niro won a Golden Globe and an Academy Award for best actor.

The King of Comedy (1982)

MAJOR CHARACTERS:
Rupert Pupkin—Robert De Niro
Jerry Langford—Jerry Lewis
Masha—Sandra Bernhard
Rita Keene—Diahnne Abbott
Television director—Martin Scorsese

The King of Comedy features another De Niro character, a childlike narcissist, who demands getting what he wants by whatever means he can concoct. The story centers on the extraordinary efforts of a man, Rupert Pupkin, to enter the world of celebrity. He is obsessed with television comedian Jerry Langford and wants to get on his show to display his own comedic ability. After failing to obtain an interview with Jerry through his office staff, Rupert and his cohort, Masha, obsessed fan of Langford, kidnap Jerry while he is walking on a New York street. Rupert and Masha take Jerry to Masha's apartment and threaten him if he does not allow Rupert to appear on his show that night. Rupert succeeds in getting on the show and does his comedy routine. He admits to the audience that he got on the show by kidnapping Jerry.

Rupert is arrested immediately after the tape of the show is aired, and he receives a relatively light prison sentence. Perhaps most significantly, Rupert gains considerable celebrity status because of his extraordinary efforts, including kidnapping Langford, to get on the show. His face appears on magazine covers, and his memoirs sell for millions. After he is released, Rupert becomes a huge star, the "King of Comedy."

The film makes a searing comment about this culture's love affair with celebrity and its creation of heroes. Moreover, the film depicts the life of a celebrity, on the one hand, and the experience of those who are outside, yearning to get in and become one of them, on the other hand. Jerry Langford, the celebrity and insider, cannot walk on the street without people accosting him, trying to get his attention, and touching him. His personal history becomes known to millions; he has essentially no privacy, and what little personal time he has is invaded by autograph seekers and fans in general. Indeed, Rupert actually finds out the location of Jerry's home in the country and arrives there with his girlfriend as if they had been invited. On the other side of the coin, Masha and Rupert, prototypical of outsiders, will stop at nothing to try to reach Jerry and become close to him or to become celebrities themselves. The film also shows the loneliness that a celebrity may suffer by being estranged from mainstream society. Moreover, the depictions of fans in the film suggest that in addition to their idolization of celebrities, fans feel envy, hostility, and hatred toward them.

The King of Comedy contains autobiographical allusions. Scorsese has said that he could identify with Pupkin with regard to his will and drive to succeed at any price.[12]

After Hours (1985)

MAJOR CHARACTERS:
    Paul Hackett—Griffin Dunne
    Marcy—Rosanna Arquette
    June—Verna Bloom
    Pepe—Thomas Chong
    Kiki—Linda Fiorentino
    Julie—Teri Garr
    Tom, the bartender—John Heard
    Neil—Richard Cheech Marin
    Gail—Catherine O'Hara

After a number of years of trying and failing to obtain the funding he needed to make *The Last Temptation of Christ*, by 1985 Scorsese was utterly frustrated. According to Scorsese, he decided to make *After Hours*, a relatively low-budget film and the property of Griffin Dunne, to show Hollywood that he could make a studio film in a relatively short time.[13]

The story involves the misadventures of another of Scorsese's lonely men, Paul Hackett, who enters into a community where he is an outsider. Because he does not belong, he is subjected to the paranoidal suspiciousness of the insiders, who eventually threaten his life.

Paul meets a young woman, Marcy, at an all-night cafeteria. She invites him to the apartment in SoHo where she is staying. Paul goes home and decides to phone her. She suggests that he come to her place although it is almost midnight. In spite of the late hour, Paul decides to take her up on her invitation.

Paul's encounter with Marcy is the first of several that he has with women in SoHo who first entice him and then frighten, abandon, and betray him. These experiences send him spirally into utter confusion, chaos, and paranoia. Indeed, from the time Paul gets into a cab to ride to SoHo and meets up with Marcy until he is back at his workplace the next morning, Paul has a series of bizarre adventures. It is as if in going to SoHo Paul enters an "Alice in Wonderland" world. The fact that these adventures occur during the hours that most people are asleep imbues Paul's experiences with a dreamlike or, more correctly, a nightmarish quality. The film blurs the boundaries between illusion and reality.

In SoHo, Paul crosses the path of a number of hysterical people who consider him not only an intruder, but indeed, the thief who has been breaking into and robbing apartments in the neighborhood. Paul must run to escape the mob and save his life. Ultimately, by virtue of another set of misadventures, Paul is deposited at his workplace the following morning.[14]

Paul loses his money, a twenty dollar bill, and almost his life during the harrowing cab ride that takes him from his home to the apartment in SoHo where Marcy is staying with her friend Kiki. He loses his shirt at Kiki's. In

Paul Hackett (Griffin Dunne) and Marcy (Rosanna Arquette) in a scene from *After Hours* (Photofest).

Marcy's room, where he expects to have sex, he smokes pot or some other drug that alters his mood. Because of his childhood memories about a hospital burn ward, Paul becomes frightened about the possibility that Marcy may have been a burn victim. He leaves Marcy without explanation and tries to get home by subway, but he is unable to do so because he does not have the full fare. Caught in a raging downpour, Paul goes into a bar where Tom, the bartender, offers to give him money for the subway. However, Tom's register is locked and he tells Paul that he left the combination for opening the lock in his apartment. Paul is desperate to get some money and offers to go to Tom's apartment and get the combination for him. Tom and Paul exchange house keys, Paul giving Tom his as a form of collateral. In the process of entering and leaving Tom's apartment, Paul attracts the attention of Tom's neighbors, who suspect that he is the burglar they have been seeking who has been vandalzing apartments in the neighborhood.

When Paul returns to the bar with the combination, he finds that the door is locked. Julie, the blonde bar waitress who is standing on the sidewalk nearby, invites him to her apartment. She entices Paul while drawing a sketch of his face. However, when Paul decides to leave, she becomes angry, and in retaliation for what she perceives as Paul's abandonment, she converts the sketch into "wanted" posters. Soon thereafter, she begins distributing the posters around the neighborhood. These posters essentially identify Paul as the infamous burglar.

After he leaves Julie's apartment, Paul returns to Marcy's and discovers her dead body in her bed; Marcy has committed suicide. Paul returns to the bar and learns from Tom that Marcy was Tom's girlfriend. Paul feels guilty and afraid because he assumes that Marcy killed herself because he left her without explanation. When he was leaving Kiki's place after finding Marcy's body, Paul saw a twenty dollar bill attached to one of Kiki's sculptures, and he grabs it. Since he has money again, Paul tries to get a cab to take him home. However, Paul loses this money as well, this time to the same cab driver who had brought him to SoHo in the first place.

Gail, another blonde woman, alights from the cab. She offers to mend his arm after she had injured it. Finding a piece of newsprint stuck to his arm, she suggests burning it off. This idea terrifies Paul, and he wants out. Gail is the driver of a "Mister Softee" ice cream truck, and she becomes convinced that Paul is the wanted burglar. She arouses the neighborhood vigilante mob to begin chase to find and hold Paul until the authorities are summoned. Paul tries to escape by going to the club Berlin, where he knows Kiki and her boyfriend are spending the evening.

When Paul first enters the club, he is grabbed by a number of young men who force him into a chair. Paul loses some of his hair because it is Mohawk haircut night. He runs from the club but is seen and chased by the vigilante mob. Paul now fears for his life. In frustration and terror, he kneels on the street, and looking up to the sky, asks "God" what he wants from him:

"I just wanted to meet a nice girl. Now I have to die for it." Tom, who earlier had befriended Paul, betrays him to the mob by telling them where Paul is.

Paul's final life-threatening encounter occurs with a blonde woman named June, who is almost alone in the club Berlin and appears to be passive and kind. Yet another sculptress whose studio is down the stairs from the club Berlin, June saves Paul from the mob by encasing him in a plaster-of-Paris, full-body covering that makes him look like one of her sculptures. However, when the danger is past and the mob has left her studio, she refuses to remove the plaster and free him. Indeed, June covers the mouth opening of the cast so that Paul cannot speak or call for help. The actual burglars enter the scene and take the plaster-encased Paul onto their truck believing it to be a work of art. As the truck races toward the uptown area, the plastered–Paul sculpture falls from the truck and onto the street directly in front of the building where Paul works. The plaster breaks apart, and Paul emerges from the cracked plaster like a chicken emerging from an egg or cocoon, symbolic of his release or redemption from a night of suffering.

After Hours interweaves sexual innuendo with religious allusions. Paul wants to meet a nice girl with whom he hopes to have sex. As his subsequent sufferings suggest, he is punished, in a religious sense, for his sins of sexual desire and sexual fantasies by incurring the fires of hell, represented by the allusions to fire and burning in the film. His trip into a wished-for "heaven," which turns into "hell," begins with a frightening cab ride. Paul enters into "hell" (or SoHo) by means of the keys Kiki hurls down to him. In other scenes, keys play a prominent role in symbolizing his sense of home and security. The imagery of the keys in the film is representative of the biblical Jesus holding the keys to the Kingdom of Heaven, which represents redemption or salvation.

In the course of his odyssey through SoHo, Paul loses his shirt, his capacity to get home, and his reputation as a good and decent man as he is persecuted by a mob of insiders from the neighborhood. Declaring him to be a burglar, the vigilantes, led by a screeching "Mister Softee" ice-cream truck, chase him, and the vehemence of the mob suggests that they want to string him up.

Beset as Scorsese was by Christian fundamentalists (and the Catholic Church) for wanting to portray the human Jesus as having desires in *The Last Temptation of Christ*, Scorsese may have felt like a mob was out for his neck. The people who strongly opposed Scorsese's making the movie seemed to be accusing him of being a burglar who was trying to rob Jesus of his divinity as well as aiming to rob them of the biblical Jesus whom they revered.

There are a number of other allusions in *After Hours* that analogize Paul Hackett's sufferings to the passions of the biblical Christ figure, reflecting Scorsese's predilection for religious imagery. While Paul is in the bar where Tom is the bartender, a neighbor knocks on the window to alert Tom to a burglary. Tom tells Paul that this is the third knock that has occurred, announcing the third burglary. In the biblical story of Jesus, before the cock crows twice, Jesus is denied by Peter three times. Tom, originally supportive and helpful, as Peter was to Jesus, eventually betrays Paul and, like Judas, tells the mob where they can find Paul to "kill" him.

Paul is betrayed as well by Julie, Gail, and June; he is shorn, wounded, and disregarded. In one scene he falls on his knees and pleads to the sky above, "What do you want from me? I'm just a word processor for Christ's sake." His appeal to the symbolic god in the heavens is reminiscent of that of Jesus who, as he was dying on the cross, asks of his God, "Why have you forsaken me?"

Paul is immobilized when he is cast into cement-like statue by June. This would-be sculpture is taken by two thieves onto their truck-van. The metaphor of the crucifixion comes to mind with regard to the two thieves who were crucified on either side of Jesus on Golgotha.

The fact that Paul is an outsider in SoHo and his encountering bizarre people who consider him a threat seem to parallel Scorsese's attempt to make *The Last Temptation of Christ*. Like Paul, Scorsese was a Hollywood outsider, and he encountered suspiciousness and opposition as if he were a thief.

Scorsese won the award for best director at Cannes for *After Hours*. Griffin Dunne was nominated for a Golden Globe as best actor in a musical or comedy.

"Mirror, Mirror" (1986)

MAJOR CHARACTERS:
    Jordan Manmouth—Sam Waterston
    Karen—Helen Shaver
    Dick Cavett—Dick Cavett
    Jordan's Phantom—Tim Robbins

In an episode in Steven Spielberg's television series, *Amazing Stories*, horror writer Jordan Manmouth arrives home after a trip and finds a young man camped outside his apartment. He tells the man to leave and goes into the apartment hoping to have a relaxing evening. There he sees a phantom reflected in a mirror; Jordan feels that this phantom wants to kill him. These frightening images haunt Jordan every time he looks at a reflective surface. Ultimately, Jordan feels that he has become the monster; that is, he perceives the phantom as his reflection when he looks in the mirror. Jordan jumps out the window to escape from it and, in effect, himself.

It appears that the horrible and frightening images that Jordan has created in his stories have come back to haunt him in his mind. Perhaps these images have been internalized and now are being projected onto reflective surfaces, including mirrors. In a related sense, it seems that Jordan has entered into the image of the phantom and is so obsessed by it that he *becomes* the phantom. This theme of a man so obsessed with and consumed by an image that he becomes one with it was depicted by Scorsese in his student short, *What's a Nice Girl Like You Doing in a Place Like This?*

The Color of Money (1986)

MAJOR CHARACTERS:
   Eddie Felson—Paul Newman
   Vincent Lauria—Tom Cruise
   Carmen—Mary Elizabeth Mastrantonio
   Janelle—Helen Shaver

The Color of Money is a sequel of sorts to *The Hustler* (1961), at least insofar as the life and career of Eddie Felson (Paul Newman) are concerned. *The Hustler* ended with pool shark Eddie Felson (also played by Paul Newman) having defeated Minnesota Fats (Jackie Gleason), the straight-pool guru, and pocketing a large wad of money. However, Eddie's former manager and the area's gambling boss, Bert Gordon (George C. Scott), demands half of his winnings or, as he threatens, Eddie will suffer broken fingers and perhaps arms as well. Eddie reminds Bert of how they contributed to Sara's (played by Piper Laurie) suicide, an event that led to Eddie's gaining the so-called "character" that Bert had said he needed in order to beat Minnesota Fats. Gordon relents on his demand for money, but he warns Eddie not to enter a big-time pool hall ever again.

The Scorsese movie reintroduces us to Eddie Felson twenty-five years older and a successful business man. Eddie watches a young man named Vincent Lauria play pool and knows that the man has a special talent. He decides to take Vincent under his wing and turn him into a first-class hustler and pool player. With Eddie's bankroll, Eddie, Vincent, and Carmen, Vincent's girlfriend, travel together for several weeks, aiming to end up in Atlantic City where a major nine-ball tournament will be held.

As he watches Vincent play, however, Eddie's own desire to play is rekindled. He tells Vincent to go his separate way, and he begins to prepare his body and mind for the tournament ahead.

Eddie and Vincent both win their early rounds and meet each other in the semifinals. Eddie wins, but before he can totally relish his victory, Vincent and Carmen come to his room and give him his share of the money. It seems that Vincent had won a lot of money by throwing his match against Eddie. The next day, Eddie forfeits his match. Later, he confronts Vincent and demands his best game. The film ends as they are about to begin their game of pure pool.

Vincent Lauria (Tom Cruise) (*Left*) and Eddie Felson (Paul Newman) prepare to play a game of pool from *The Color of Money* (Photofest).

Both Mastrantonio and Newman received Golden Globe nominations; Newman won the Academy Award for best actor for his portrayal of Eddie Felson.

The Last Temptation of Christ (1988)

MAJOR CHARACTERS:
    Jesus—Willem Dafoe
    Mary Magdalene—Barbara Hershey
    Judas—Harvey Keitel
    Zealot—Paul Greco
    Pontius Pilate—David Bowie
    Mary, mother of Jesus—Verna Bloom
    Peter, an Apostle—Victor Argo
    Centurion—Steve Shill
    Saul/Paul—Harry Dean Stanton
    Devil in the guise of a girl angel—Juliette Caron
    John, an Apostle—Michael Been

John the Baptist—Andre Gregory
Jeroboam—Barry Miller

The film was based on the book *The Last Temptation of Christ* by Nikos Kazantzakis. It is a fictional story that shows the human side of the man whom Christians venerate as the Son of God. The film depicts Jesus as searching for his place in the mystery of life, beginning to recognize his divinity, preaching, and finally, accepting his death by crucifixion. At this stage, the story diverges strongly from the biblical accounts of Jesus. In the Kazantzakis story as well as the film, while Jesus is suffering on the cross, he is tempted by the devil to come down to earth and begin a totally human life with Mary Magdalene. The film ends years later with Jesus, as an old man, realizing anew his divine mission as saviour and resuming his place on the cross. The film and its implications with regard to the Scorsese opus are discussed in detail in Chapter 11. This fictional portrayal of the Christ-figure was important to Scorsese, and he strove to obtain studio funding for the film for some years.

The Last Temptation of Christ earned Scorsese his second Academy Award nomination for best director. Barbara Hershey received a Golden Globe nomination.

"Life Lessons" (1989)

MAJOR CHARACTERS:
Lionel Dobie—Nick Nolte
Paulette—Rosanna Arquette
Phillip Fowler—Patrick O'Neal

"Life Lessons" is Scorsese's contribution to *New York Stories* (1989) (segment 1), which also includes short films made by Woody Allen and Francis Ford Coppola. The film features a fiftyish and well-known New York artist, Lionel Dobie. Dobie shares his extensive studio space with his twenty-two-year-old assistant, Paulette, a would-be artist.

Realizing that she does not have the talent to become a good artist, Paulette wants to move out and return home, but Lionel selfishly tries to persuade her to stay. He needs her and the sexual tension she evokes in him to produce his artistic creations. She decides that she will stay if she and Lionel stop all sexual activity. Lionel agrees to her terms. Nevertheless, as she tries to live her own life on her terms, Lionel watches her every move, gives her unwanted advice, and interferes with her decisions. Ultimately, Paulette decides that she must leave to preserve her identity. Coincidentally, at about the time that Paulette leaves, Lionel meets another fledgling artist at a party, a young woman, who is excited about the prospect of moving in with the great artist and learning from his life lessons.

GoodFellas (1990)

MAJOR CHARACTERS:

    Jimmy, the "Gent," Conway—Robert De Niro
    Henry Hill—Ray Liotta
    Tommy DeVito—Joe Pesci
    Paulie Cicero—Paul Sorvino
    Karen Hill—Lorraine Bracco
    Frankie Carbone—Frank Sivero
    Billy Batts—Frank Vincent
    Tutti Cicero—Frank DiLeo

GoodFellas chronicles three decades of the life of a family of gangsters who live and run their operations in New York City. The film is based on a true story, *Wiseguy*, by Nicholas Pileggi. The term "goodfellas" is another word for wiseguys or "one of us." The focal characters of the film are Henry Hill, Jimmy the "Gent" Conway, and Tommy DeVito.

The film depicts the attraction that gangsters have to people who have very little in the way of prestige and material goods. It shows, specifically, how Henry Hill, as a boy and adolescent, idealizes the gangsters in his neighborhood and wants to be one of them, to belong to a group that he perceives as very special.

Henry does, indeed, become a wiseguy and meets Jimmy Conway, a man noted for his expertise in hijacking, and Tommy DeVito, a psychopath who has an explosive temper. As a young man, Henry makes a lot of money and attracts his wife-to-be, Karen, because in her eyes he is an exciting guy whom people respect.

After a number of years of living the criminal life, the three men, Henry, Jimmy, and Tommy, have become greedy, in effect, addicted to the money and power that has been available to them. Henry also becomes addicted to drugs. Eventually, their greed destroys them as well as the gangster family. Henry turns state's evidence and enters the witness protection program. Tommy gets killed because he broke a rule of the mob. Jimmy goes to prison.

Thematically, this film shows that gangsterism creates its own church, so to speak. Its members adhere to a common belief system, spend much of their time together, and feel that they are special—better than other people—because of their membership in this elite society. This group of insiders, moreover, feels contempt for and is suspicious about those outside their group.

From a biographical perspective, Scorsese grew up in a neighborhood that had gangsters who were viewed as having special power and privilege. Scorsese has acknowledged his attraction to the criminal life, and as he stated, he assumes that a number of other people are similarly attracted to the mob life.[15]

GoodFellas was nominated for six Academy Awards including best directing for Scorsese and best writing (screenplay based on material from another medium) for Scorsese and Nicholas Pileggi. Joe Pesci won an Academy Award as best supporting actor. The movie also received five Golden Globe nominations including one for best picture (drama); Scorsese was nominated for film direction and for writing (together with Nicholas Pileggi). Bracco and Pesci were similarly cited.

Cape Fear (1991)

MAJOR CHARACTERS:
>Max Cady—Robert De Niro
>Sam Bowden—Nick Nolte
>Leigh Bowden—Jessica Lange
>Danielle—Juliette Lewis
>Claude Kersek, private detective—Joe Don Baker
>Lori Davis—Illeana Douglas
>Lee Heller, Cady's attorney—Gregory Peck
>Lieutenant Elgart—Robert Mitchum
>Judge—Martin Balsam
>Tom Broadbent—Fred Dalton Thompson

The 1991 film is Scorsese's remake of the 1961 thriller, *Cape Fear*, that starred Gregory Peck as Sam Bowden, an attorney, and Robert Mitchum as Max Cady, a sadistic ex-con who is bent on gaining revenge against Bowden, the man he holds responsible for his imprisonment. In Scorsese's film, Robert De Niro plays the role of Cady; Nick Nolte portrays Sam Bowden.

Released from prison after serving a fourteen-year term for aggravated sexual assault of a sixteen-year-old girl, Cady arrives in the town of South Essex (presumably in North Carolina) where the well-to-do Bowden lives with his wife, Leigh, and his fifteen-year-old daughter, Danielle (or Danny). Cady first makes himself evident to Bowden, appearing outside the shop where the Bowdens have gone for ice cream after seeing a movie. The next day Cady appears at Sam's car and reminds Sam of their former association.

The story is set in July, on the days immediately before and after the Fourth. Because Danny was suspended from school for smoking marijuana, she has to attend summer school classes to avoid expulsion. Sam and Leigh have had marital problems and although they have undergone counseling, Leigh is still angry with Sam for his past sexual liaisons. Danny isolates herself when she hears her parents quarreling. A precocious and restless teenager who has begun to be aware of her budding sexuality, Danny displays her nubile body around and outside the house by wearing clothes in a casual but provocative way. The family likes to vacation on their houseboat moored in an isolated section of a river on Cape Fear, but when Sam proposes that they take two weeks off and go to their houseboat—his initial idea to get some distance from Cady—Leigh begs off, citing that she wants to work on her travel agency business and that Danny needs to finish her summer classes. Leigh has a low opinion of Sam's work as an attorney, referring to his knowing how to "fight dirty." Early in the story, it is apparent that Danny idealizes her father; she tells him that she believes that he could have boxed successfully and defeated the "loser" in the movie theater (who was Cady) who annoyed them with his cigar smoke and loud and boisterous laughter the night before.

Cady begins to carry out his plan to avenge himself by destroying Sam, his reputation, and his family. He poisons the family dog, frightens Leigh by appearing seemingly out of nowhere, beats and rapes Sam's friend, Lori, and lures Danny into a private and seductive encounter with him.

Cady, moreover, sets out to blacken Bowden's professional reputation and to strip him of the respect of his colleagues. Unbeknownst to Bowden, Cady taperecords Bowden making a threat to him and uses this recording in court to obtain a restraining order against Bowden. Since Bowden foolishly had paid three bullies to beat up on Cady after he made the threat, an action recommended by Sam's private detective, Kersek, as a way to force Cady to leave town, Cady appears in court bruised and seemingly wounded. Cady's attorney, Lee Heller, (who Sam had hoped to retain for himself to get a restraining order against Cady), files a complaint against Bowden with the American Bar Association ethics committee, accusing Sam of threatening and harming Cady. Bowden thus faces disbarment on the charge of moral turpitude.

At every turn of the drama, each move that Sam makes to try to rid himself of Cady and the danger that he represents is countered by Cady. Indeed, Cady gets the upper hand every time Sam takes an action against him. Frustrated and terrified, Sam wants Kersek to help him subdue Cady. They set up a trap so Cady will believe that Sam has gone to Atlanta to appear at a hearing of the ethics committee. The viewer sees that Cady takes steps to make certain that Sam is out of town and, thus, his wife and daughter appear to be alone in their home. Sam and Kersek expect Cady to break into the house with the intention of harming Leigh and Danny.

Kersek sets up trip wires throughout the house, including at all of the entry points, to alert him when Cady tries to break in. Kersek sits guard in the living room with a gun in his hand. Despite these elaborate precautions, Cady gets inside the Bowden house and kills the maid, Graecela, as well as Kersek with his own gun.

From their bedroom, Sam and Leigh hear the gunshot and rush downstairs. They find the bodies of the two victims in pools of blood. Sam steps into the murder scene, gets blood on his shoes and clothing, and handles the gun. Leigh and Sam do not call the police, however, because they believe that Sam will be accused of the murders.

The three Bowdens flee from their home and make their way to their houseboat moored in Cape Fear. As the Bowdens drive off toward the river, the viewer sees that Cady has strapped himself to the undercarriage of their SUV. Thus, as the family flees toward their isolated hideaway, they are bringing Cady along with them to their secret hideaway. Sam calls the police from the dock and tells them about the murders at his home. He refuses to turn himself in, and he becomes a fugitive from justice.

The Bowdens get to their houseboat, moored in an isolated cove, and as the women are settling in for a long stay while Sam stands outside with a gun, Cady appears and takes Sam's gun from him. In the ensuing struggle, Sam is knocked unconscious. Cady goes inside the houseboat and imprisons the Bowdens as he was once imprisoned. In addition, Cady cuts the boat loose from its moorings.

While Sam is unconscious, Cady threatens the two women with rape. A ferocious struggle ensues. Ultimately, what subdues Cady is what might be termed an "act of God" rather than the actions of the Bowdens alone. As the unanchored boat is tossed to and fro by wind and driving rain, it begins to break up as it crashes against rocks. These violent motions cause the Bowdens and Cady to slip, fall, and topple about inside the houseboat. Cady loses control of the gun and the handcuffs with which he had planned to manacle Sam. This action gives Sam the opportunity to grab the handcuffs and use them to attach Cady's leg to a pole in the boat. Leigh and Danny jump into the river and swim to safety.

Scorsese reformulated several aspects of the original *Cape Fear*, some of which affect the action sequences, and others the characterizations. For example, in the 1991 film, the Bowdens speak of having been to a marital counselor and Leigh Bowden has a travel agency business. The idea of a couple going to marital counseling or a woman owning her own business would not have been consonant with the cultural mainstream of the 1961 film.

In the 1961 version of the film, moreover, Sam Bowden was an eyewitness to Cady's crime, and he is depicted as a good and honorable man who did his duty in helping to prosecute and convict Cady. This earlier rendition of Bowden is of a man who has done nothing unethical: he feels no guilt, and he is understandably justified in protecting himself and his family from the evil Cady. The viewer is entirely sympathetic to Bowden in that story.

In the 1991 film, Bowden was Cady's attorney, and he withheld information from the court. This information about Cady's victim having been promiscuous, if revealed, might have exonerated Cady or at least might have contributed to his receiving a lighter sentence. Scorsese showed his psychological acuity in reformulating the character of Sam Bowden as feeling guilty. Adding the dimension of guilt to the characterization of Bowden provides for the presence of conflict within him and the exacerbation of his emotional distress. The sympathy of the audience for Sam is similarly conflicted. Sam Bowden is and feels guilty for suppressing information that would have benefited his client, that is, for his betrayal of Cady. Sam defends his action on the basis of the brutality with which Cady beat and raped his teenaged victim. Nevertheless, Sam violated his oath as a defense attorney, and, in effect, acted as Cady's judge and jury. At the outset of the drama, Bowden knows what he did, but he does not realize that Cady knows as well. When he defended Cady originally, Cady was illiterate, and Bowden believes that Cady was and is simply too ignorant to know the truth.

When Cady first makes himself evident to Bowden, appearing outside the shop where the Bowdens had gone for ice cream, although it is not clear whether Sam knows who he is, Sam seems to feel uncomfortable. The next day, Cady appears at Sam's car and has a conversation with him. That night, when Leigh awakens from a dream, she sees a man (Cady) sitting on the wall that bounds their property, his appearance illuminated in the night sky by the Fourth of July fireworks display. Having been alerted by Leigh to the presence of the man who, he presumes, is Cady, near his property, Sam becomes angry as well as alarmed and talks to his law partner, Tom, the next day about getting a restraining order against Cady. Tom recommends that Sam engage Lee Heller, the "best criminal lawyer in the state." Sam agrees to contact him. In this conversation, Sam reveals to Tom that he "buried" information that could have helped his client, but he still does not believe that Cady knows anything about this matter. Tom's reaction to Sam's revelation indicates his disdain of Sam. In a subsequent encounter between Cady and Bowden that takes place in downtown New Essex, Sam offers Cady $10,000 to leave town and to "compensate" Cady for his fourteen years of "suffering." Under the guise of trying to encourage him to get out of town, this offer is, in reality, Bowden's attempt to assuage his guilt, and Cady realizes this. Sam's feeling guilty for having done something that was unethical and caused his client undue suffering exacerbates his fear that his secret will be discovered by colleagues, his family, and the legal profession, a discovery that could lead not only to his being shamed but also to his disbarment. Although Sam consciously believes that Cady is unaware of what Sam did, Sam unconsciously has a sense that Cady knows something. Sam is concerned that his former client might be planning to harass and, perhaps, harm him in retaliation. Sam fears about his unethical behavior being discovered by his social milieu and being perceived as one who has fallen in their esteem, in turn, contribute to his reckless and foolish behavior in dueling with his brilliant adversary.

Scorsese and De Niro also reformulated the character of Max Cady so that he is much more horrifying than the original character played by Mitchum. In Scorsese's film, Cady is a religious fanatic, diabolically clever, and seemingly psychotic. The Mitchum character, although a violent and sadistic man, lacks the fanatical and diabolical qualities that De Niro and Scorsese added to their characterization of Cady. Both of the Cady characters are bent on revenge, but adding the religious fanaticism imbues the

De Niro character with a sense of self-righteousness and relentlessness because he fancies himself as the avenging angel of God.

Both Robert De Niro and Juliette Lewis received Golden Globe nominations for their portrayals in *Cape Fear*.

The Age of Innocence (1993)

MAJOR CHARACTERS:

> Newland Archer—Daniel Day-Lewis
> Ellen Olenska—Michelle Pfeiffer
> May Welland—Winona Ryder
> Mrs. Welland—Geraldine Chaplin
> Mrs. Mingott—Miriam Margolyes
> Regina Beaufort—Mary Beth Hurt
> Julius Beaufort—Stuart Wilson

Based on the novel by Edith Wharton, *The Age of Innocence* is a costume drama. The setting is fashionable New York society during the 1870s. Joanne Woodward serves as the narrator of the film. Scorsese's movie remains faithful to the Wharton novel, and he artfully replicated the costumes, food, manners, utensils and decorations used at the dining tables of the time.

Newland Archer, a self-controlled and dignified member of this elite society, is the major male character; the Countess Ellen Olenska is the female lead. Newland is engaged to marry May Welland, Ellen's cousin.

Ellen has just returned from having spent many years in Europe as the wife of the Count Olenska. She has left her husband and arrived back in New York to live near her family. Her family is bracing itself for the scandal that may develop because of Ellen's unorthodox behavior in leaving her husband.

Newland and Ellen meet and eventually fall in love, although this is never stated explicitly. In spite of his feelings for Ellen, Newland goes forward with his plan to marry May. Moreover, it becomes clear that Ellen would not have asked Newland to betray his engagement since this would have hurt her cousin May.

About a year or two after the wedding, Newland and Ellen have occasion to be alone with one another again. It is apparent that their feelings for each other are strong, but neither can face the prospect of destroying Newland's marriage. Nevertheless, Newland suggests to Ellen that she become his mistress. At about this time, May realizes that her husband and Ellen have amorous feelings for each other. She purposely tells Ellen that she is pregnant, although she is not certain about this, and Ellen decides to leave for Europe and remain there. As it happens, May is actually pregnant. When Newland is finally ready to confront the truth and tell his wife that he is in love with Ellen, May tells him about her pregnancy and Ellen's planned departure.

Once Newland knows about May's pregnancy, he realizes that there is no hope for a relationship with Ellen, and he accepts his destiny as a husband and father.

Consistent with the mores of that time and place as well as class and position, the characters keep their emotions in check, thus maintaining an air of controlled decorum at all times. Much is left unsaid in this milieu; symbols and signs have special meaning, known only to the insiders.

In discussing the film, Scorsese applauded Archer for his sense of responsibility to his family.[16] This laudatory comment by Scorsese is remarkable since Archer invited Ellen to become his mistress in spite of the fact that he was married to May. Indeed, the storyline suggests that Ellen and Archer would have consummated their relationship if Ellen had not decided to leave for Europe after she learned about May's pregnancy. Scorsese's comment about Archer suggests that Scorsese is unable to perceive Ellen as the true hero(ine) of the story, the one who refuses to dishonor herself and her family by engaging in a sexual liaison with Archer.

The Age of Innocence received five Academy Award nominations, including one for best screenplay (based on material from another medium) for Scorsese and Jay Cocks. The film was nominated for a Golden Globe as best picture (drama), and Scorsese received a nomination for best director. Michele Pfeiffer and Winona Ryder were nominated as best actress and best supporting actress, respectively; Ryder won the award in her category.

Casino (1995)

MAJOR CHARACTERS:
- Sam Rothstein—Robert De Niro
- Ginger—Sharon Stone
- Nicky Santoro—Joe Pesci
- Lester Diamond—James Woods
- Billy Sherbert—Don Rickles
- Andy Stone—Alan King
- Jennifer Santoro—Melissa Prophet
- Frank Marino—Frank Vincent
- Don Ward—John Bloom

Scorsese's 1995 gangster movie, *Casino*, adapted from a true story of the same title by Nicholas Pileggi, has a religious motif. The film depicts the mob as having broadened its domain to Las Vegas in 1988. The focal character, Sam "Ace" Rothstein, is given a share of paradise, as symbolized by the Tangiers, a 62.7 million Vegas hotel and gambling casino. Sam's gangster pal, Nicky Santoro, a psychopath who was originally hired by the mob bosses to protect Sam, decides to set up an independent crime ring in Las Vegas and live there. Both Sam and Nicky serve as narrators in the film.

The casino and its system of control, exercised by the mob bosses from the midwest, is an ecclesiastical system of sorts. This "church" worships gambling and money; its sacraments include skims to the mob bosses and payoffs to the right politicians in Nevada. Keeping the church stable requires the right balance of give-and-take among the bosses, the workers, the police, and the politicians. Paradise or heaven on earth, as defined by getting unlimited amounts of money from the suckers who came to the casino to gamble, is lost as the demigods—Rothstein and Santoro—become hungrier and hungrier for the forbidden fruit, greedier and greedier for unrestrained power and megalomaniacal control. *Casino* is especially masterful in its depiction of a system built on greed. Inevitably, the greed breeds violence, which once unleashed, spins out of control. In the narrative, Nicky relates that they "fucked it up," and, ultimately, destroyed their paradise on earth.

Sharon Stone won a Golden Globe as best actress in a drama; Scorsese received a nomination for the film direction of *Casino*.

A Century of Cinema: A Personal Journey with Martin Scorsese through American Movies (1995)

In this four-hour documentary Scorsese offers his personal view of American films through the 1950s. *A Century of Cinema* consists of three parts, all narrated by Scorsese: Part I is titled the "Director as Storyteller" and features westerns (a favorite of Scorsese when he was a boy), gangster films, and musicals. Part II is titled The Director as Illusionist and Smuggler;" and Part III is The Director as Iconoclast."

Collaborating with cowriter and codirector Michael Henry Wilson, Scorsese, a learned student and teacher/historian of cinema, presents the work of a number of filmmakers. Using archival footage as well as interviews, he discusses the visions of noted directors including that of Frank Capra, John Cassavetes, Francis Ford Coppola, John Ford, Howard Hawks, Fritz Lang, George Lucas, Arthur Penn, Nicholas Ray, Douglas Sirk, King Vidor, Orson Welles, and Billy Wilder. Using film clips from the movies that most moved and intrigued him, Scorsese relates how a number of films affected his work as a director.

Kundun (1997)

MAJOR CHARACTERS:
    the adult Dalai Lama—Tetzin Thuthob Tsarong
    Dalai Lama, age twelve—Gyurme Tethong

Dalai Lama, age five—Tulku Jamyang Kunga Yenzio
Dalai Lama, age two—Tenzin Yeshi Paichang
Mother—Tencho Gyalpo
Father—Tsewang Migyur
Messenger—Lobsang Gyatso
Reting Rimpoche—Sonam Phuntsok
Taktra Rimpoche—Tsewang Jigme Tsarong
Ling Rimpoche—Tenzin Trinley

A religious and historical epic, *Kundun* opens by portraying the early life of the fourteenth Dalai Lama and ends with the spiritual leader as an adult leaving Tibet and seeking exile in India. Scorsese used Chinese and Tibetan people as actors to add to the film's air of authenticity and historical accuracy. This film is an apt example of Scorsese's cinematic neorealism, that is, the blurring of the boundaries between documentary and fiction

The Dalai Lama is considered to be the reincarnation of the Buddha of Compassion. The film's opening captions inform viewers that the sons of Genghis Khan gave the Dalai Lama his name, which means "Oceans of Wisdom." Moreover, viewers are reminded that the Tibetans have practiced nonviolence for more than 1,000 years.

In 1933 the thirteenth Dalai Lama died, and a search is begun to find the child who would be the next spiritual leader. A holy man finds a two-year-old child, living in a remote village with his parents and siblings, who the man believes is the next reincarnated Buddha. Two years later the child is brought to the Buddhist monastery in Lhasa where he is trained as a monk and head of state. The Chinese invade Tibet when the boy is fourteen. The Dalai Lama attempts to form a coalition with the Chinese. Finally, in 1957, with his people suffering under Chinese rule and his religion in jeopardy, the Dalai Lama leaves Tibet and seeks asylum in India.

Bringing Out the Dead (1999)

MAJOR CHARACTERS:

Frank Pierce—Nicolas Cage
Mary Burke—Patricia Arquette
Larry—John Goodman
Marcus—Ving Rhames
Tom Walls—Tom Sizemore
Mr. Burke—Cullen O. Johnson

Bringing Out the Dead was adapted from the novel by Joe Connelly, who based his book on his personal experiences as a paramedic working in East Harlem. The story covers a two-day period during the early 1990s in the life of paramedic Frank Pierce. Frank works the night shift, driving his ambulance through the seedier streets of New York City where addicts abound.

The story revolves around Frank feeling utterly exhausted and hallucinating that he sees the ghost of a seriously ill woman named Rose whom he had been unable to save. He blames himself for her death in spite of the fact that there was nothing he could have done to save her.

Frank believes that he has the power over life and death. He talks about the "high" that he feels when he saves someone. However, when he fails to save a dying person, Frank feels depressed. Frank's tendency to play God crystallizes around the life-and-death struggle of Mr. Burke, who suffers a heart attack and cardiac arrest. While trying to resuscitate the old man, Frank comes into contact with his daughter, Mary. At the hospital, Mr. Burke codes a number of times, and each time he is intubated and kept alive. On one of these occasions, Frank hears Mr. Burke say that he does not want to be intubated but to be allowed to die. Frank undertakes the task of removing the heart monitors so the old man will expire as he wishes. This act, according to Scorsese in the trailer to the film, means that Frank has reached the "heart of compassion."

Frank goes to Mary's apartment to tell her that her father has died. He imagines that he sees Rose (in Mary's body), who tells him that her death was not his fault and that no one asked him to suffer. The film ends with Frank and Mary lying on her bed while she comforts the long-suffering Frank in a Pieta-like pose. A progressively intense white light shines upon the pair as the scene slowly dissolves. This closing suggests Scorsese's intention of depicting Frank as a compassionate, saviour-like figure, who attains redemption.

Il Mio Viaggio in Italia (2001)

The title, translated, is *My Voyage to Italy*. The film is a four-hour documentary presented by Scorsese who discusses and explains modern Italian cinema. As Scorsese recounts, when he was a boy, he and his family watched Italian postwar movies on the family's sixteen-inch black-and-white television set. This experience enabled Scorsese to connect with his familial roots as well as with the values of his Italian heritage and it influenced him in deciding to become a filmmaker.

The documentary offers Scorsese's perspective of Italian cinema made from the mid–1940s to the 1960s and it discusses how these films influenced Scorsese as well as his view on how this early Italian cinema affected the world of film in general. The great works surveyed by Scorsese include Rossellini's *Roma Cita Aperti* and *Paisa*, both of which depict a history of survival and self-sacrifice by the people of Italy for the sake of freedom. According to Gonzales, "for Scorsese, the clarity of Rossellini's vision becomes a near-religious experience."[17] A number of the films Scorsese discusses are artistic products that also make political statements.

An exposition of Italian neorealism, which enabled the dissolution of the boundaries between documenetaries and fictional films, is included. In addition to the films directed by Roberto Rossellini, Scorsese presents a number by Fredico Fellini as well as those featuring the acting of Vittorio DeSica, Anna Magnani, and Ingrid Bergman In addition, Scorsese includes lengthy excerpts of the films that most moved him.

Holden remarks that this documentary was a labor of love for Scorsese and that the films he chose represent "compassion, that trust in the spiritual, whose source Mr. Scorsese locates in the soil, on the streets, and in the culture and religious traditions of Italy is a quality that extends to his own films."[18]

The documentary won the William K. Everson History of Film Award from the National Board of Review.

Gangs of New York (2002)

MAJOR CHARACTERS:

    Amsterdam Vallon—Leonardo DiCaprio
    Bill "the Butcher" Cutting—Daniel Day-Lewis
    Jenny Everdeane—Cameron Diaz
    Priest Vallon—Liam Neeson
    William Tweed—Jim Broadbent
    Walter "Monk" McGinn—Brendan Gleeson
    P. T. Barnum—Roger Ashton-Griffiths
    Happy or Uncle Jack—John C. Reilly
    Johnny—Henry Thomas

The story of *Gangs of New York* is drawn from the book, *The Gangs of New York: An Informal History of the Underworld*, written by Herbert Asbury. The movie is set during 1846 to 1863 in New York's notorious Five Points area. Although the Civil War is raging, the people of the underclass who live in Five Points are dealing with a war of their own, one involving rival gangs, who are vying for control of the streets, rampant political corruption, and day-to-day living that is filled with squalor and starvation.

The Civil War has an impact on the people in the Five Points area because the federal government had passed the first draft law, which stipulates that all able-bodied men are subject to being drafted into the Union army. However, men who can pay $300 can escape the draft. The attempt to draft those who did not have $300, that is, the poor, led to the infamous draft riots that occurred during July 13 to 17, 1863. During this period, some of the bloodiest riots in the city's history occurred. Mobs controlled much of Manhattan. Working-class and poor Irish Catholics were rioting against the police and federal troops. This mob violence is depicted in the film.

At the opening of the movie, the head of the Irish tribe known as the "Dead Rabbits," Priest Vallon, is killed by the head of the gang of Nativists, Bill "the Butcher" Cutting. Vallon's young son, Amsterdam, witnesses the murder of his father. Amsterdam spends the next sixteen years in a reform prison. Having outlawed the Dead Rabbits, Bill assumes control of the streets and acquires even greater power when he makes a deal with the corrupt politician, William Tweed. When Amsterdam is released from prison, he is bent on avenging his father's death. Ultimately, he unites the growing horde of Irish immigrants into an army, reunites his father's gang, and engages in a battle against Bill Cutting and the Nativists. In that battle, Amsterdam kills Cutting. (See Chapter 2 for a detailed discussion of the plot and themes.)

Gangs of New York received ten Academy Award nominations including one for best picture, film direction (Scorsese), actor in a leading role (Daniel Day-Lewis), art direction, cinematography, film editing (Thelma Schoonmaker), screenplay written directly for the screen, costume design, original song, and sound. The film also received five Golden Globe nominations; Day-Lewis was awarded a Golden Globe for his portrayal of Bill "the Butcher" Cutting, and Scorsese won his first Golden Globe as director.

4

Narcissism and Male Sexuality

This chapter explains two psychoanalytic terms used to describe, in part, the personality and behaviors of a number of male characters who play focal roles in Scorsese's films and who are discussed in chapters 5, 6, and 7. The first of these terms is *narcissistic*; the other is *phallic*. Since men play leading roles in almost all of Scorsese's films, the masculine pronoun is used in the following discussion.

Narcissism can be defined simply as "self-regard or self-love." Culturally, we tend to think of narcissism in negative terms and narcissistic as describing people who are selfish and self-centered. Unabashed or immature narcissism—expressed as arrogance, selfishness, having a pronounced sense of entitlement, and an exaggerated demandingness—is appropriate for young children. From a developmental perspective, within a healthy family milieu, the immature narcissism of children undergoes transformation to healthy forms of narcissism—for example, self-confidence—in the adult. Therefore, when describing narcissism as a personality feature in adults, this feature must be seen as being on a continuum from healthy and mature to disturbed, unhealthy, or immature (or childlike).[1]

At one end of the spectrum, a person whose narcissism is at a healthy or mature level has solid self-esteem, and confidence, takes care of himself, and is more-or-less comfortable with himself in a wide variety of social situations. Such a person is not easily slighted or injured by another person's rejection or criticism. When criticized or rejected, a healthy adult may feel hurt momentarily or for a short time. However, an emotionally-mature person has enough psychological reserves (*reserves* can be thought of as "a healthy sense of self or self-esteem" to step back from the situation, place the matter into perspective, heal himself from the feeling of hurt, and go on with his life without resentment. The psychologically mature person will not be undone emotionally by such inevitable injuries, will not dwell on them, and will not react ragefully and vengefully toward the perpetrator of the insult or criticism.

In general, narcissism is described as unhealthy or disturbed in an adult personality when there is excessive and extreme self-concern and a childlike level of selfishness. These childlike features in the adult indicate that the person's self-esteem and confidence are shaky; the person feels insecure about his self-worth. Such persons defend against this unsteadiness with grandiose and omnipotent fantasies, arrogance, a sense of entitlement, a need to display himself, and an exaggerated demand for attention. A person whose narcissism is at a childlike level perceives the world almost entirely according to his own sense of reality; he sees himself as the center of the universe and views actions as affecting him alone. He is not able to step into the footsteps of another and empathize with the other person's experience. The character of Jimmy Doyle in *New York, New York* is an apt example of a man whose narcissism is at a childlike level. He is extraordinarily demanding of attention and needs to be on center stage and applauded on a consistent basis.

People whose narcissism is immature or childlike may also come to believe that they are godlike, becoming consumed with fantasies of invulnerability and omnipotence. All of the gangster characters in *GoodFellas*, for example, Henry Hill, Jimmy Conway, and Tommy DeVito, and those in *Casino*, Sam Rothstein and Nicky Santoro, and Bill "the Butcher" Cutting in *Gangs of New York* are prime examples of the type of narcissist who imagines that he has unlimited power with which he can control the world. Using common parlance, these characters (or people such as those represented by these characters) can be called "control freaks."

A person whose narcissism is at an immature level is easily injured by slights and criticisms and may react to hurts with narcissistic rage and a wish for revenge and retaliation. Narcissistic rage is the reaction of a person who feels attacked and injured at the core of his self. The more vulnerable the person is, that is, the more immature is his level of narcissism, the greater the rage is likely to be. In the extreme, rage is expressed as one's unremitting desire to get even, or gain revenge against those who have injured him. Narcissistic rage can become out of control and violent.

Some people focus their narcissism on intellectual achievement and accomplishments, others on their physical attributes. Almost all of Scorsese's central male characters are narcissistic in the sense that their narcissism is childlike or immature, and most of these characters are also phallic. Those men whose personalities show both features may be termed "phallic-narcissistic."

The phallus is a representation or symbol of the penis. The narcissism of these phallic men, that is, the source of their greatest pride and their sense of self-worth, derives from their imagined virility and power; their personalities are organized in terms of fantasies of phallic power and supremacy.[2] In the extreme, an emphasis on phallic supremacy or what is commonly termed, "macho sexuality," can devolve into sexual dominance and violence.

The character of Rupert Pupkin in The *King of Comedy* is representative of a man whose narcissism is at a childlike level, and he is somewhat phallic. Rupert craves to be on center stage and receive the unbounded attention and applause of millions. He reacts to the rejection by Jerry by evolving a plan so that he gets what he demands and, thus, show his girlfriend, Rita, that he is a potent man.

Decades ago, psychoanalyst Wilhelm Reich described the "phallic-narcissistic character" as "self-confident, often arrogant.... Usually haughty, either cold and reserved or defensively aggressive" and in the behavior toward the love object (that is, women), there is always an admixture of more or less disguised sadistic traits."[3] Indeed, phallic-narcissistic men often feel contempt for women. Moreover, according to Reich, the narcissism of these characters appears as exaggerated displays of self-confidence and superiority, and if their vanity is hurt, they may react either with coldness or with aggression.

Vincent Lauria in *The Color of Money* struts around pool tables with a haughty and arrogant display of self-confidence; his pool stick, which he sometimes wields as if it were a sword, is symbolic of the phallus. When he feels rejected by Eddie, that is, his vanity is hurt, he reacts seemingly with little affect, but he is determined to get even (aggression) and succeeds in doing so.

Reich goes on to make the important point that the exaggerated aggressive behavior of these men serves a defensive function. What this means is that these men typically have low self-esteem and deep-seated insecurities about their potency as men, in effect, their manhood. They defend against coming to terms with these insecurities and doubts as well as against showing them to the world by exaggerated and sometimes aggressive as well as exhibitionistic displays of their superiority. Reich states, "[T]he pride in the real or fantasied phallus goes hand in hand with a strong phallic aggression. To the unconscious of the man of this type, the penis is not in the service of love but is an instrument of aggression and vengeance."[4] Such a man intensely fears seeming to be passive, which he associates with appearing to be feminine or a homosexual. In such phallic-narcissistic men, the sexual act, unconsciously, serves to prove to women how potent they are, but at the same time sexual intercourse means "piercing or destroying the woman, ... degrading her."[5]

There is a scene in *Who's That Knocking at My Door?* that is illustrative of a phallic-narcissistic character showing contempt for a woman and degrading her. In this scene, J.R. has just had sex with a woman, and she is lying naked in a bed. J.R. takes a deck of playing cards, bends the pack, and then lets go of the cards. The cards fly every which way over the woman and the bed. This act is symbolic of J.R.'s capacity to spurt his semen all over the woman, and thus, it represents his fantasied mastery over her.

In spite of their contempt for women, phallic-narcissistic men are commonly desired by and attractive to women because they appear to have all of the traits of masculinity, including supreme self-confidence. A good example of this tendency occurs in the encounter between Ben Eberhardt and Alice in *Alice Doesn't Live Here Anymore*. Alice perceives Ben as an attractive and charming man. He appeals to her vanity, telling Alice that he really likes her singing, and appeals to her loneliness with his seeming interest in her. Ben succeeds in getting Alice to have sex with him. Alice soon discovers that Ben is not only a philanderer but also a violent man, a batterer. Ben insists on getting what he wants, that is, Alice as a sexual partner, in spite of the fact that he is married and has a young son. Later, Ben reacts violently when he realizes that his wife is trying to interfere with his having a sexual relationship with Alice. He reacts by threatening his wife with a knife. He also threatens Alice lest she even think about abandoning him.

Another example in the Scorsese opus of a female character who is attracted to a phallic-narcissistic man is Lori in *Cape Fear*. Lori is nursing hurt feelings because of Sam Bowden's rejection of her by drinking too much. Max Cady takes advantage of her vulnerability and comes on to Lori with interest and empathy. Throughout this encounter, Cady is planning to beat and rape her.

In more recent psychoanalytic thought but entirely in line with the findings of Reich, Person reports on clinical studies that have shown that men's wishful fantasies of phallic supremacy—the penis as especially large and invested with mastery as well as women as available on demand—exist together with dreaded fantasies and anxieties of inadequacy, the unavailability of sexual objects or rejection by them. These fears translate into castration anxiety.[6] Homosexuality is another dread of phallic-narcissists.

It stands to reason that men who have a great need to show that they are immensely powerful tend to be those who are the most insecure about their physical endowment, their performance, their capacity to attract and hold onto women as sexual objects, and their overall power in the world. In other words, the men who are most insecure with regard to their phallic power defend against feeling shame and showing their insecurities by exhibiting to the world that they are strong and powerful with exaggerated displays of their phallic supremacy.

Phallic-narcissistic men will feel injured easily if they experience a threat to their potency. An example of such a threat is that of a woman, who is the man's sexual object, having an apparent interest in another man. A man such as that, represented by the character of Jake LaMotta, feels threatened when his sexual object is unavailable or when he feels rejected by her. When he feels insulted and humiliated about his phallic significance because of this kind of threat, he may react with extreme narcissistic rage. This dynamic occurs in *Raging Bull* when Vickie LaMotta makes an innocuous comment about another fighter being good-looking. Jake becomes enraged and out-of-control. In another case in that film, Jake beats up his brother as well as his wife because he suspects that they have had sex together. In Scorsese's films, we see this level of violent behavior also in the character of Travis Bickle in *Taxi Driver* when he is rejected by Betsy. After this rejection, Travis fragments, or falls apart, and goes on a killing spree.

Some of Scorsese's characters express their phallic significance by showing off their superior strength by beating, raping, and demeaning women. The characters of Jake LaMotta (*Raging Bull*) and Max Cady (*Cape Fear*) are prime examples of phallic-narcissistic men who engage in this kind of violent behavior. Indeed, Cady is particularly savage toward Lori, taking a bite of flesh from her face in the course of his horrific beating and rape of her.

The madonna-whore complex, which determines J.R.'s (*Who's That Knocking at My Door?*) and Charlie's (*Mean Streets*) attitudes toward women, as well as the attitudes of the other male characters in these films, is consistent with the features of phallic-narcissistic character described above.

In the mind of the phallic-narcissist, sexual women are perceived as dangerous and they must be debased or forced to submit to their power.[7] The madonna-whore complex dictates that a phallic-narcissistic man can marry only a virgin because a woman's virginity indicates that she has not been sexual and, therefore, that she is not dangerous. If the woman is not a virgin, then a phallic-narcissist debases her by calling her a whore. In such instances, the man thus feels free to have sex with her, that is, a nonvirgin, on his terms or to rape her. Both J.R. and Charlie demean the women with whom they are involved. Charlie, for example, calls his girlfriend, Teresa, a "cunt"; J.R. calls the Girl, who had been date-raped, a whore. In *Mean Streets*, Tony shows his friends his caged female tiger. The tiger is symbolic of the dangerousness of women. One of the guys refers to the tiger as a "good girl," and admonishes her not to "bite." Tony shows his power over the tiger and her submission to him by keeping her caged.

For a number of Scorsese's phallic-narcissistic characters, using a gun (symbolic of penis or phallus) is the way to ensure their sense of phallic superiority. This is true for Travis Bickle in *Taxi Driver* and Scorsese's gangster characters. Bill Cutting (*Gangs of New York*) demonstrates his phallic supremacy by using knives skillfully to wound or kill his perceived enemies. Jimmy Doyle (*New York, New York*) uses his saxophone as a symbol of his fantasied superiority, and he dominates his wife at every turn. Jimmy's demeaning, controlling behavior toward his wife, Francine, is indicative of his expressing his power over her. His infidelities and his attempts to surpass Francine with regard to success and fame are also indicators of his phallic-narcissism.

According to psychoanalytic thought, the phallic stage of development (3 to 7 years of age, approximately) refers to the period of life when children organize their sexual thoughts in terms of either having a penis or not having one. In other words, it is the developmental period during which children develop a sense of their sexual identity. From a developmental point of view, when boys reach the phallic-narcissistic level, "the boy's penis becomes a highly valued body part, his main source of narcissistic and autoerotic gratification, and the focus of his phallic exhibitionistic wishes."[8] It is during this process that, ideally, the boy develops a strong identification with his father. This period of development occurs prior to the oedipal period. During the preoedipal or phallic-narcissistic period, the boy relates in terms of two-person dynamics (for example, he and his father). In the oedipal period, triadic or triangular relationships develop (for example, he and his mother and his father).

When we encounter phallic-narcissistic men in reality or in fiction, we can surmise that some aspect of their development went awry. It can be said to some degree at least, that the psychological or emotional development of these men was arrested at the phallic stage.[9] Thus, some phallic-narcissistic characters behave as if they were little boys who have just discovered that they have penises and want to show off this discovery to the world. Johnny Boy (*Mean Streets*) is an example of such a personality. He is continually showing off, wields a gun indiscriminately, and, in general, behaves as if he were a cocky little boy.

In the next three chapters, the personalities and behaviors of Scorsese's male characters who are phallic-narcissists are examined in the context of their respective film stories.

5

Rageful Warriors and Batterers

These next three chapters—5, 6, and 7—examine the personalities and behaviors of those male characters whose narcissism is at a childlike level. In a number of cases, the characters are phallic-narcissists. The behaviors, motivations, and relationships (or lack thereof) of these men are seen as linked to and driven by their individual psychology as well as the circumstances of their lives. Based on the definitions developed in Chapter 4, these characters exhibit disturbed narcissism, in part, in the form of extreme self-concern and selfishness. Moreover, each perceives and defines the world almost entirely according to his own subjective view, thus creating what may be termed each man's narcissistically perceived universe. Each man's personal perceptions, which may devolve into paranoia, and self-interest are paramount in motivating his actions. Narcissism has a number of faces, and these characters exhibit it in different ways. However, underlying the psychology of a number of these "men" are insecurities and doubts about their sense of self, their manhood, and their place in the world.

In attending to the individual psychology of these phallic-narcissists, we can appreciate each man's vulnerabilities, particularly with regard to power and potency. In addition, an analysis of these characters' overall psychology allows for an appreciation of the linkage of aggression and sexuality as well as the basis for paranoia with regard to violence. Also examined is the role of fantasies in each man's sense of himself and of his place in his social milieu.

Each of the first three Scorsese characters can be described as a "rageful warrior" because each sees himself as fighting a battle. Travis Bickle (*Taxi Driver*), Jake LaMotta (*Raging Bull*), and Max Cady (*Cape Fear*) are violent and take a warlike stance in preparing for their battle or battles. Each of the three trains and builds his body into a fighting machine. The fourth character, Ben Eberhardt (*Alice Doesn't Live Here Anymore*), is similarly violent, but because he plays a relatively small role in the film, his personality is less well-defined than the others discussed in this chapter. Each of the four of these "men" uses lethal weapons and is prepared to kill. Each of them fuses and confuses sexuality with violence. Of the four, three actually batter women in their respective films: LaMotta, Cady, and Eberhardt; Bickle does not.

TRAVIS BICKLE

Robert De Niro plays Travis Bickle, the 26-year-old focal character in *Taxi Driver* (1976). Travis is a psychologically vulnerable man who, under emotional stress, devolves into violence. He is an obsessive diarist, writing his thoughts into a notebook, and he narrates his experiences in the form of a voice-over throughout the film.

Travis cannot sleep at all. He spends his nights riding buses and the New York subways. When he applies for a job as a taxi driver, he explains to the dispatcher who is interviewing him that he is doing so because of his sleeplessness and that instead of riding around at night aimlessly, he might as well get paid for it by driving a cab. He assures the dispatcher that he will drive "anytime anywhere" and that he just wants to work long hours. Privately, he hopes that working long and hard will help him sleep and provide him with distraction from his "morbid self-attention." Travis avoids the question of previous employment, and we never discover if he had worked before and, if so, what the nature of this work was. The interview reveals that he is an ex–Marine, honorably discharged in May of 1973, that he has little education, and, flashing a pleased smile, that his driving license is "clean, real clean, just like my conscience." We assume he is a Vietnam veteran, although as Schrader, the film's screenwriter explained, it was not his intention to make Travis a Vietnam vet.[1]

Travis begins working, driving literally anyone who approaches his cab anywhere all over town, even to the most dangerous and undesirable areas, in twelve-hour shifts from six in the evening until six or later in the mornings, six and sometimes seven days a week. Even with this grueling work schedule, however, Travis is unable to sleep.

As depicted, Travis is the epitome of the loner, feeling isolated, alienated, and estranged from the human race. He is limited psychologically, culturally, and, perhaps, intellectually as well, and he is intensely lonely. He writes, "Loneliness has followed me my whole life everywhere.... There is no escape. I'm God's lonely man." He also demonstrates through his behavior, that it is difficult for him to relate to people. He writes a once-a-year letter to his parents but refuses to send them his address. He has difficulties connecting with fellow cabbies, and although he attempts to date Betsy, he shows a lack of both empathy and reality-testing by taking her to a porno film when they are out on a date. This action indicates that Travis lacks the understanding that this type of film is singularly inappropriate for his idealized "woman in white."

Travis seems not to know much about ordinary life, as if he were an innocent babe who has been hibernating in a cocoon. He is an observer of life rather than a participant and is much like a peeping Tom who peers out at the world through the windows of his cab or sits witness to the sometimes bizarre goings-on in the back seat. The dearth of information about Travis, with which the viewer contends, imbues him with an aura of inscrutability. Travis is, indeed, secretive, hiding behind a mask with which he presents himself to the world. He seems to revel in appearing to be both simplistic and philosophical, ignorant about general cultural affairs but having insight about people. Betsy describes him as a "walking contradiction," seeming to be both "prophet and pusher." Sport sees him as a "real cowboy." Iris wonders if he is a "narc."

Consistent with his enigmatic reserve and aura of inscrutability, Travis presents a number of contradictions. For example, he pops pills and drinks from his pocket flask all day long. Travis's obvious dependency on and abuse of drugs and alcohol flies in the face of his condemning and demonizing people who use drugs as "dopers." As another example, although he sees himself as having a "real" clean conscience and his external world as very dirty, like an "open sewer," Travis spends a good deal of his free time watching porno films in a "Show & Tell" theater. On the bases of his asexuality as well as his attendance at porno films, it appears that his one pseudosexual outlet is derived from watching others having sex. However, there is no indication of his ejaculating from watching erotica. Instead, it appears that his sexual energy is trapped or pent-up. Travis may be impotent, or he may fear, consciously or unconsciously, that he is impotent.

Travis's cell-like apartment, moreover, is hardly the epitome of good taste and cleanliness. The apartment windows are barred; its walls and door are soiled; and it is furnished in an haphazard and disorganized fashion with only minimal necessities strewn about. His mattress on a small cot is bare; an electric bulb that provides his only light is without a shade. Even when he is earning $300 or $350 a week, and even more when he goes off the meter, Travis does not spend money on improving his living conditions. He eats junk food; his wardrobe is limited; he knows nothing of politics, books, or music; and he has no friends. The way he lives is an indication of the general state of his mind—small, constricted, and consumed with thoughts about the dirt and smut of the city all about him and whose "smell" gives him headaches.

Travis can be described as having a solipsistic (that is, defined entirely by his own mind) and Manichean (or black and white) sense of reality defined by his being good and clean, while his milieu which is peopled by the "animals" who "come out at night.... whores, skunk pussies, buggers, queens, fairies, dopers ... [is] sick and venal." In effect, Travis has split his world into two sharply dichotomized halves—one, wholly clean and white, the other, dirty and black—and there is for him absolutely no gray, no mixing, no integration possible. This subjective perception of his social milieu is both narcissistic and paranoidal, a view that is not only self-serving but also one that pits good versus evil.

Travis experiences this venal milieu as external to him, that is, other-than-him, and he keeps it in this state by demonizing others to the extreme. Although indicating by his words that he is repulsed and disgusted by what he sees on the streets, particularly after dark, he chooses to live and work in this milieu, keeping the evil world within the periphery of his experience so that he can continually objectify this world as "not-me" and intensify his hatred of it.

Travis writes in his diary: "All I needed was a sense of someplace to go ... to become a person." These words suggest that he lacks a sense of purpose and "place" as well as a sense of feeling connected to other people. His self-proclaimed need of a place to go and becoming a person appear to be met when Travis seizes upon and becomes obsessed with Betsy (Cybill Shepherd), a pretty and wholesome-looking blonde woman whom he sees one day walking on the street and entering the campaign headquarters of Senator Charles Palantine, a presidential candidate. Travis characterizes her as an "angel" in a white dress and who, according to him, appears "out of this filthy mass." He writes in his diary that "she is alone, they cannot touch her." This description indicates that Travis perceives Betsy as entirely different from the "dirt and filth" of his milieu; she represents the glorious alternative to his otherwise dreary life. In his mind, if Betsy becomes his companion and friend, not only would his loneliness be assuaged but her angelic presence would match his sense of himself as "clean, real clean" because she is like him.

After watching her for some time through the window of his cab while she works at her job, Travis goes to the Palantine headquarters office and asks Betsy to come out for coffee and pie at a nearby cafeteria. He tries to make a connection with her, telling her she is beautiful, that she is lonely and unhappy, and that she needs a friend, as he does. Displaying what she interprets as his keen insight about human nature, Travis rather pretentiously criticizes her coworker, Tom, as "silly" and disrespectful of her while, he says, between the two of them—that is, Betsy and Travis—there is a connection, "an impulse we were both following." Flattered and charmed by his unabashed attention and admiring gaze and intrigued by his enigmatic style, Betsy agrees to go with Travis on a date to a movie later that week. By placing Betsy on a pedestal and fantasizing that he and she are one and connected to one another, Travis's sense of himself is inflated.

After the fiasco at the porno film when Betsy walked out on him, Travis

5. Rageful Warriors and Batterers

phones her repeatedly, wanting to see her again and assuring her that they would go somewhere else next time. She speaks to him the first time he calls, but, after that, she refuses to take his calls or to accept the deliveries of flowers he sends to her office. We can imagine that Betsy believes that Travis does not know her at all and that all he wants is to have sex with her.

Frustrated and angry, Travis goes to the campaign headquarters and confronts Betsy about her refusal to talk to him. She does not want to talk to him, and a male coworker comes to her assistance to force him to leave. Travis loses his temper, and, as he is ushered out of the building unceremoniously, he screams ragefully to Betsy: "You're in hell, and you're gonna die in hell like the others." He writes and speaks that "she is like the others—cold and distant—a lot of people are like that—women for sure." With these words Travis indicates that, in his mind, Betsy has become bad like the rest of them; using the word "hell" suggests her venality. He tell us that the bouquets of flowers that he sent to Betsy, now rotting in his apartment, are making him sick.

After Betsy's humiliating rejection which Travis experiences as a betrayal, he literally snaps, or fragments, and becomes totally enraged. He begins to prepare himself for revenge. He feels injured by her refusing to talk with him, disdaining him as it were, and her prior idolized state is turned on its head. She becomes, in his disturbed mind, entirely bad like the rest of his external world. She has acquired this change in status, actually the opposite of the former, *because* she rejected him. His demonization of her is indicative of his reaction to feeling humiliated as being inadequate. He is deflated by feeling judged by her. Betsy's rejection taps into Travis's own feelings of inadequacy (as a man) and impotency and, indeed, exacerbates them. Travis defends his sense of self from these uncomfortable feelings by making her the one who is bad, that is, casting her out from his imagined sense of himself as real clean. His view of Betsy, which undergoes a switch from his first encounter with her to her rejection of him, is an indication of his tendency to split or dichotomize the world into black and white or good and bad. He is paranoid about that part of the world that he perceives as black, dirty, and bad. Moreover, as he is so intensely and narcissistically injured and humiliated by Betsy's rejection, it is apparent that he has extraordinary insecurities. The potential for a narcissistic rage response in terms of violent behavior is, in turn, extraordinarily high.

As Travis is depicted, with having headaches that torture him, being consumed with "bad thoughts," and having an inability to relate effectively with other people, it appears that he is not only emotionally disturbed but also subject to psychotic episodes. He sees himself as inadequate—no friends, a lousy job, days spilling over into others with no hope for change—and he is probably depressed. When he sends an anniversary/birthday card to his parents, he lies about his life, writing that he has an important and sensitive job with the government that requires secrecy, that he is dating a girl named

Betsy, and that they would be proud of him. These lies suggest that he fears if his parents know the truth about his actual life, he would be perceived by them as a failure and, perhaps, as an impotent man. Being perceived as impotent by his social milieu is Travis's worst dread.

Soon after he suffers Betsy's rejection, a troubled-looking Travis tells his cabbie cohort, Wizard, that things "got me real down" and that " I just wanna go out and really, really do something—I got some bad ideas in my head." His wanting to do something, seemingly driven by bad thoughts, suggests that Travis is thinking about some form of violence that will gain him not only revenge against Betsy and the others who are like her (and who, in his mind, threaten him) but also glory and a sense of accomplishment. Travis's "bad ideas" about really doing something are for him the ways to counter his paranoidal feelings of being seen as inadequate and to show his social milieu that he is a potent man.

Travis buys guns: a .44 magnum, a .38 snub nose revolver, a Colt .25 automatic, and a .380 Walther. In the context of the story, it appears that Travis gets the idea of using guns to not only avenge himself but also to strike out and clean up the dirt when one of his passengers talks about killing his unfaithful wife, who he states is having an affair with a "negro," with a .44 magnum. Other events that trigger Travis's use of weapons are Palantine's words, which Travis hears on television, "that the people are beginning to rule," and seeing the young prostitute, Iris, for the second time trying to pick up "tricks." After this series of events, all of which contribute to the collapse of Travis's fragile equilibrium, he writes in his diary: "My life has taken another turn ... there is a change." Travis gets himself in top physical shape for the battle that he is planning by changing his diet, engaging in vigorous muscle-building exercises, and practicing with his guns at an indoor firing range.

After buying his guns, Travis goes a theater to watch a porno film. In one scene of the film, one of the participants says, "look at the size of that," referring to the man's penis, and describes it as becoming "harder and harder" and "throbbing." Travis brings his hand up to his face and moves his fingers in a scissor-like motion as if he were identifying shooting a cocked gun with the hardened and throbbing penis, which is apparently on the screen. He says: "The idea had been growing in my brain for some time. True force— all the king's men ... cannot put it back together again." It is apparent that Travis has linked the expression of sexual energy with brute force. In his mind, using "true force" to accomplish his goal has become the way to prove his manhood, his potency. For Travis, sexuality and violence have become entwined.

Back in his apartment in front of the mirror, Travis holds the large and hard magnum revolver, admiring his image. It is as if he is admiring his penis, long and hard and throbbing in delight. Gazing at his image with obvious pleasure, Travis feels powerful and imagines himself, grandiosely, as an

5. Rageful Warriors and Batterers   81

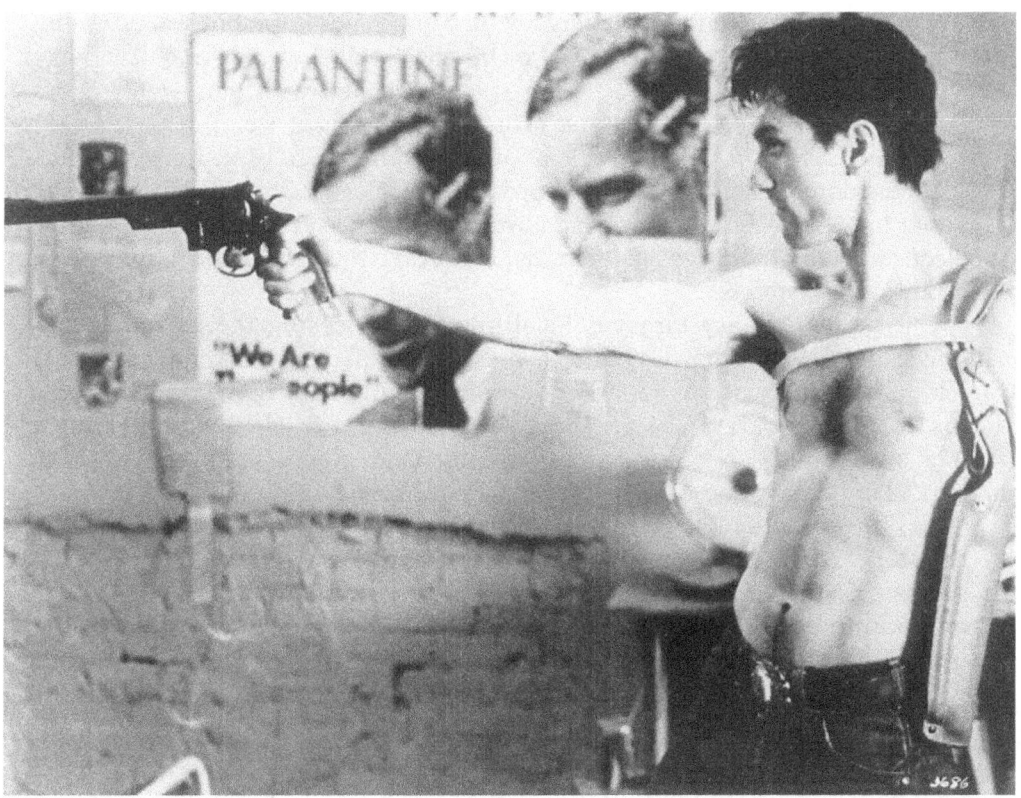

Travis Bickle (Robert De Niro), after his transformation into a warrior, practices drawing his gun and prepares for battle against imaginary enemies, from *Taxi Driver*.

omnipotent warrior and a veritable crusader for good. It seems that Travis's pent-up sexual energy has finally found an outlet. His mission, as the omniscient savior that he imagines himself to be, is to cleanse his milieu of its filth by bloody, violent means. These mirror scenes indicate that Travis is a phallic-narcissist and that he has regressed, psychologically, to an early stage of development.

Using a double shoulder holster and a device he created that permits quick access to the gun he has hidden up his arm, Travis practices challenging his imagined opponents and beating them to the draw in front of his mirror. With four guns and a Bowie knife fastened onto his body, he transforms himself into a veritable combat machine. To his fantasized enemy in the mirror, Travis says, "Your move ... you talking to me? ...Listen you fuckers, here is a man who would not take it any more, a man who stood up against the scum, cunts, and dogs, the filth, the skum.... You're dead." From a psychological perspective, his talking to the image in the mirror is an indication of Travis's solipsism. Moreover, the mirror functions literally to affirm

Travis's grandiose narcissistic fantasy of being an omnipotent warrior. This is how Travis wants to be perceived by his social milieu, which includes Betsy. The image in the mirror—a potent warrior, armed with guns—affirms his fantasy of phallic supremacy and grossly inflates his sense of self.

When Travis fragments, or falls apart psychologically, he imagines himself megalomaniacally as the one ordained to cleanse the filth he perceives about him—as if he were a priest administering the sacrament of baptism to cleanse original sin. In this vein, earlier Travis had welcomed the rain as cleansing the streets.

Travis's primary target is Palantine. After "casing the joint," that is, attending a Palantine rally and, in a seemingly friendly manner, engaging with a Secret Service agent and questioning him about the weapons he and his colleagues carry, Travis goes to another and bigger rally sporting a Mohawk haircut and dark glasses. His intention is to assassinate the presidential candidate and others who may be in his way.

The reason Travis targets Palantine is understandable in the context of the story. During the time that Travis worships Betsy and perceives her as all-good, in his mind Palantine is good as well because of her association with and admiration of the presidential candidate. Coincidentally, during this period, Palantine and his aide ride in Travis's cab. Travis tells Palantine that what he hopes he will do, if he wins the election, is to clean up the streets of the filth and scum. At this stage, it is clear from his enthusiasm, when he discovers that his passenger is Palantine, that Travis has a positive view of the man. After Betsy is demonized in Travis's sick mind, however, anyone she admires and is associated with, including Palantine, is also demonized and cast into the category of dirt and filth, like the rest of his universe. Moreover, when he hears Palantine speaking about the people ruling, Travis probably interprets these remarks as indicating the Palantine values them, the people in his milieu whom Travis perceives as bad and those responsible for the dirt and filth all about him. In addition, in Travis's mind, shooting a high-profile figure will give him notoriety and attention and then the world will recognize him as a man of action, forceful and potent.

Frustrated in his attempt to shoot his primary target, Palantine, because of the extensive Secret Service protection, Travis switches gears and moves to his secondary target, the pimp, whom he blames for forcing Iris, a twelve-and-a-half-year-old whore into the disgusting and dirty life of prostitution. Again, in this context, Travis demonstrates that he sees himself as Iris's savior, the redeemer of sin, by virtue of the violence he has planned that will cause massive suffering and shedding of blood, his and that of others.

The experiences that Travis has with Iris are representative of his imagining himself, megalomaniacally, as a warring crusader for good, in effect, a Christlike savior, one willing to sacrifice himself for the sake of good. Travis first encounters Iris when she rushes into his cab one night and asks him to

5. Rageful Warriors and Batterers

take off. Before Travis can do so, however, her pimp, Matthew (or Sport), pulls her out of the car, forcibly. Travis interprets her entering his cab as her trying to get away from Matthew and going to Travis for help in doing so.

Travis next sees Iris one night as she tries to pick up tricks. When Travis again sees Iris, as both are walking on the street, he wants to locate her place in the neighborhood. She, oblivious about his intention, asks him only whether he wants some action, and when he appears to be interested, she directs him to Matthew. Travis makes a deal with Matthew and then follows Iris to the building and room where she sees her customers. Travis is appalled by her young age and refers back to their first encounter during which she was seemingly trying to get away from her pimp. During the fifteen minutes that Travis has purchased in her gaudy sex parlor festooned with a panoply of lit candles, he stops her from removing her scanty blouse and from undoing his zipper. Instead of having sex with her, he tries to convince her that she ought to leave her life as a prostitute and return to her home and parents. Since their time together is running out, she agrees to have breakfast with him the following day. In the cafeteria where they meet, Travis offers her money so that she can leave Matthew, and before going on his mission to kill Palantine, Travis mails the money to her.

After his frustrated attempt to murder Palantine, Travis goes to the area where Iris plies her trade. He first shoots Matthew and then enters the building and shoots the man who serves as the timekeeper for Iris and, next, the customer who is in Iris's room. Travis's shooting spree leaves three bloodied bodies strewn about and Travis lying injured in the room. When the police enter the scene with their guns drawn, Travis puts his bloody hand to his head, his finger cocked to his head, and he mimics the sound of a gun shooting his brains out.

In the finale, we hear by virtue of an voice-over the words written by Iris's parents to Travis in a letter expressing their profound gratitude to him for rescuing their daughter and contributing to her return to them. The newspapers clippings on the wall of Travis's apartment show that he has been hailed as a hero. After lying in a coma and recovering from his wounds, Travis is applauded in the media for his courage in killing gangsters who were keeping girls like Iris in virtual captivity as prostitutes.

In the next scene, some three months later, Travis is back at his cabbie job, and he picks up Betsy as a customer. He refers to Palantine having won the nomination and says that he hopes that he will win the election, now only seventeen days away. Betsy comments that she read about Travis in the newspapers and asks him how he is. He pooh-poohs his exploits and says that he just has some "stiffness." As she alights from the cab, it appears that she may want to connect with him again and asks him the amount of the fare. Travis pulls down the meter handle and drives away saying, "No problem." Travis's disinterested and rejecting attitude toward Betsy is his way of saying, "Now that I'm a somebody, I don't need you anymore," and it represents, for Travis, a vindication for her rejection of him. He is now in the driver's seat, so to speak, recognized and affirmed as a real man, indeed, a courageous hero by the social milieu.

This ambiguous ending represents both or either reality or fantasy. As fantasy, the ending is Travis's wish-fulfillment of his narcissistic and megalomaniacal fantasies and is, perhaps, a dream. As reality, Scorsese tells us that Travis attains redemption because of the perception of others. In this context, the ending can be understood as a cynical comment on how society and the media create heroes and celebrities even when the people who attain heroic status are mentally disturbed or perverts.

Travis's extensive knowledge of and acquisition of guns suggests that he has had combat experience. We imagine that he saw action in Vietnam, and we are left to wonder if this experience exposed him to trauma which, in turn, contributes to his anxiety and depression as well as the headaches he has everyday.

The depiction of the two women—Betsy who is virginal and madonna-like at first and is then transformed in Travis's mind to one who is bad and dirty and Iris, who changes her life of a prostitute to one who is clean—is indicative of his whore-madonna complex. There are scenes in the film that suggest that Travis is racist as well.

From an autobiographical perspective, Scorsese identified with Travis, saying in an interview: "I know this guy Travis.... I know the killing feeling, the feeling of really being angry."[2] In another interview, Scorsese acknowledged: "You feel you understand the rage ... pain of romantic rejection."[3] Scorsese's use of the mirror in this and other films probably derives from his personal experience. When Scorsese was a boy, he reenacted his movie heroes that he had seen on the screen and fantasied being them in front of a mirror. From a psychological perspective, a mirror serves to affirm one's wished-for fantasies, for example, about being seen as a strong and powerful man. In other words, one's image in the mirror reflects back the grandiose fantasy that one has in his mind. This process had the effect of pumping up a boy or man who feels small and powerless.

Jake LaMotta

As depicted in *Raging Bull* (1980), the character of Jake LaMotta (Robert De Niro) is a brutal and violent man, capable of meting out as well as absorbing tremendous punishment. He has a fiery temper that can snap without warning, and he is easily incited to murderous rage.

A particular feature that distinguished LaMotta as a fighter was his endurance. He did not box in the classic sense but, rather, charged in much like a bull does, getting close to his opponent's fists and head with seeming disregard for the effects on him of charging in that fashion. His style might be described as being akin to that of kamikaze pilots, as if he is willing to pulverize his opponent even if it means suicide for him. Using this fighting style, he often knocked out his opponents, but in the process endured horrific punishment and pain. Amazingly, he never went down to the mat and suffered a knock-out. The film shows two of his matches which are particularly indicative of LaMotta's steel-like determination not to go down. One of these is his 1947 match with Billy Fox. In the film, Jake assents to the demands of the mobsters who control boxing to throw this fight. He does so with the promise that he will be given a title match in return. Jake does, indeed, throw the match, but he does it in such an obvious way that he is investigated by the boxing commission. During the fight LaMotta essentially invites Fox to hit him again and again as he leaves himself open to the inferior fighter's punches. Although absorbing punch after punch and offering little or no defense, Jake never falls to the mat; he simply endures Fox's horrible barrage.

Before the fight, knowing that he is going to lose the fight, he declares, "I don't go down for nobody." This statement makes clear LaMotta's intention that losing the fight did not include his falling and appearing to be knocked out. After the fight, as the spectators boo because of the obvious fix, Jake exclaims to his brother, "They want me to go down too?" Losing the fight on a decision and losing by a knock-out (KO) are two very different experiences for the fighter. As the events in a boxing ring are on public display, in Jake's mind, if he were to be knocked out, he feels that he would be seen as an utter failure, an impotent man, by all those who observe the fight.

A second time in the film when LaMotta's extraordinary endurance is evident occurs in his sixth match (during the 1950s) with Sugar Ray Robinson, a fight that cost Jake the middleweight crown. Jake suffers a bloody, vicious beating that is almost too violent to watch. He staggers against the ropes and suffers a number of cuts on his face, and his blood flows down his torso and onto his legs. At times, Robinson's punches to the barely upright LaMotta cause blood from facial cuts to squirt onto spectators in the front rows. During this assault, LaMotta taunts Ray to hit him more, though he is barely standing against the ropes, defenseless and bloody. The fight is stopped by someone in Jake's corner, although Jake denies the stoppage immediately afterward, seemingly wanting the carnage to continue. Sugar Ray is awarded the victory on a technical knock-out (TKO), but Jake says to Ray: "I never went down—you never got me down."

Jake's capacity for enduring great pain and punishment—as if his body were made of impenetrable steel that could not be bent or toppled—is the key to an appreciation of his psychological makeup and his sense of himself as a potent man. The character of Jake can be described as one whose sense of self is organized in terms of a narcissistic fantasy of omnipotence that renders his body indestructible. LaMotta's obvious resolve to never go down, although enduring horrific beatings, is reminiscent of the resoluteness of a child who refuses to cry "uncle, when he is being beaten," never "gives in," and never admits being the loser in a contest. Rather, taking it like a man and not acknowledging defeat is, in Jake's mind, being a winner of sorts, the endurance being the indicator of his omnipotence. From another point of view, his enduring horrific beatings is indicative of Jake's self-hatred and self-destructiveness, in effect, of a subconscious wish to be punished because he feels that he deserves to be punished, a theme that emerges later in the film.

After the third fight with Robinson in Detroit in 1943, a match that Jake loses, his brother Joey (Joe Pesci) exclaims that Jake was "robbed" of the decision. Jake responds: "I've done a lot of bad things, Joey. Maybe it's coming back to me.... I'm a jinx, maybe." LaMotta's sense of being a bad person, that is, his self-loathing and his feeling guilt about having done bad things, is a psychological, two-way street explaining his violence toward others as well as his self-destructiveness. Jake's violence toward others derives from his projecting his internalized sense of badness onto others, thus perceiving others as bad. This projection results in his feeling paranoid about others who, he believes, present a threat to him. His self-destructiveness derives from his feeling that he deserves to be punished and that this self-directed punishment may expiate his guilt.

LaMotta, consumed with doubts about his self-worth and his manhood, has an explosive temper that is triggered by seemingly minor provocations. The explosiveness of his rage, often sudden and murderous, is linked with

Jake LaMotta (Robert De Niro) in the boxing ring, from *Raging Bull* (Photofest).

his insecurities as a potent man. His temper or rage flare up when he was narcissistically injured; that is, something happens that causes him to feel that his sense of self as a real man is threatened or, from a related perspective, that his fantasy of omnipotence might be toppled. Given his internalized sense of being no good, an external threat taps into his negative feelings about himself and, indeed, exacerbates his self-loathing as well as his paranoia. He defends against this discomforting feeling by exploding—that is, a narcissistic rage response—into violence directed against imagined enemies. There is no question that the character of LaMotta is a phallic-narcissist.

In an early scene, Jake's temper flares up in an interaction with his first wife, Irma (played by Lori Anne Flax). As she is preparing a steak for him, they argue about how much the meat should be cooked. After his repeated demands that she is overcooking the meat, his wife hurls the steak onto his plate that is set in front of him at the kitchen table. Jake explodes, upending the table, screaming like an animal and threatening his wife. It seems that the woman's "crime" was to disobey his demand at the moment he made it. With his second wife, Vickie (Cathy Moriarty), he is imperious as well, ordering her about as if she were a servant and physically abusing her at will. Jake's exerting power and control over weaker women suggests that, in his mind, expressing his strength and power firms up and defends his sense of being an omnipotent man. LaMotta's explosive and blind rage is consistent with the idea that Jake's body was a gun that was always cocked, ready to explode its firepower and destroy the person whom he regards as his enemy even if the other person were not an opponent in the boxing ring.

As depicted in the film, although Jake's self-worth is linked with his success in the boxing ring, it also derives from his perceptions about his second wife's loyalty to him. Jake becomes obsessed with the blonde and beautiful Vickie from the time he first sees her when she is only fifteen years old. Winning her heart and having her affection exclusively for himself is, in his mind, an indication that he is a real and potent man. Jake is insanely jealous, indeed, paranoid, about Vickie and her fidelity to him. An indication of this paranoia occurs in the film when Jake approaches a match with a young fighter named Janiro. Vickie makes an offhand comment that Janiro is "good-looking." It appears that she did so on the basis of something she had heard or read about the fighter. However, Jake becomes obsessed and paranoid that Vickie knows Janiro. Later, during the fight, LaMotta viciously smashes the young fighter's face repeatedly so that his former good looks are obliterated. This behavior is indicative of Jake's insecurities about his masculinity; that is, he feels threatened because he believes that Vickie is attracted to the other man. In other scenes, Jake explodes in fury when Vickie kisses Jake's brother and a friend on their mouths. Jake's paranoia ultimately convinces him that his brother has had sex with his wife. Jake hits both Vickie and Joey, destroying his relationship with his brother.

It seems apparent that Jake's insecurities, manifesting in the form of paranoia, are linked to homoerotic dreads, that is, his fear of being impotent or of having no self-worth as a man, in effect, the opposite of an imagined omnipotence. There is an allusion to Jake's homoerotic dreads in the film. In an early scene with his brother, Jake comments on his small hands, like those of a "girl," he says. "What does it matter?" his brother asks. Jake responds that he will never be able to fight the best there is, namely, Joe Louis and, thereby, show that he is the better fighter (although, realistically, he and Louis were in different weight categories). Then he demands that Joey hit him hard in his face. When his brother demurs, Jake refers to his fear about being a "faggot." After some fisticuffs between the brothers, Jake pinches Joey's cheek.

The concluding scenes of the film show that Jake retires from boxing during the mid–1950s and goes to live in Miami with his wife and three children. He is seen talking to a reporter to whom he says that he will no longer have to worry about his weight. He opens a nightclub using his name on the marquee, seemingly enjoying being the center of attention. However, he abuses alcohol and has sex with a number of women. His wife leaves him in response to his infidelities. He is arrested for having served alcohol to minors in his club and for contributing to corrupting the morals of a fourteen-year-old girl. He serves time in the Dade Country stockade. In a scene where he has been placed in solitary confinement, he hits his fists and his head on the stone walls of his cell. He refers to himself as "dummy" and "stupid" and proclaims, "I'm not an animal." Later in 1958, in New York City, he is depicted doing comedy routines in nightclubs. The end of the film suggests that he was afforded redemption, and, as the proverbial blind man in the Bible, ultimately he was able to achieve some sight, that is, self-awareness.

Given Jake's murderous rage and his capacity for sudden and violent responses to threats to his imagined sense of impotence, it is as if he perceives his body as a lethal weapon, loaded to fire and kill on a moment's notice. In his mind, sexual potency and his capacity for violence are intertwined. He defends against his insecurities as a man by using his power to hurt others as well as by his childlike demand that he be recognized as the ultimate boss, the one whom others, particularly the women in his life, have to obey. In the mind of this character, women have to be submissive to him to affirm his greater power as a man or his phallic supremacy.

Applying a religious perspective, the film likens the tremendous punishment that LaMotta endures to the suffering of the biblical Christ on the cross. In this context, the film chronicles fourteen of LaMotta's fights; there are fourteen stations of the cross that mark the steps of the passion of Jesus on the path to his crucifixion. Accordingly, LaMotta's redemption from his "sins" is attained by virtue of his enormous suffering and the shedding of his blood.

Scorsese has made statements that suggest he identified with LaMotta's self-destructive tendencies. The director has spoken about the mental and physical crisis that he suffered just before he began making *Raging Bull*. In this context, Scorsese said: "I went through a serious crisis.... I was lucky; I survived; the crisis passed. My suicide period was over.... To want to kill yourself over work, to dream of a tragic death...."[4]

In a televised interview, Scorsese indicated that he empathized with LaMotta's highly constrained life.[5] In effect, Jake's world consisted of the gym, the boxing ring, and the rooms of his home. Living within such a limited milieu, Jake's experience, perceptions, and attitudes were also limited. In Scorsese's experience, the fighter's severely constrained world was reminiscent of the limited world of Little Italy.

The biblical reference that appears on the screen at the end of the film about the blind man who is able to see refers not only to his character but to Scorsese himself, suggesting that not only LaMotta but also Scorsese are redeemed. Moreover, the statement from the Bible gives expression to Scorsese's belief about judging the behavior of other people. As stated earlier, Scorsese places his characters in a particular time and place and sees their behavior as affected by their experience within that milieu. Essentially, Scorsese asks, "How do you know what you would have done if you had been in the other person's shoes?"

Scorsese was also able to identify with LaMotta's capacity to endure punishment. As Scorsese has said, as a boy in the tough neighborhood of Little Italy, "The only way I was able to defend myself was to be able to take punishment. Then I got a lot of respect. They said, 'Oh, he's okay. He can take it.'"[6] It appears that the young Martin learned to endure punishment to feel that he belonged within the group of boys in his community and to be seen as one of them.

MAX CADY

Max Cady (Robert De Niro) in the 1991 remake of the 1960s thriller, *Cape Fear*, is the most diabolical of Martin Scorsese's film characters. Released after serving a fourteen-year imprisonment for aggravated sexual assault of a sixteen-year-old girl, Cady believes that his court-appointed attorney, Sam Bowden (Nick Nolte), had not provided him with an adequate defense. While he was imprisoned in a brutal penitentiary in Georgia, Cady studied law in general and his case in particular and learned that Bowden had suppressed information that would have shown that his rape victim had had a history of promiscuity. Cady believes that if this information had been revealed during his trial, it might have led to his being acquitted or, at least, to his having received a significantly reduced sentence.

After he gains his freedom, Cady arrives in the southern town of New Essex (presumably in Georgia) with a plan to settle in this town where the well-to-do Bowden has a successful law practice and lives with his wife, Leigh (Jessica Lange), and their fifteen-year-old daughter, Danielle or Danny (Juliette Lewis). Because of his imprisonment, Cady suffered the loss of his wife and daughter and the loss of his freedom and sense of belonging to the human race. Moreover, he suffered humiliation and loss of his self-respect as a man because he was subjected to repeated acts of forced sexual victimization. He is determined to avenge himself by forcing Bowden to "learn about loss."

Confronting Bowden directly from the outset of the film, indeed, getting into his face, Cady carries out a relentless plan of revenge and retribution. Cady's self-righteous indignation is given moral authority by virtue of the biblical references he quotes liberally and with which he has tattooed his upper body. As directed by Scorsese and acted by Robert De Niro, Cady is a brilliant sadist, a sexual pervert, and a psychopathic killer. The relentlessness of Max Cady is indicative of one who is so consumed with narcissistic rage that he pursues his quarry with single-minded purpose and is entirely bereft of sympathy, pity, and any capacity for forgiveness. His all-consuming rage and sense of self-righteousness obliterates his admitting even a thread of personal responsibility for the rape he committed as well as for the fact that seven years were added to his sentence by the parole board because he was suspected of the brutal murder of an inmate.

In formulating the character of Max Cady, Scorsese links narcissistic rage with relentless and self-righteous revenge and links aggression and competition for power with sexual perversion. As a phallic-narcissist, Cady uses his penis as an instrument with which to inflict pain and punishment on women. Cady's vindictiveness is driven by narcissistic rage that derives from what he perceives as attacks on his self that he suffered in prison and against which he was helpless to defend himself. In his mind, Sam Bowden is solely responsibility for all of the suffering that he has endured, suffering that includes having been branded by his wife and family as a pervert.

The fearsome and dangerous Max Cady (Robert De Niro), showing some of his elaborate tattoos, in *Cape Fear* (Photofest).

In addition to Cady's fury that he was "sacrificed" by his counselor, a psychological theme that underscores Cady's hatred of Bowden is the allusion that Cady is "white trash" or inferior to Bowden. Cady believes that Bowden sees him as an inferior and a hillbilly—Sam describes him to Leigh as a "Pentecostal cracker"—and is enraged with Bowden for this perception of him. Cady defends against feeling inferior by aggressively competing with Sam and proving that he is actually superior to him, indeed, more-than-human or godlike. He competes with Sam for the affection of the females in his life, Leigh, Danny, and Sam's friend, Lori, as well as intellectually. Cady strives to attain all that Bowden is and has. He has not only become literate but also knowledgeable about the law. Cady describes an early conversation he has with Bowden as "two lawyers ... talking shop" and in another scene refers to the two of them as "colleagues." During the dramatic climax on the Bowdens' houseboat, Cady says to Bowden, "If you're not better than me, I can have what you have." In his twisted mind, Cady imagines that if he takes people and things away from Sam, he, Cady, will take them unto himself and become not only like but also more than Bowden.

As the illusory avenging angel of the Lord who comes down from heaven to exact "an eye for an eye and a tooth for a tooth," Cady is determined to strip Bowden of all that is dear to him, as if this will compensate Cady for everything that has been taken from him. First, he poisons Leigh's beloved dog, Benjamin. Then he rapes, brutally beats, and cannibalizes Sam's friend and companion, Lori, apparently knowing that she will not press charges against him because of the humiliation that she would suffer in open court if she did so. Biting and tearing into Lori's face is Cady's imagined incorporation (or taking into himself) of a person Sam cares about. Since Cady, mistakenly, believes that Sam and Lori have had sex, his brutal rape of her is his way of showing that he is more powerful than Sam. These actions leave Sam no doubt that Cady is intent on hurting his wife and daughter and, perhaps, himself as well. In a similar vein, Cady sets out to blacken Bowden's professional reputation and to strip him of the respect of his colleagues.

Cady defines himself in terms of a fantasy of himself as the great avenger who comes to make right a great wrong. Indeed, as if he imagines that he has a sacred duty to do so, he is intent on saving or redeeming Sam, whom he perceives as a great sinner, by subjecting him to great suffering. Consonant with Cady's grandiose sense of himself, Scorsese imbues the psychotic Cady with superhuman qualities. Cady has used his time in prison to prepare himself for the ferocious battle that he fights with Bowden. He proudly proclaims that when he was confined in his eight-by-nine foot cell, he was "surrounded by people less than human; my mission was to become more than human." With exercise he has built his body into a fortress of omnipotent strength such that he is able to not only withstand the attack of the three bullies who use sticks, rods, and chains to beat him, but he succeeds in subduing them. As another example, when he is doused with boiling water by Danny on the houseboat, Cady shows that he is impervious to heat by burning a candle and letting the molten wax flow onto his hand and down his arm.

In addition to having gained legal expertise and reciting biblical references by memory, Cady is uncanny in outsmarting Bowden, the police, the judge, and the private detective, Kersek. As if by magic, Cady poisons Benjamin, the dog, in the Bowden house without being seen or leaving any trace of having been in the house. He again seemingly practices black magic by entering the Bowden home and murdering both the maid and Kersek although the house had been wired to alert its inhabitants to an intruder. In a number of scenes, the camera substitutes for Cady's eyes; that is, the viewer sees people and events as if he or she were seeing these through Cady's eyes, thus, leaving the impression that Cady is omnipresent, watching every move of the Bowdens, his gaze even penetrating the walls of their home.

Cady is also exquisitely and diabolically empathic in knowing how his victims feel and, as a result, of knowing how to trick them and lure them into his various traps. In short, he senses how people "tick" and how to "get to" them. Cady knows what Bowden did to him, and he knows that Bowden feels guilt about it and fears a disclosure. Cady intuits that Sam's fear and sense of superiority cause Bowden to underestimate Cady's knowledge and skills. Cady uses his psychological understanding of Sam to predict Sam's actions and "beat him to the punch." Hiring Lee Heller, a well-known and respected attorney, and obtaining a restraining order against Sam before Sam can do so are indications of Cady's remarkable prescience.

As another example, Cady knows that Lori is in love with Sam. By design, he encounters her at a bar and learns that she feels hurt and angry because Sam stood her up for a racquetball game. As she drowns her sorrows by drinking too much, Cady offers her companionship and the prospect of sexual excitement. Enticed by the friendly and fun-loving Cady, she, recklessly, invites this complete stranger to her apartment for what she assumes is sexual play and, in her mind, a way of getting even with Sam for ignoring her. There, in her apartment, Cady easily restrains her and then savagely beats, rapes, and cannibalizes her. In Cady's mind, these horrific acts affirm his phallic supremacy not only with regard to Lori but, more importantly, with regard to Sam.

Similarly, posing as Danny's high school drama teacher for one of her summer courses, Cady telephones the vulnerable teenager and speaks to her in an empathic manner about typical adolescent concerns, for example, feeling awkward and dealing with parents who lack an understanding of her feelings. Having made an emotional connection with her by phone, he lures Danny into believing that the next morning's class will be held in the basement area of her school rather than in a regular classroom. Alone with Cady in the otherwise deserted theater, Danny feels sexually stimulated by the older man's sensuality and provocative allusions as well as by his offering her marijuana and speaking to her knowingly of the "negativity" at home and of the turmoil she feels. He appeals to her desire to be wanted and to feel special by saying that in her he has found a "companion for the long walk to the light." Cady's invitation to Danny to join with him and eat from the forbidden fruit, as it were, enables him to seduce her into a sensual kiss and symbolic fellatio. Danny realizes eventually that Cady is not her drama teacher but, rather, the man her parents had warned her about, or the "big bad wolf," as Cady refers to himself. Although she is frightened, she is also excited and thus is drawn into Cady's trap of feeling an emotional connection to him. By tempting the vulnerable teenager, Cady has successfully competed with Sam for Danny's allegiance, and in this way he drives a wedge between Danny and her father. In this encounter with Danny, Cady shows that he is a clever and pathological liar. Presenting himself as a gentle and thoughtful man, Cady denies to Danny that he had anything to do with the death of the Bowden's dog and asserts with a straight face that he wishes only to help her father, not to hurt him.

Scorsese uses the seemingly omnipotent qualities of Cady particularly effectively during the chilling climax on and about the houseboat. After he is set ablaze by Danny who squirts lighter fluid in his face as he is smoking a cigar, Cady jumps into the river screaming in pain. Consistent with the fantasized invincibility of Cady's godlike figure, a few minutes later Cady, whose face is now scarred by the burns, rises from the water, an act symbolic of a resurrection, ready to attack again. From a psychological point of view, the apparently invincible Cady leaves his victims feeling entirely helpless and more and more terrorized, and the viewers share in this terror. Even Sam recognizes Cady's seemingly superhuman capabilities. After the family has taken flight, Sam telephones the police to report the murders of the detective and his maid that had occurred in his home. He describes to the police that his fleeing the murder scene is excusable because of a "force majeure," that is, an unforeseeable "act of God," that cancels all obligations.

Scorsese increases the tension and the terror progressively by depicting Cady as outsmarting Bowden at each subsequent twist of the drama that spirals into abject horror for the family. As Bowden competes with Cady at every stage, Cady outmaneuvers him, and Sam becomes more and more enraged, terrified, and careless. For example, Kersek and Bowden evolve a trap with which they plan to capture and kill Cady. They guess that Cady will try to enter the Bowden home during the two-day period when, as they have set it up, to all appearances Sam is out of town defending himself at the American Bar Association hearing. Sam buys a gun that Kersek holds as he sits guard downstairs while the family sleeps upstairs and Kersek waits for Cady to make his move. This ill-conceived plan devolves into Cady entering the house unnoticed and murdering the maid and then Kersek (with the piano wire that Cady stole during an earlier and undetected visit to the Bowden home) while the Bowdens are asleep. Compounding his miscalculations of Cady's genius, instead of reporting the crimes and waiting for the police, Sam grabs the gun in Kersek's hand, slips into the pool of blood around the body—thus leaving signs that he was involved in the murders. He and his family drive off in their SUV intending to flee to and hide in their houseboat.

In doing so, Sam becomes a fugitive from the law. In addition, since Cady has strapped himself to the undercarriage of their vehicle, instead of escaping from Cady, Sam unwittingly brings him along with the family to a remote location. In this way, Cady succeeds in isolating the family from outside intercession, and in the isolated and storm-ridden Cape Fear, Cady fully assumes the role of God as depicted in the Book of Job and subjects the family to the ultimate test of faith to determine how strong or how weak they are as the biblical God so subjected Job.

Cady appears on the houseboat and, having stripped Sam's gun from him, he threatens Bowden with ultimate loss, that is, the destruction, psychological as well as physical, of his wife and child as Cady had himself lost his family. The literal and figurative imprisonment of the Bowdens on their boat, helpless, contained, and isolated from the world at large, is symbolic of how Cady felt in his prison cell. As the god that he fantasizes he is, omnipotent and omniscient, he forces Sam, standing in the witness box as the accused prisoner, to confess his crime or sin of having suppressed the information that Cady believes would have saved him from imprisonment. Cady proclaims that he is Virgil and that Sam is in the "ninth circle of traitors." In this scene, Cady acts as the ultimate judge and forces Leigh and Danny, who witness Sam's confession, to act as jurors. Grandiosely, Cady judges Bowden as guilty of "betrayal of God, of his fellow man, and of his country." More to the point, he finds Sam "guilty of judging me and selling me out." In imposing his sentence on Sam he declares: "Now you will truly learn about loss, loss of freedom, loss of humanity. Now you and I will truly be the same." It is at this stage that Cady orders the parents to get on their knees and remove their clothing. In the context of the story, it appears that Cady's diabolical plan is to force the parents, naked and manacled or otherwise restrained, to watch him savage their daughter and listen to her screams, during which he imagines that they will beg him, while they are kneeling before their "god," to stop and offer him their bodies as substitutes for Danny's. In this way, as he was reduced to animalistic behavior, a loss of his humanity, while he was in prison, Cady plans to force Sam and Leigh to regress and act in an animalistic way. Similarly, as he was subjected to a humiliating full-body strip search by the police at Sam's intercession, an event witnessed by Sam behind a one-way mirror, Cady intends his victims to be utterly humiliated and degraded.

During the harrowing final stage of the struggle with Cady, the three Bowdens literally rise to the occasion and each tries to protect the others from Cady. Earlier Sam, Leigh, and Danny were often argumentative, distant from one another, and unempathic; however, when they are confronted with the prospect of personal destruction by the sadistic Cady, they show their cohesiveness as a family, their courage, and their selfless love for each other. Even Danny, who initially feels pleasure that Cady had seemingly come after her, realizes the danger that he represents to herself and to her parents and takes direct action to hurt or kill him. Leigh and Sam work in unison to save their daughter, and Sam finds a hidden reservoir of strength and resolve in subduing Cady with a rock.

In the context of the religious theme set forth by Scorsese, Bowden's betrayal of Cady is necessary if there is to be any redemption, not unlike Judas's betrayal of Jesus which was necessary if Jesus was to become the Redeemer. (See Chapter 11 for a discussion of *The Last Temptation of Christ*.) As depicted, the Bowdens gain redemption to continue their lives on Earth while Cady, psychotic to the end, believes that he has gained ultimate salvation proclaiming, as he is drowning, that he is "bound for the Promised Land." His eyes focus on Sam's until the last moment of his life, a sight that one imagines, as Danny's narrated recollection of these events suggest, will remain in Sam's consciousness, or at least in his nightmares, forever.

In addition to the themes of "divine" justice and retribution, the film illustrates a spiritual theme of Scorsese, namely, the power of the selfless love of the Bowdens, that is evoked when they are on the houseboat confronted with imminent danger, in defeating the devil, as it were.

BEN EBERHARDT

Ben Eberhardt (Harvey Keitel) in *Alice Doesn't Live Here Anymore* (1974) appears as a charming and sexually attractive man when he first encounters Alice at the bar where she is a singer. Using his wiles, he appeals to her ego by telling her that he really likes her singing. Alice is lonely, and Ben, who is fully aware of her loneliness, tries to take advantage of her vulnerability. He is insistent on spending time alone with her and is seemingly unwilling to take "no" for an answer. Indeed, after one encounter, he drives her home, but she goes into her motel, leaving Ben outside. Ben responds to Alice's refusal to continue their "talk" inside by using his hand to mimic a gun whose trigger he pulls. Ben's message is clear: "I'll get you."

Alice, lonely and eager for a relationship with man, finally surrenders and begins having sex with Ben. After a week or so of sleeping with Ben, Alice discovers that he is married and has a child. She learns this about Ben when his wife, Rita, comes to the motel to talk with Alice. Alice tells Rita that she will stop seeing Ben immediately. Suddenly, Ben appears outside Alice's door. He is enraged and threatening, shouting loudly and uncontrollably at his wife. Using his fist, Ben breaks through the glass panel of the locked door to let himself in.

As a phallic-narcissist, Ben must have his sexual object, Alice, available on demand. Rita is threatening Ben's continuing to have what he wants, and Ben perceives this as a challenge to his phallic supremacy. Utterly enraged, Ben produces a knife and threatens to cut Rita if she does not get out. After he chases Rita out, he threatens Alice and demands that they meet that evening as usual. When Alice tries to calm him down, he screams that she must not tell him what to do and says that he will "bust" her "jaw" if she ever does that again. This exchange indicates the extraordinary response of a phallic-narcissist to anyone who attempts to control him. Alice responds to this harrowing encounter with the almost-maniacal Ben by quickly leaving the area with her son, Tommy.

Interestingly, Ben had told Alice when they first met that the way he makes a living is to fill bullet casings with powder. This occupation seems to be symbolic of Ben's proclivity for violence.

These four characters represent male aggression taken to an extreme. Moreover, Cady and Bickle are probably psychotic and the other two seem to become psychotic when they are enraged. In depicting these violent men in his films, Scorsese seemingly was giving vent to his own rage about the frustrations and injustices that he felt he had suffered in his life. He knew from his own experience the "killing feeling, the feeling of really being angry," and perhaps by depicting these extreme emotions on the screen, Scorsese was quieting his own.[7] All of these characters live limited and constrained lives, and, thus, their internal worlds or mindsets are also limited. As alluded to earlier, Scorsese applies a nonjudgmental approach to these violent men, and he understands their behavior as part and parcel of where they come from, to paraphrase the director.

6

Demigods

This chapter considers Henry Hill and his gangster pals or "wiseguys" in *GoodFellas*, Sam "Ace" Rothstein and Nicky Santoro in *Casino*, Bill "the Butcher" Cutting in *Gangs of New York*, Rupert Pupkin in *The King of Comedy*, and Frank Pierce in *Bringing Out the Dead*. These characters are termed "demigods" because they imagine that they are gods of a sort, having the capacity to affect the life and death of others.

A number of these characters—particularly the gangsters in *GoodFellas, Casino,* and *Gangs of New York*—use unbridled force and violence to get what they want, becoming addicted to the "high" associated with power. Rupert Pupkin is less violent and aggressive than the gangsters, but he, nevertheless, selfishly pursues his self-interests, disregarding the needs and desires of others. The variety of characterizations shows that a man's fantasy of being godlike can be used to achieve both malevolent and, in the case of Frank Pierce, benevolent ends as well.

THE GOODFELLAS

The focal characters of *GoodFellas* (1990) are Henry Hill (Ray Liotta), Jimmy, the "Gent" Conway (Robert De Niro), and Tommy De Vito (Joe Pesci). *GoodFellas* is psychologically astute in its portrayal of how one's sense of self derives from and depends on that person's connection to his social milieu—often a family—in which one is embedded and upon which one depends for emotional sustenance. These emotional or psychological "supplies" include a sense of belonging, feeling affirmed, and offering idealization, or something or someone in which one can believe fervently and from which one derives a sense of security. In the case of Henry Hill, the "family" to which he strives to belong is the criminal mob in his neighborhood.

The story opens around 1955. Henry Hill informs the viewers—via a voice-over—that, as a youngster living in a poor, working-class family, he noticed that the gangsters in his neighborhood were the people who were most respected and admired by others in his milieu. A flashback shows that Henry got a part-time job at the cab stand across the street from his home, this location being a hangout for the mobsters. Eventually this evolves into a full-time job with the gangsters, and Henry stops going to school altogether during his teens.

Henry looks up to these gangsters rather than to his laborer father because their life seems glamorous and affords them seemingly unlimited amounts of money to buy fancy clothes and cars. He sees these men as powerful, able to get for themselves everything one could want. As established in the film, Henry is drawn to join the gang, to become one of them, because membership offers him security and a sense of belonging to an elite class within his milieu—"movie stars with muscle," as he terms it—that boost his self-esteem and sense of self-worth. This family of gangsters seem more attractive to Henry than his biological family, which has struggled to make ends meet. Henry's father, who is often angry and abusive because he has five mouths to feed on a limited salary, is, for Henry, less idealizable than Paulie Cicero (Paul Sorvino), who is the gang boss in the neighborhood.

As a boy looking up to men as role models, Henry wants to emulate the gangsters. Henry describes his experience when he was a young teenager:

> I always wanted to be a gangster. To me, being a gangster was better than being President of the United States.... I knew I wanted to be a part of them. It was there that I belonged. It meant being somebody in a neighborhood full of nobodies. They could do what they wanted. I could go anywhere and do anything.... I belonged. I was a part of something. They treated me like a grownup.

This sense of belonging to something bigger than himself, in effect, a family of sorts, is a key dimension in appreciating Henry's psychological makeup. He derives emotional sustenance from belonging, and that boosts his burgeoning sense of self and inflates his grandiosity.

At thirteen, Henry was learning how to score day after day, making more money than most grown men. He meets Jimmy Conway soon after joining the gang.

A "big man" respected by the gang, Jimmy is noted for his hijacking expertise and success and for his cleverness in paying off the right people, including the cops.

A scene that shows how "belonging" provides Henry with emotional support and admiration occurs after he is arrested and arraigned for selling contraband cigarettes. First, his gangster friends send an attorney to court and get him off, showing that he has value in their eyes and that they will protect him. Later, as Henry is leaving the court, the gang members, including Paulie, greet him with applause—"You broke your cherry," he is told—

6. Demigods

Jimmy Conway (Robert De Niro, *center*) talking with fellow gangsters Henry Hill (Ray Liotta, *left*) and Frenchy (Mike Starr, *right*) in a scene from *Good-Fellas* (Photofest).

as if he has just become a man or graduated from high school, and Jimmy tells him that they are proud of him for keeping his mouth shut and not selling out his friends.

As Henry grows up and becomes more and more a member of the goodfellas, he looks down on people like his father who work regular jobs and earn regular money. To him, such people are suckers. It is evident that Henry's sense of self is organized in terms of his feeling superior to others. From the perspective of phallic narcissism, Henry's becoming a member of the gang serves to affirm his imagined phallic supremacy.

While Jimmy seems to be most identified with making big scores (and lots of money), another gang member, Tommy De Vito, is noted for his explosive violence. He reacts with murderous rage to anyone who questions him, injures his very fragile facade even by joking, or is perceived by Tommy as being an enemy of sorts. Tommy retaliates brutally, usually with his gun. As depicted, Tommy is an out-of-control lunatic, a psychopath.

The story focuses attention on Henry's involvement with Karen (Lorraine Bracco), the woman who becomes his wife. Upon meeting Henry as a young man, Karen relates that she was impressed with his power. According to Karen, Henry is able to get a ringside table at the Copacabana without a reservation, people cater to him, and everyone seems to know him. Henry wines and dines her and always has a lot of money. She finds him to be an "exciting" guy to whom everyone wants to be nice. When Henry first brandishes a gun and then gives it to her to hide, she says, "I got to admit, it turned me on." Karen's experience informs us of the attractiveness and excitement of power, indeed, of omnipotence, of being able to do and to have what ordinary people cannot. This depiction is a comment on the cultural tendency to idolize material wealth and power in any form and the cultural wishful fantasy of having unlimited power and wealth.

Eventually, after Henry and Karen marry, she realizes that he is a gangster and expresses her concern that he will end up in prison. Henry assures her that he will not and reveals his grandiosity and sense of megalomaniacal control when he says to her, "No one goes to jail unless they want to. They make themselves get caught. They don't have things organized. I've got things organized with these guys." Karen tells us that Henry's criminal activities seemed to be normal and not criminal. She rationalizes that the kind of work Henry does simply shows that he is enterprising, and she is proud of the money he brought in. Moreover, as she recounts, the "family members" were so very close during those years; there were never any outsiders involved in their activities. The extended family of gangsters, with their spouses and children, celebrated birthdays and anniversaries and go on vacations together. This closeness makes their criminal activities seem normal. This normalization of even criminal activities by virtue of "family" support is an important psychological feature of belonging to a social milieu that affirms the behavior of its members.

After a time, Henry's and Karen's dream-fantasy begins to devolve into a nightmare. Along with Jimmy's active intervention, Tommy kills Billy Batts, a "made" man, "made" referring to a certification of sorts by the Mafia to one who has been granted special rights. The rules of the Mafia dictate that a made member of the family—who had to be 100 percent Italian—could not be "whacked" unless one obtained permission from the bosses. Tommy explodes into murderous rage and kills Batts because he feels insulted by a comment made by Billy. Because he fully ignored the rules of the family, eventually, Tommy is executed by the mob bosses in retaliation for killing Billy.

The killing of Batts is an indication of what is happening to all three of them—Henry, Jimmy, and Tommy. Having had the license to do whatever they wanted for years, outside of the laws of society and of ordinary men, all three of them have become megalomaniacal. They have a fantasy of themselves as gods, able to do anything they wish. Their megalomania now extends to breaking "family" rules. It is evident that they are greedy for money, sex, and power. Less obvious is that they have become addicted to these "substances." Like addicts who abuse chemical substances, gangsters like Henry, Jimmy, and Tommy get a "high" from exercising their power. However, as they progress in forcing their will on others, they come to need more and more power, and thus, they become more and more violent to feel the "high." Henry, Jimmy, and Tommy are out of control and utterly without restraints, even in terms of abiding by the rules of the mob family. For example, Tommy shoots a young go-pher in the bar they frequent simply because he didn't move fast enough for him.

Compared to his more psychopathic brethren, Tommy and Jimmy, Henry is relatively tame, expressing his megalomania in terms of drugs and sex rather than killing people who get in his way. Henry becomes addicted to dealing and using drugs. He expresses his fantasy of phallic supremacy by having an adulterous relationship and then setting up his girlfriend in a fancy apartment. When Karen discovers Henry's betrayal, problems and fights develop between them. Henry leaves Karen and his children and goes to live with his girlfriend. However, Karen appeals to Jimmy and Paulie for help, and they convince him that he must go back to his family and do the right thing. Essentially, they tell him that he can do what he wants with regard to his sexual activities, but he must give the appearances of being loyal to his wife. Giving the appearance of fidelity to one's family—particularly if one has children—is one of the unwritten rules of the mob.

Henry spends several years in prison for roughing up a gangster in Florida who owed money to gang members. During his years in prison Henry increases his involvement with and use of cocaine. Although warned by Paulie, his father figure, to stay away from drugs, after he is released Henry establishes an extended network of buying, distributing, and selling drugs across state lines. Both his wife and his girlfriend became users, and both of them as well as Jimmy are involved in the highly profitable operation.

The characterization and behavior of Jimmy also shows how his greed or addiction to power and money takes over his sense of allegiance to the family. He runs an operation—the Lufthansa theft at the JFK airport—that involves a number of gangsters. The theft nets $6 million in cash, and as Henry Hill describes it, "more than enough to go around." Yet, because of Jimmy's greed and the extent of his addiction, he becomes paranoid. Fearing that one of the participants might talk and implicate him, and also wanting all of the money for himself, Jimmy sets out to kill everyone involved in the airport heist.

Eventually, Henry's drug ring is broken up by narcotics agents, and Henry loses the support and respect of Paulie. In addition, Henry fears that Jimmy is planning to have him killed. Henry is aware of Jimmy's paranoia and realizes that Jimmy might think that Henry will implicate him in the narcotics operation. Suddenly and for the first time since he joined the gang, Henry does not feel safe. He enters the federal witness protection program, and as a witness for the prosecution, he implicates Paulie and Jimmy in a courtroom.

In the final scene, Henry is seen living an ordinary life in a suburb somewhere in the United States. He has regrets about what he felt he needed to do to save his life: "The hardest thing was leaving the life. I still love the life. We were movie stars with muscle. We had it all for the asking." The film ends with the ghost of Tommy shooting his gun directly at the camera. Perhaps this represents Henry's worst dread, a nightmare really, of there being a contract out on him. This fear arises from his betrayal of his family and the guilt that he feels about doing so.

GoodFellas shows what belonging to a family of gangsters means psychologically. Having an unrestricted license to get whatever they wanted—money for clothes, jewelry, houses, and furnishings—without working for the money, these men feel that they are superior to other men in the neighborhood whom they consider beneath them. Their sense of phallic supremacy coupled with their fantasy of omnipotence grossly inflates their sense of personal worth and esteem, of being "real" and potent men.

For these gangsters, violence in the form of theft, extortion, and murder become convoluted with their feeling that they are omnipotent, gods of a sort. These men have psychological as well as cultural deficits that they try to fill in, as it were, by using money, sex, power, and violent behavior to express their personal and highly exaggerated fantasies of entitlement and unlimited material success. Henry, Jimmy, and Tommy become megalomaniacal, imagining that they are gods. As the film portrays, they also become hopeless addicts, their craving for a "high" via having power over the life and death of others progressively gets out of control. Ultimately, they destroy the "good life" that they had created as well as themselves.

The film has autobiographical elements particularly with regard to Scorsese's early experiences among the boys and men in Little Italy whose activities were on the fringe of gangsterism or who were actual gangsters. In addition, Henry's wish to be part of something bigger than himself, something like belonging to a "family" that offered security, is reminiscent of Scorsese's desire to be a part of the church. In this context, first being an altar boy—joining the family, as it were—and then aspiring to be a priest offered the young Scorsese the promise of ultimate security in the form of salvation.

With regard to other works in the Scorsese opus, *GoodFellas* contains more finely-articulated themes about narcissism, materialism, and greed than he first expressed in his student film, *It's Not Just You, Murray*! Although, on a narcissistic level, the gangster life may seem attractive because of peoples' wishful fantasies of superiority and omnipotence, that is, people wishing that they have the power to get whatever they wish, Scorsese shows that with such a lifestyle, greed and paranoia will destroy the gangsters from within. Scorsese also shows that there is no honor among thieves, that they will eventually turn against each other and breach whatever loyalties once existed among them.

Sam "Ace" Rothstein

Rothstein (Robert DeNiro) is the focal character in Scorsese's 1995 gangster movie, *Casino*. He is an obsessive who has a special skill in gathering esoteric information on sports teams and statistics. At the opening of the film, Sam has established a reputation as a superb handicapper and has made big money for the mob. He is rewarded with the management of the Tangiers, a casino in Las Vegas. Sam demands complete control of the operation of the casino and receives carte blanche from the bosses. Ever an obsessive about order and details, he runs a tight, high-quality operation, and he seemingly knows how to keep the police and the political figures content.

Sam creates a near-perfect world for himself: a casino with a good reputation whose profits were bountiful, a luxurious home with landscaped grounds, tailored clothes, and expensive cars and jewelry. Sam strives to give the appearance of propriety. He loves the attention he gets for being a big man in Vegas, and he demands and receives respect from his milieu, even becoming a member of the country club. This attention and applause feeds Sam's fantasy of his phallic supremacy.

Sam falls in love, or perhaps, more correctly, becomes obsessed with, Ginger (Sharon Stone), a hustler and whore, whom he imagines is the perfect adornment for him in his paradise on earth. Charming, sophisticated, and beautiful, Ginger is not in love with Sam but, rather, with her pimp, Lester Diamond (James Woods). Sam knows about her attachment to Lester but, believing that she would prefer him to Lester because of the material things he could give her, he asks her to marry him. Ginger is persuaded to agree to his proposal because, as a symbol of his love and trust in her, Sam gives her access to the key to his safe deposit box that contains two million in cash and a cache of jewels. In addition, Sam provides Ginger with an extensive and elaborate wardrobe and other beautiful things, as if she were a queen, to buy her loyalty. However, Sam gives Ginger little or nothing in the way of emotional support. Sam's foolish surrender of control of his safe deposit box to Ginger suggests that he has a fantasy that he is such a good catch that any woman whom he would marry would remain loyal to him. His absolute trust in Ginger is childlike and incongruent with his age and his experience. However, his behavior is understandable from the perspective that having a beautiful woman as his wife feeds Sam's narcissism and sense of himself as a potent man.

Interestingly however, as Nicky (Joe Pesci), Sam's gangster pal, relates, Sam cover his bets with Ginger by having a child with her, Amy, before they get married. Although Ginger is so attached to Lester that she feels compelled to call Lester on her wedding day and Sam finds her on the phone in tears, he believes, foolishly, that he can trust her with his life as well as with his money. Lester, meanwhile, knows that he can manipulate Ginger at will with sweet words and drugs. Although she abuses alcohol and drugs, Ginger represents

Ginger Rothstein (Sharon Stone) and her husband, Sam Rothstein (Robert De Niro), in a scene from *Casino* (Photofest).

to Sam the perfect companion to complement his grandiose fantasy of personal success, the ultimate evidence, as it were, that he has made it and has it all. In other words, having Ginger as his wife feeds Sam's sense of phallic supremacy.

After Nicky moves his operation to Las Vegas, he establishes his own loan sharking and extortion rackets buttressed by beating up and murdering people who refuse to cooperate with him. As a "made" man, Nicky feels he can do as he pleases, and he starts running bookie operations inside the casinos. His activities come to the attention of law enforcement officials, and he is banned from every casino in Vegas. In response, Nicky, with his brother Dominick, import a gang of their own, and the crew acts as if Vegas were the "wild west." Nicky runs a crime ring that includes robbing high rollers, casino bosses, and bookmakers. He even opens his own restaurant. Nicky revels in his new world of "broads," "booze," and drugs, but he incurs the suspicion of the FBI, who begin tapping his phone and following his activities.

Over time, Ginger becomes a coke addict as well as a drunk, and her behavior embarrasses Sam. The more Sam tries to control her, the more she seeks the succor of Lester Diamond. On one occasion, Lester arrives in town to get $25,000 from Ginger, and she gives him the money. Sam is enraged, feeling threatened by Ginger's continuing attachment to Lester. He orders his men to beat up Lester to frighten him into leaving town. This action, in turn, distresses Ginger, and she withdraws further from Sam. Sam, jealous and obsessive about holding onto her, tries to control her more by having her wear a beeper.

As the story progresses, Sam and Nicky become more and more addicted to money, power, and violence and increasingly paranoid. The two men begin to unravel as Ginger is doing so with alcohol and drugs. Even the casino workers take progressively greater advantage of the system. It is expected that everyone involved in the casino operation will do some skimming, but as long as the bosses keep getting their cut, the system will remain intact. Eventually, however, the bags of money that are delivered to the bosses get lighter and lighter. In response, the midwest bosses send an emissary, the underboss of Kansas City, to Vegas to stop the skimming of their profits. This man, however, comes under the scrutiny of the FBI, and surveillance cameras and telephone taps record his activities and his interactions with the bosses.

Sam has a fantasy of himself as being very, very smart, actually omniscient; his downfall is due to his demand that his way is the only way. He makes the mistake of firing an employee who is related to a politician who, in turn, has connections to the county gaming commission. As the omniscient god of his universe, as Sam imagines himself to be, he absolutely refuses to compromise with the politician in any form. The frustrated politician says to Sam as he prepares to leave the casino: "You act like you're at home. You are our guests." The politician retaliates against Sam because of his lack of cooperation; Sam's application for a licensing permit is rejected by the gambling commission.

This rejection of Sam's application enrages Sam. For him the rejection is an insult, a repudiation of the grandiosely positive image of himself that he has worked to create. Sam responds to the rejection—a blow to his phallic narcissism—by engaging in the unthinkable in the world of the mob: He goes on television, speaks to reporters, and, in general, attracts publicity to himself and the operation of the casino. Sam is obsessed with being right and being seen in that light by the Vegas milieu. His seeking publicity to prove that the gaming commission acted inappropriately and unjustly is an indicator of his obsessiveness about preserving his grandiose image as well as his pride. In addition, Sam—whose narcissism is at a childlike level—thoroughly enjoys the spotlight and the massive public attention that he generates. Sam is consumed with a narcissistic fantasy that he is a god in his own right, totally ignoring the fact that the bosses gave him whatever power he enjoys and that it is their money that is at stake, not his.

Both Sam and Nicky, each addicted to money and power, each imagining that he can do whatever he pleases, spin out of control, blaming each other for the troubles that the operation is suffering. Sam assumes the role of entertainment director of the casino, develops an ongoing television show, and sues the gambling commission. The bosses want him to walk away; he refuses to do so because his pride is at stake.

Sam and Ginger's marriage continues to fall apart. She leaves Sam, taking their young daughter with her to Los Angeles, where she meets Lester. Sam is beside himself and demands that she return the child. Ginger appeals to Nicky for mediation and help. Nicky intervenes and effects a reconciliation of sorts between Ginger and Sam. However, soon thereafter, Ginger and Nicky begin having a sexual affair. Nicky's taking another gangster's wife, although inflating his fantasy of phallic supremacy, is a breach of the rules of the mob. Ginger eventually takes the key to Sam's safe deposit box, gets all of the money, and leaves him. Soon thereafter, she dies from a "hot" dose of drugs in Los Angeles. Because Nicky overextended his reach, even as a made man, Nicky and his brother are beaten severely and buried in the desert while they are still alive. The FBI arrest the bosses. Sam is subjected to a car bombing, but in his obsessive style, he escapes because of the precautions that he had taken to have a metal plate installed under the driver's seat. The Tangiers collapses, and big corporations take over the casinos. Sam, one of the sole survivors of the destruction of paradise, goes back to work as a handicapper in San Diego. The film suggests that he has learned his lesson about the danger of pride and has returned to live on Earth as a more humble man.

From a psychological perspective, this story of gangsters has much in common with *GoodFellas*. Sam and Nicky fantasize that they are like gods. Metaphorically, Sam and Nicky disobeyed the rules of paradise, as it were, and ate from the tree of knowledge. Ultimately, they are punished for their "sins" of greed and pride. The gangsters' greed for money, power, and control devolves into an addiction, and they become megalomaniacal. Similar to the earlier film, *Casino* shows that as these addicts try to grab more and more power, they become progressively more paranoid and more violent. The violence once unleashed, however, becomes circular and cannot be controlled. The greed, selfishness, and violence destroys them and their paradise. The focus on the destructiveness of greed is a theme that is consistent with Scorsese's values.

Scorsese could identify with the self-destructiveness inherent in Ginger's (as well as Henry Hill's) abusing drugs because he had fallen prey to them earlier in his life. The theme of betrayal in the film, that is, Sam appears to be the hapless victim of Ginger's treachery as well as Nicky's betrayal of Sam, is portrayed also in *GoodFellas*. Scorsese seems to be saying that there is no honor among thieves and that, in effect, loyalty disappears in the face of greed.

Bill "The Butcher" Cutting

Bill Cutting (Daniel Day-Lewis) is the gang leader of the Confederation of the American Natives in *Gangs of New York* (2002). He is, in effect, a mob boss of an earlier era as compared to the gangsters in *GoodFellas* and

Casino. He strives for absolute power and control—features associated with phallic narcissism—over the Five Points area of New York City. As he says, the five streets—Mulberry, Worth, Cross, Orange, Little Water—are representative of five fingers, and if he has them all, they comprise a "fist." Bill makes a fist of his hand; this is symbolic of his complete power and dominance over all the people of the area.

Bill considers himself a true American and, thus, superior to the Irish immigrants, whom he calls the "bastard sons of Erin" and "sons of Irish bitches." His hatred derives from religious bigotry—the immigrants are Roman Catholics and he is Protestant—as well as from the Nativists' fear that these newcomers to America or, as Bill calls them, trespassers, will take jobs and opportunities away from the real Americans. Bill defines a "real American" as one who will fight and perhaps give his life to his country. Bill's father, he recounts, died in 1814 fighting the British, presumably in the War of 1812.

Bill Cutting is literally a butcher, and he is particularly adroit in using knives and cleavers when he butchers animals. He applies these skills in his butchering of men, knowing how to wound a man so he will suffer a slow death. He also knows how to apply a fatal blow that will lead to a relatively quick death.

The movie begins in 1846 with a ferocious battle involving hand-to-hand combat between people who use knives, razors, cleavers, axes, and other

Bill "the Butcher" Cutting (Daniel Day-Lewis) and his gang of Nativists prepare for battle in *Gangs of New York* (Photofest).

instruments of a similar ilk. The battle involves a conglomerate of Irish tribes, led by Priest Vallon (Liam Neeson), and the Nativists, led by Cutting. Vallon's tribe is named the Dead Rabbits. The battle will decide who, Vallon or Cutting, will hold sway over the Five Points area in lower Manhattan.

Bill strikes a mortal blow and fells Vallon. Bill tells the wounded Vallon that his death will be swift. Nevertheless, Vallon asks Bill to "finish it," and Bill uses a knife to hasten his death. Bill calls out to the various gang members who are still fighting to see that their "king," if you will, has fallen. The death of Vallon heralds the rise of Cutting as the undisputed ruler of Five Points. Cutting outlaws the Dead Rabbits and decrees that Vallon's young son, Amsterdam (Leonardo DiCaprio), who witnessed the killing, be handed over to the law, presumably so that he will be shipped off to reform prison.

Bill attains complete power in the area. He has the police under his thumb, and he forms an alliance with William Tweed (Jim Broadbent) and his corrupt Tammany Hall political machine. Bill provides the muscle so that Tweed can gain political advantage and control the people of the area. Bill is well paid for his services. Tweed and his cronies provide "protection" and promises of social services to the unknowing and starving immigrants in return for their votes when an election occurs.

The gangsters in Five Points steal and plunder and all of them are forced to share their booty with Bill. One scene shows houses that are ablaze and are allowed to burn so that gang members can loot them. As in all cases of thievery in "murderers' alley," the spoils are given to Bill. All of the gangsters kowtow to Bill, wanting to remain in his favor, out of fear of his knives and his propensity to kill men he considers his enemies without warning. Indeed, everyone in Five Points pays homage to Bill, who is considered a king of sorts. Half-naked women lie at his feet while he is entertained during a show; young men do his bidding without question. His arrogance is plainly displayed in his telling Amsterdam, when they first meet, that Amsterdam has to pay (by giving him booty) for the "pleasure of my company." Bill even decides what events will be celebrated and how to celebrate them. He decrees that each year there will be a celebration of the great battle of 1846 when Vallon was killed.

Bill uses fear as his weapon to maintain his megalomaniacal control over the people in Five Points. He says in this context, "Fear is what preserves the order of things." Bill explains that he has "stayed alive this long," forty-seven years, "because of fear, the spectacle of fearsome acts. Somebody steals from me, I cut off his hands; he offends me, I cut out his tongue; he rises against me, I cut off his head, stick it on a pole, raise it high up so all on the streets can see."

Bill fancies himself as having the power of life and death over the people in Five Points. However, there is some truth to his fantasy of himself as omnipotent. In one scene, Tweed tells Bill that it would look good to the wealthy uptown people, who fear the rampant gangsterism in Five Points, if four men from the Points were hanged. These hangings would indicate to the rich and powerful New Yorkers that Tammany Hall was meting out punishment to criminals. Bill chooses the four men, and they are hanged in the public square.

Amsterdam Vallon is released from reform prison about sixteen years after the battle of 1846, and he returns to Five Points incognito. Another young man named Johnny recognizes him as Vallon's son and claims to have tried to help him escape from the Nativists sixteen years earlier. Johnny (Henry Thomas) is a petty criminal who works for Bill, and he encourages Amsterdam to join him. Amsterdam does so and shows his superior skill in fighting and stealing. It is not clear in the film whether Amsterdam joins up with Cutting so that he can more easily get to the man who killed his father or whether he joins in the thievery to survive. Bill takes a liking to Amsterdam who demonstrates unusual risk-taking and courage, and Amsterdam seems to admire Bill. On one occasion, Amsterdam saves Bill's life when a man tries to shoot Bill with a pistol. Bill begins to think of Amsterdam as a son.

Soon thereafter, Bill learns Amsterdam's true identity from Johnny. Johnny is jealous that both Bill and Jenny (Cameron Diaz), a young pickpocket, have taken a strong liking to Amsterdam, and Johnny betrays Amsterdam in retaliation. Bill is enraged, feeling that he has been played for a fool by Amsterdam.

At the celebration of the battle of 1846, Bill shows his arrogance as well rage toward Amsterdam during a knife-throwing exhibition. At this stage of the action, Bill is aware that Amsterdam and Jenny have become lovers. Bill asks Jenny, his former assistant and one-time lover, to join him on the stage. Wanting to demonstrate his superior power (phallic supremacy) in comparison to Amsterdam, Bill hurls the knives at Jenny quickly and unexpectedly and comes so close to hitting her body that Amsterdam, who is in the audience, is frightened. Indeed, the last knife Bill throws nicks Jenny in the neck.

Bill's hatred of the Irish immigrants is obsessive and self-serving, and ultimately, it contributes to his downfall. In hating the Irish and considering them as inferior, Bill raises himself up and feeds his grandiose fantasy of himself and the Nativists as superior. In other words, Bill's bigotry toward the Irish serves his infantile narcissistic demands and preserves his self-image of superiority.

As more and more Irish arrive on the shores of New York, Tweed, who is interested only in votes, suggests that Bill recruit them and get their votes. Bill refuses to do so, remaining mired in his self-centered hatred of the Irish rather than looking to the future of what their numbers will mean in terms of their voting power. Bill explains self-righteously that his father was a true American, and he will not dishonor his father's memory by helping or aligning himself with the "trespassers" in any way. Because of Bill's refusal, Tweed turns to Amsterdam, once his position as the leader of the Irish is established, to recruit the votes of the thousands of new Americans.

Bill's consuming hatred of the Irish leads, moreover, to his betraying his own code regarding honorable combat, that is, looking his opponent in the eye when he strikes him. The new Irish voters, now organized by Amsterdam Vallon, elect their candidate, McGinn, as sheriff. Bill is enraged that an Irishman has been elected because it indicates that he has lost some of his power and control over Five Points. He approaches McGinn as if he means to challenge him. McGinn suggests that they go inside and have a talk. When he turns his back on Bill, Bill hurls a knife and kills him. In undertaking this cowardly act, Bill seems to have lost any semblance of good sense. In killing an elected official, even Tweed thinks that Bill has gone too far. It seems that Bill's infantile narcissism, his fantasy that he is a god and, thus, that he can do whatever he wishes and suffer no reprisal, has gotten utterly out of control.

The killing of McGinn incites the people of Five Points against Bill, and the Irish organize themselves, with Amsterdam as their leader, to fight the Nativists in a battle. In this battle, Bill is killed by Amsterdam. Thus, Bill's infantile narcissism, his greedy pursuit of power and sense of superiority over the Irish, leads to his demise.

Like many of the other phallic-narcissists who are gun-toting killers considered in these chapter, Bill's weapons serve as his phallic-substitutes. He demonstrates his extraordinary skill in knife-throwing not only in battles but in a public exhibition. His behavior with sexual women seems to be unemotional and uncaring, viewing women as things. However, he had taken in Jenny Everdeane when she was twelve as well as her mother and took care of them "in his own way." This expression by Jenny does not make clear what the basis of their relationship was except that he did impregnate her. Jenny explains to Amsterdam that Bill did not touch her until she asked him to and that the scars on her stomach were caused when the baby was cut out of her. She tells Amsterdam that after that occurred, Bill did not want her anymore because he does not "fancy" women who are scarred. In light of the circumstances surrounding Jenny's scarring, it seems that Bill is particularly arrogant in his disdain of Jenny.

The movie, *Gangs of New York*, and its autobiographical implications were discussed in Chapter 2.

RUPERT PUPKIN

The character of Rupert Pupkin (Robert De Niro) in Scorsese's 1983 movie *The King of Comedy* captures the essence of people who have the capacity for violence and imagine that they can attain what they wish by any means whatsoever. Although he lacks the brutal aggressiveness of psychopathic mobsters and is no battle-scarred warrior, Rupert does declare a war of sorts to get what he wants.

6. Demigods

Rupert is utterly obsessed by his wish to become a famous comedian like his idol, television star Jerry Langford (Jerry Lewis), and he lives in a fantasy world. He imagines having lunch with Jerry Langford in a restaurant and fantasizes that the star pleads with Rupert to take over his television show as a favor to him. During this imagined conversation, Rupert repeatedly begs off, citing busyness, but eventually accedes to Jerry's request. Continuing the fantasy, a fan interrupts the duo seeking Rupert's autograph. Rupert's delusions of grandeur are even more apparent when, during this fantasy scenario, a caricaturist comes by their table to show them his drawing of the heads of the two men. Rupert remarks to the artist: "There's only one problem. You made his bigger."

In his apartment Rupert has life-size cutouts of Jerry Langford and of Liza Minnelli, and he imagines that he is on a television show with the two of them sitting on either side of him. Rupert sees himself performing before a mural of a large studio audience and hearing thunderous applause from them. In this scenario, he is a famous TV star, the king of comedy, and millions adore him.

At one level, Rupert epitomizes the ambitious American striving not just for success but also for acclaim and enormous wealth. He is obsessed with

Rupert Pupkin (Robert De Niro) (*left*) having an imaginary lunch with his idol, Jerry Langford (Jerry Lewis), in a fantasy scenario from *The King of Comedy*. (Photofest)

and idolizes celebrities, clamoring at stage doors with others for their autographs, and he wants nothing less than to be one of them. However, the thirty-four-year-old Rupert has crossed the fantasy-reality boundary. He does not just daydream and wish to be a celebrity, his fantasies have become real to him. Moreover, he not only idealizes Jerry, but he tries to merge with him. He has studied the life and career of Jerry, mimicking his jokes and delivery, and he imagines that he is Langford. Indeed, in the opening scenes of the film, Rupert is dressed like Jerry. Rupert's wished-for merger with Jerry is, unconsciously, an attempt to counter and defend against his sense of powerlessness. His fantasy of merging with the star provides Rupert with an illusory sense of omnipotence that feeds his infantile narcissistic demands.

The dramatic action turns on an interaction that Rupert has with Jerry Langford early on in the story. One evening, after his show ends, Jerry tries to walk from the stage entrance to his waiting limousine. He makes his way through a crowd of screaming fans, a number of whom want to touch him. Rupert is standing near Jerry's car. Another fanatic, a woman named Masha (Sandra Bernhard), jumps into the back seat of Jerry's car from the unguarded side and grabs Jerry when he enters from the other. Shocked by Masha's appearance, Jerry leaps out of the car and runs back into the crowd. Rupert, acting as if he were Jerry's bodyguard, helps to keep the crowd away as Jerry gets back into his car after Masha has been removed from it. Rupert enters the car as well, sitting next to Jerry in the back seat. In the way of explaining his presence, Rupert reminds Jerry that he helped him fend off fans, showing Jerry the cut on his hand, a wound Rupert incurred during the melee. Jerry hands Rupert his monogrammed handkerchief to clean up the small amount of blood the cut produced. Rupert keeps the handkerchief as a treasured souvenir. They chat as the limousine drives to Jerry's apartment. Rupert tells Jerry that he is a comedian, that he is "dynamite" and ready for his big break. As a way to get rid of him, Jerry tells Rupert to call his office the next day. Rupert takes this statement as a promise that Jerry will give him an audition.

Actually believing that he is on the threshold of his big break, Rupert immediately goes to see Rita Keene (Diahnne Abbott), bar waitress who was a cheerleader during Rupert's high school years. Although he has not seen her in years, Rita has been Rupert's secret sweetheart, something of which she is unaware. In seeking out Rita, Rupert is looking for a sexual companion who will mirror and admire him as a potent man. Rupert has a strong wish for Rita to see him as successful; her approval and applause would boost his self-esteem and inflate his grandiose fantasy of himself a giant celebrity who receives the idolization of millions of viewers.

Rupert eats dinner with Rita and shows her the signatures of celebrities that he has preserved in his autograph book. Predictably, he slips into delusions of grandeur, telling her, for example, that he is a personal friend of Woody Allen and that he is going to make it big in Hollywood and get a house in Malibu. He points out to her his own signature in the book as if he were a celebrity.

The one-to-one interaction with Jerry has pushed Rupert to the brink of insanity. He tells Masha, his colleague in the celebrity-hounding mania, for example, that he has a "real relationship" with Jerry, not a fantasy-based one such as *she* has. Incredibly, Rupert invites Rita to spend a weekend with him at Jerry Langford's country home, implying that he and Jerry are close friends and that Jerry has invited him for the weekend.

Scorsese provides us with some understanding of Rupert's motivation for his fantasies and delusions. In a fantasy scenario entirely enacted in his mind where Rupert has become the king of comedy, Rupert marries his high-school sweetheart, Rita, who is queen of the show, on national television. In this film sequence, Rupert imagines that there is a mystery guest on the show, namely, his former high school principal, George Cap, who had failed him (presumably because of Rupert's bad grades). Before millions of viewers, Cap apologizes to Rupert for believing that he would not "amount to a hill of beans." Cap says, "But we were wrong and you were right. We'd like to apologize and beg your forgiveness," and he thanks Rupert for the "meaning [he has] given to our lives."

This fantasy sequence informs us that Rupert has created scenarios of greatness to counter his almost nonexistent self-worth, the humiliations he has suffered because of his repeated failures in the real world, and the shame of feeling like a failure. The psychological basis of Rupert's need to be seen as greater than he perceives himself to be is reminiscent of Henry Hill's desperate need to feel that he was a somebody by belonging to a family of successful gangsters. Rupert wants to join what he perceives to be the celebrity family for the same reason—to feel that he is a somebody and that he belongs—except that Rupert, unlike Henry, is an adult. As a grown man, Rupert has accomplished little with his life—he works as a delivery boy and lives with his mother, and thus, he probably feels very insecure about his manhood. Moreover, he probably endured great humiliation when he was in high school where he was treated as if he were a failure. Rupert's fantasies, which appear to be at a psychotic level, have the effect of aggrandizing a greatly impoverished sense of himself. Without these fantasies, Rupert would feel that he is a dismal failure, a nothing, and he would fear that he would be seen as such by everyone in his world, including Rita, the woman he most wants for himself. From the perspective of phallic narcissism, undoubtedly Rupert feels that he lacks power both to attract a sexual object as well as to attain success in the real world.

Believing that he received a personal invitation for an audition by Jerry to be on his show, Rupert goes to the studio to see Jerry. He gets as far as the production assistant who requests that he drop off a tape of his comedy routine. Rupert makes the tape in his apartment, using canned voices and applause from his collection of previously-taped shows, and he adds his own comedy routine as if he were a guest on Jerry's show.

After delivering the tape and while waiting in the reception-area of the studio, Rupert engages in another daydream in which he imagines that he is sitting with Jerry and that, after listening to Rupert's tape, Jerry tells Rupert that he is a genius and asks him just how he does it. In the fantasy scenario, Rupert responds that he uses the awful things that have happened to him and turns them into events that are comedic. This statement provides an inkling of the humiliations that Rupert has suffered in his life. Rupert continues his daydream and fantasizes that Jerry says that he envies Rupert's great talent and that Jerry invites him to his home for the weekend. In response, Rupert tells Jerry that he would like to bring along with him a very special young lady. Rupert has Rita in mind as his companion for the weekend.

The reverie ends when Jerry's production assistant comes back to the reception area and returns the tape to Rupert after having listened to it. She tells Rupert that he has potential but that he is not ready for the Jerry Langford show. She advises him to get more experience by performing his act in clubs and, thus, improving his comedic skills. Rupert has no respect for the production assistant, totally ignores what she has said, and, having been informed that Jerry is out, he decides to sit and wait in the reception area for Jerry to return to the studio so that Jerry can listen to the tape. However, soon thereafter, he is ushered out by the security guard.

While Rupert waits for Jerry outside the building, Masha comes by and tells him that Jerry is actually upstairs in the building. Rupert goes back up and barges into a number of office suites looking for Jerry. Rupert is caught by the security guards and is thrown out of the building. Totally denying reality, he tells Masha that he was not thrown out but, rather, claims that he was invited to Jerry's country home for the weekend.

In a totally delusional state, Rupert goes to Jerry's estate, taking Rita and several packed suitcases. At the doorway of Jerry's home, he tells the house boy that he was invited for the weekend. As the servant tries to reach Jerry to advise him about the uninvited guests, Rupert shows off to Rita just how well he knows Jerry. He points out a number of displayed photographs of Jerry, some from his youth, and tells her when they were taken, thus showing that he has investigated and studied the intimate details of Jerry's life.

Having received the call from his houseboy, Jerry returns home from the golf course and demands that Rupert leave. Rupert reacts as if his personal friend, Jerry, were making a joke. Rupert refers to the (comedy) material in his briefcase that he has brought along for the two of them to work on together. Jerry calls him a moron and screams that he wants him out of his home. Rupert feels utterly humiliated and demeaned in the presence of Rita, who now realizes that what Rupert told her about his relationship with Jerry is a figment of his imagination.

Jerry's actions have disturbed Rupert's fantasies. Not only did Jerry order Rupert to leave, but he also admits to Rupert that he said that he would listen to Rupert's tape in the car the night they met just to get rid of him.

6. Demigods

Because of Jerry's words, Rupert feels a massive sense of narcissistic injury, humiliation, and rage. Rupert now believes that Jerry is not on his side at all and that he must take matters into his own hands. In other words, Rupert's former idealization of and wish for merger with Jerry has been turned on its head; Rupert feels betrayed and now perceives Jerry as his enemy.

Rupert and Masha evolve a plan to kidnap Jerry as he is walking along the street. Wielding a toy gun, they threaten Jerry and force him into their car. They take him into Masha's apartment under duress, and they tie him to a chair. Rupert laments to Jerry, "Why couldn't you just listen to my tape." Jerry, believing that his life is in danger, apologizes and promises to do so if they will free him. However, Rupert has enough sense to realize that he has crossed the line into lawlessness. Moreover, Rupert refuses to free Jerry because he believes that in kidnapping Jerry, he has concocted the perfect plan for getting himself on Jerry's show.

Jerry is forced at gunpoint to call his producer, Bert Thomas, and tell him that his life is in danger if he does not comply with Rupert's directives. Jerry tells Bert that a man calling himself "King" must be allowed to come on the show that evening as the first guest and perform his routine. Moreover, Jerry warns Bert that he will not be released until after the taped show is aired later that evening. Although the police and the FBI arrive at the studio, they take no action against Rupert because they believe that Jerry's life is at stake. Rupert is allowed to do his comedy performance, and the authorities wait with him until the broadcast is about to be wired.

While Rupert is away at the studio, Masha, who is also delusional, makes dinner for herself and Jerry. Meanwhile, Jerry is taped to a chair looking very much like a mummy. Masha acknowledges her love for him, sits on his lap, and sings to him as if she were Liza Minnelli. She also begins taking off her clothes, imagining that they are going to make love. Jerry manages to break free and then realizes that the gun is a toy. He rushes to his studio.

As his comedy spot on the show is about to be aired, Rupert, accompanied by FBI agents, goes to Rita's bar and tunes into the show on the television so that he and Rita can watch his routine. Since Rita can now see that Rupert actually was on Jerry's show, Rupert is able to prove to Rita that he is a success.

In his comedy act, Rupert refers to the inattention of his parents and teachers that he suffered all of his life, and he tells the viewing audience that the only way he could break his cycle of failures and get on the show was to hijack Jerry Langford and strap him to a chair. Rupert concludes by saying to the audience that it is "Better to be king for a night than a schmuck for a lifetime."

Rupert's comedy act and the story about the kidnapping is seen and heard by millions of people. Although he is sentenced to six years in a minimum-security prison, Rupert's face appears on national magazine covers, and he sells his memoirs for a million dollars. He is released after two years and nine months. His agent reports that his memoirs will become a major motion picture. Upon his release, Rupert resumes his show business career as the king of comedy.

Rupert Pupkin is Travis Bickle in comedic garb and without the blood. Both characters are loners and perceive themselves as losers. Both live in hovels, have minimal-type jobs, and are failures at relationships. In other words, both Travis and Rupert have not been successful in the real world. Both are severely obsessed—one with dirt, the other with celebrity. Because both have psychological deficits that include lacking a cohesive sense of self and a sense of being potent men, both of these characters are vulnerable to fragmenting (or falling apart) and becoming insane under the stress of incurring severe narcissistic injury. Each reacts to his respective injuries with humiliation, shame, and narcissistic rage. Each becomes violent, albeit in significantly different ways. The violent actions of both Travis and Rupert indicate that each has a grandiose fantasy of himself that defends against his insecurities as a potent man. Each feels entitled to do as he wishes, and each takes the law into his own hands.

However, Rupert does not use a real gun and bullets and, thus, no one gets killed in *The King of Comedy*. Nevertheless, both Rupert and Travis are psychotically obsessed and paranoid about their respective social milieus, the seamier side of New York in Travis's case, and the world of show business in Rupert's. Both films end with the respective characters getting their wish-fulfillments, realizing in apparent reality what both men have dreamed or fantasized about. Although the endings of both films may represent fantasies, the ending scenes suggest that both Travis and Rupert attain redemption, albeit this occurs because of the perception of others. As depicted, both attain fame in a culture that admires heroes to such an extreme that it raises to celebrity status people who not only lack creativity but, also, may be utterly selfish as well as psychologically disturbed.

For both Rupert and Travis, how each of them feels that he is perceived by the woman of his dreams, Rita and Betsy, respectively, is an essential feature of the motivation for their behavior. Each of these destructive characters yearns to be seen as a success, and each manipulates events in order to force their wished-for perception to win out. The viewer is less likely to see Rupert's behavior as aberrant compared with that of Travis because Rupert's rage is less muted. However, the attempt at lovemaking by the deranged Masha is no less an attempted rape, the kidnapping of Jerry no less an act of forcing one's will onto another, than other more-violent behavior committed by Travis or the gangsters at gunpoint.

There are autobiographical elements in the characterizations of both Rupert and Jerry Langford. As noted earlier, Scorsese can empathize and identify with Pupkin's enormous ambition to succeed (and to be seen as a success), regardless of the cost, and he has probably experienced the price of celebrity status, particularly with regard to the loss of his privacy.[1] In addition, since the film provides the psychological basis of Rupert's ambition—feelings of inadequacy and wishing to be recognized as a success—so cogently, it raises the question of the motivation for Scorsese's ambition. Scorsese, like Rupert, probably felt inadequate and not respected within the social milieu of Little Italy. Given the limitations of that community, it was important for Scorsese to break out from its boundaries and achieve success in the larger world beyond that milieu.

Frank Pierce

The focal character of *Bringing Out the Dead* is Frank Pierce (Nicolas Cage), a five-year paramedic, who works the night shift driving his ambulance through the seedier streets of New York City.

Each night Frank faces the daunting task of trying to save people who are dying from drug overdoses or knife and gunshot wounds that are the result of homicide or suicide attempts. In other words, his patients are drawn largely from the dregs of society, and he tries to have compassion for these people who live on the margins of mainstream society. Frank has no capacity to separate himself psychologically from the feelings of others. Having no self-boundaries to speak of, he absorbs the suffering of the patients he picks up as if he were a "grief mop."

Frank has reached his breakingpoint, and he needs time off. He tells of feeling trapped if he ends up in the back of the vehicle with dying patients. He drinks on the job and hallucinates seeing the ghosts of those who have died on his watch. He relates that "now the ghosts didn't wait for me to sleep." He has used up all of his sick time, and he is repeatedly late for work, hoping to be fired. However, even after he has been warned about lateness and comes in late intentionally, he is not fired but, rather, sent out again into the world of the near-dead, a world that is haunting him.

Frank is especially haunted by what he hallucinates is the ghost of a woman named Rose, an eighteen-year-old asthmatic and homeless woman who had died on his watch. He feels responsible for her death although he could do nothing to save her. He hallucinates seeing her face on the bodies of hookers who walk the streets. Frank gives us a glimpse of his experience: "Five or six in the morning is the worst time for me, just before dawn—just when you're lulled in thinking it would be safe to close your eyes for one minute. That's when I first found Rose. She was on the sidewalk not breathing." He speaks of the bodies of the dead he has seen leaving their mark, feeling humiliated for his witnessing.

Frank is consumed with what he believes is his power over life and death; he seems to believe that he is infinite, like a god. He says in this context:

> Saving someone's life is like falling in love. The best drug in the world. For days, sometimes weeks, afterwards you walk in the street making infinite whatever you see. Once, for a few weeks, I couldn't feel the earth.

Everything I touched seemed lighter. You wonder if you have become immortal.... God has passed through you. Why deny that, for a moment there, God was you?

Frank tells us that when things go wrong and the patient dies, spreading the blame is a survival tactic of paramedics because "no one wants to play the God of hellfire." This expression suggests that Frank sees himself as a punishing and cruel god when he cannot save some people, even if he does everything he can to avert death. He is in despair about the death of Rose, his sense of self is near-collapse as indicated by his hallucinations of her. Moreover, when Frank loses patients, his need for narcissistic exhibitionism of his healing capacity suffers immeasurably, and he feels guilt and shame.

Drugs and addicts permeate the mise-en-scene of *Bringing Out the Dead*. A number of the street people who become patients of the paramedics are on drugs: Mary is an ex-addict who returns to a supplier's apartment to get a drug to let her sleep, and Frank drinks heavily and uses drugs during his period of near-collapse.

Following the addiction theme with which the film is imbued and Frank's statement that saving people is the "best drug in the world," it appears that Frank has become addicted to the "high" from the adrenaline rush associated with a lifesaving act. The "high" contributes to his imagining that he has performed miracles and that he has the godlike capacity to heal. Such a megalomaniacal fantasy inflates his sense of self and boosts his self-esteem. However, when his efforts fail and a person dies, Frank becomes depressed and anxious as his fantasy of being a godlike healer is turned on its head, as it were. There is no thrill, no rush, when people die, and when we first see him after months of saving no one, he is behaving like an addict who is in the throes of withdrawal.

Frank's tendency to play God and get his adrenaline rush crystallizes around the life-and-death struggle of old Mr. Burke. After suffering a cardiac arrest while at home and falling into a state of being brain-dead, Burke is resuscitated by Frank's extraordinary efforts. Rushed to the hospital, Burke codes seventeen times in two days, and the nurses and doctors resuscitate him each time. Burke's daughter, Mary (Patricia Arquette), and Frank encounter each other during her father's life-and-death struggle, and Frank tries to give her hope that her father will survive. However, Frank is present during one of the times that Mr. Burke codes, and Frank believes that he hears the old man demanding that he not be intubated. When he has the opportunity to do so, Frank takes matters into his own hands. Without attracting attention, he enters the intensive care unit where Mr. Burke is being monitored. Frank removes the monitors on Burke's chest and attaches them to his chest so that no alarm will sound. He removes the respiratory hose that is keeping Mr. Burke alive and breathes into it himself until the man expires.

6. Demigods

Mary Burke (Patricia Arquette) and paramedic Frank Pierce (Nicolas Cage) in a scene from *Bringing Out the Dead* (Photofest).

Then he reattaches the heart monitors onto Mr. Burke and the now-alerted hospital personnel arrive on the scene and pronounce the old man dead.

Soon thereafter Frank goes to Mary's apartment to tell her that her father has died. Mary invites him inside, and they lie together on her bed, she cradling Frank in her arms in a Pieta-like pose.

Like Travis Bickle, the world that Frank Pierce inhabits, his social milieu, is defined by the boundaries of his job, which, in turn, is defined by the streets through which his vehicle travels. He seems to have no life outside of this milieu, no wife, no friends, no support system. Both Travis and Frank live a solipsistic existence. Both films—*Bringing Out the Dead* and *Taxi Driver*—deal with life and death in the seedier sections of the city. Furthermore, like Travis, Frank believes, grandiosely, that he has the personal power and the responsibility to change things as well as the omniscience to know how things should be changed.

In the interviews included in the special edition video of the film, Scorsese comments that although he grew up in a decent family, they lived in a neighborhood that was less than a block from the Bowery, and he saw the derelicts, the dregs of society, that is, people who are just waiting to die. According to Scorsese, because of the human misery that he witnessed as a child, he has been conflicted between feeling compassion for the unfortunate, on the one hand, and feeling repulsed by them, on the other hand. The director speaks of a similar conflict in his character and the necessity for Frank to get past his ego or pride to reach the "heart of compassion."[2]

It appears that Scorsese's notion of Frank getting past pride and to the "heart of compassion" is expressed by Frank's "pulling the plug" on Mr. Burke. Although the portrayal by Cage engenders a sense that Frank is compassionate, it can be argued that Frank hears what he wants to hear, that is, that Mr. Burke wants to die. Moreover, given his hallucinatory tendencies, Frank is hardly in a position of being able to trust his senses. It is clear that Frank takes the matter of when and how Mr. Burke dies into his own hands, an action that is indicative of his unconscious fantasies of omnipotence and omniscience. Indeed, rather than having gotten past his own ego or childlike narcissism, it appears that Frank has simply reformulated his megalomaniac fantasy to include allowing some of his patients to die.

It is useful to examine the religious allusions in the film to appreciate the linkage between Scorsese's intentions in creating his characterization of Frank and the character's god-complex. The religiosity of the film is suggested by its symbolism: a cross superimposed on a blood-red background. This symbol appears on the paperback edition of the book and the casing of the video. In addition, the director's comments on pride and compassion are commensurate with beliefs within the Christian tradition. Frank, who seemingly represents Jesus, suffers and bleeds because of the sins of humankind. He is, metaphorically, on the cross, feeling helpless and alone. He has performed a number of "miracles," restoring to life people who were nearly-dead. This godlike power has boosted his sense of self. In imagining that he is like a god, he has committed the "sin" of pride. However, now that power and the thrill associated with it are seemingly gone and Frank is in despair, his sense of self is in a state of near-collapse as indicated by his suffering about Rose's demise and his hallucinations of her. He is "saved" because he is able to transcend his self-interest, his pride as Scorsese describes it, and allow Mr. Burke to die as he believes the old man actually wishes. In the end, Frank is redeemed from his suffering and his sin, comforted by Mary (Burke) in a Pieta-like pose.

Frank Pierce is in some ways an unlikely companion to the other characters considered in this chapter. Frank is not violent nor entirely self-centered as are the other characters. He wishes no ill-will toward his patients, and, indeed, he wants to save them. However, in expending so much of his mental and physical energy in trying to save dying patients, Frank is destroying himself.

Frank Pierce is included in this chapter to make the point that even those who may seem to be benevolent may fall into the trap of imaginings that they are omniscient or omnipotent. Such a fantasy in the mind of a benevolent character may lead him to self-destructive behavior. This occurs because when the fantasy of being godlike is shattered, as it inevitably must, the person may turn his narcissistic rage toward himself. Frank does so when he is unable to save patients who are dying.

7

Boys in Men's Clothing

The film characters examined in this chapter—J.R., in *Who's That Knocking at on My Door,* Charlie and Johnny Boy in *Mean Streets,* Jimmy Doyle in *New York, New York* Eddie Felson and Vincent Lauria in *The Color of Money,* and Lionel Dobie in "Life Lessons"—are self-centered and arrogant men who behave as if they were little boys. Although less violently aggressive than the men discussed in the two previous chapters, they are, on the whole, irritating and cocky, and they think only about themselves. A number of them are outright punks and thugs; others who are more mature define themselves largely in terms of their talents and skills. These men live in a narcissistically perceived universe (defined by their personal perceptions of themselves and others) and defined by macho images of manhood. They dismiss or demean anything that disturbs the mental image or fantasy that they have constructed of themselves as potent and successful men, a fantasy that they want others in their milieu to see, affirm, and applaud. They tend to feel superior to women as well as to other men outside their social circle, whom they perceive as lesser beings. On the whole, these male characters are representative of phallic narcissists.

J.R.

J.R. (Harvey Keitel) is the male lead in *Who's That Knocking at My Door?* (1967). This early film of Scorsese is his personalized account of the limited life and psyche of young men who grow up within the boundaries of Little Italy (New York City) and the Catholic church.

J.R., who is essentially Scorsese's alter ego, is a young adult, who is in-between jobs, owes money, and spends a good deal of his time with friends in and out of the 8th Ward Pleasure Club. He likes John Wayne westerns and other tough-guy movies. J.R. has no visible means of support, and it appears that he lives in his mother's home. Attesting to the Catholic influence on J.R.'s and Scorsese's value system, the apartment is rife with religious statues.

J.R. and his friends, who are homophobic, sexist, and racist, spend their days and nights drinking and getting drunk, playing cards, and gambling, fooling around with women, whom they call whores, roughhousing and fighting with each other, and even toying with a loaded gun. It seems evident that J.R. is a man who has not grown up and has no promise of a mature future stretching before him.

When J.R. is first seen on the screen he appears to be a good-natured and fun-loving guy who has not grown up and who identifies with a macho image of manhood. J.R.'s psychological world is confined and constrained by the values of Little Italy and the Catholic Church. Within this subjective world of macho men, J.R. has a sense of himself as an adequate or "real" man who fits in with the other guys in his immediate social circle. Anything that does not conform to this macho image of himself is shunned and demeaned, a way of protecting and thus defending himself from any disturbance of his image of himself as a potent man. Less consciously, J.R. probably suffers from insecurities about his masculinity.

The focal issue of the film, shown in flashback sequences, is J.R.'s relationship with "the Girl," (played by Zina Bethune). With her long, golden hair and sweet demeanor, this is the type of girl whom a guy like J.R. treats with respect and perhaps takes home to meet his mother. We learn that in J.R.'s mind, there are two types of women: virgins and whores. Indeed, J.R. is explicit in making a distinction between "broads" and "girls" : a "broad isn't exactly a virgin, you play around with a broad, you don't marry a broad." Making this distinction allows J.R. to be sexual with women at will, both in fantasy and in reality, and feel comfortable that his behavior is consonant with that of the other men in his milieu. This misogynous attitude also serves as a defense to guard against his insecurities as a man.

The Girl, who he assumes is a virgin, is a beautiful and intelligent white Anglo-Saxon Protestant. She appears to have had a broader cultural experience then he has. J.R. takes her to his mother's apartment for some necking and fooling around. He stops, however, from "going all the way," attributing this reticence for sexual intercourse to the fact that he loves her and that he is "old-fashioned." It is clear that in his mind, he would have sexual intercourse with a girl like this only if they were married.

Having come to understand J.R.'s view of "girls" and "broads," and because she and J.R. are falling in love, the Girl tells him that she is not a virgin. She explains that she was raped by a boy she had trusted and that this happened some time ago. Via graphic images that Scorsese creates on the screen, we see that the rapist had driven her down a long road to a secluded area. Once the Girl realizes that her date intends to force himself on her, she tries to run, but he grabs her, subdues her, and pushes her forcibly back into the car where he rapes her. The Girl tells J.R. that after the rape she had felt dirty and ashamed.

J.R. is shocked by the story and says that he can't believe it, that it doesn't make any sense. In his self-righteous mind, if she were a good girl, she would not have let the boy take her to a secluded area. Clearly, J.R. places responsibility for the rape entirely on the Girl's shoulders. She should have known better and not have trusted the boy, he says. Since it did happen, he concludes that she must have brought it on herself. Indeed, he wonders out loud if her account is true and if perhaps she told the other guy the same story that she told him. The Girl leaves without saying a word.

The Girl's story has disturbed J.R.'s narcissistically perceived world with its concrete and self-righteous definitions of right and wrong. J.R. replays the scenes of the rape in his mind over and over, and because he is aroused by his mental images of the Girl's naked body, he concludes that the Girl is a broad, a dirty woman.

After a night of heavy drinking and fooling around with his male friends and women brought in for having "fun," J.R. rethinks what he did and said to the Girl. He goes to her apartment, waking her at six-thirty in the morning. He apologizes for what he had said to her and adds that he forgives her and is willing to marry her anyway. The Girl says no, that she cannot marry him on that basis. J.R. is enraged because of her rejection of what he considers a generous offer, and he vehemently expresses his feelings, calling her a broad and a whore. Incredibly, he chides her for letting him into her apartment at that early hour of the morning. She tells him to leave, to "go home." We can imagine that the Girl's rejection has disturbed J.R.'s narcissistic equilibrium. He feels humiliated because her rejection evoked his phallic insecurities.

J.R. goes to the church confessional, where erotic and religious images commingle in his mind. He prays to Christ, and, as he kisses a crucifix, he attains, in fantasy, the bloody stigmata of Jesus. Although J.R. would like to see himself as Jesus incarnate, he does not have the capacity to empathize with the Girl and truly forgive, accept, and love her as the biblical Jesus did Mary Magdalene. Quite simply, J.R. cannot get beyond his limited sense of personal selfhood, derived from his roots, and his madonna-whore complex.

The ludicrousness of the double standard that J.R. applies to men and women—men can sin and continue to be seen as "real" men, women cannot sin without falling from grace—escapes his mental capacity and experience. In his mind, he and other men who drink to excess, gamble, and rape women can go to confession and cleanse themselves; a woman is tainted forever by an act committed by a man such as he. These values about men, women, and sin are consistent with those of the other men in J. R.'s social circle. He abides by these values because his sense of himself as a potent man derives from and depends on his identifying with the other phallic-narcissistic men in the cultural milieu in which he is embedded.

Scorsese presents a picture of his Sicilian-American-Catholic culture in this film. In an interview, Scorsese described how women were viewed in his culture:

"Women were separate entities, and the madonna-whore dichotomy encouraged fear of them, distrust, ... they didn't seem like real human beings."[1]

This statement of Scorsese suggests that he suffered from the same phallic-narcissistic disturbance as J.R. does, at least when he was a young man.

CHARLIE AND JOHNNY BOY

Mean Streets (1973) continues and expands the theme of showing the life of young men who are limited and constrained, literally and figuratively, by the boundaries of Little Italy. The two focal characters of the film are Charlie (Harvey Keitel) and Johnny Boy (Robert De Niro).

Charlie, a stand-in for Scorsese, is in emotional turmoil. He is materialistic, enjoying the relatively easy worklife he has, a people-pleaser who wants to be liked by everyone, and he is religious, as least insofar as sin and penance are concerned. He is dependent on his uncle Giovanni (Cesare Danova), the gangster boss of the neighborhood, for his job as a collector, and he is hopeful that Giovanni will secure his future by giving him a restaurant to run. The restaurant will soon be available because the current owner cannot continue to make his loan payments to Giovanni. In other words, Charlie will be given the management of a restaurant that will become available because of extortion. Charlie is respectful and diffident to his uncle, trying to remain in his favor, while lying to him about some of his activities. Giovanni has advised Charlie to stay away from Johnny Boy and Johnny's epileptic cousin, Teresa (Amy Robinson). Nevertheless, Charlie is in a sexual relationship with Teresa, and he is a good friend to Johnny Boy.

Johnny Boy is the proverbial spoiled brat who thinks the world is his oyster, catering exclusively to his needs and wants. He is unstable psychologically, a cocky, enraged, and violent adolescent who only wants to play but, nevertheless, wants to enjoy the fruits of adult life. Of the five characters who provide the action in the film, Johnny Boy is the least mature. Indeed, compared to the other "four honorable men," even his name, Johnny Boy, is indicative of his juvenile character. He engages in violent and dangerous behavior, for example, placing explosives in a mail box and shooting a gun from the rooftop of a building, without ever considering the implications of his behavior to other people. These dangerous activities amuse the childlike Johnny.

Johnny seems to be unable to maintain relationships and engage in reciprocal behavior with both men and women. His only sexual contacts with women are the proverbial one-night stands. He poisons his friendships with men because of his unpredictable and dangerous behavior. Moreover and significantly, he loses his male friends because he does not honor his word in a world that places a high premium on men's honor.

The core of Johnny Boy's trouble in the context of the story is that he has borrowed money from men in his neighborhood and has not honored his commitments to pay it back. Indeed, he is a pathological liar and schemer, his behavior flying in the face of the code that defines manhood in this tightly knit social milieu. After having borrowed money from a number of men in the neighborhood, he avoids his creditors and continues to flaunt his money at the local bar as if he were a "big" man loaded with money. Johnny Boy utterly desecrates the code of honorable men by lying and dismissing his responsibility for paying off his debts; his word means nothing.

For Johnny Boy, having money and spending it freely serve to inflate his ego and protect him from acknowledging his insecurities about his potency as a man.

The relationship between Charlie and Johnny is complicated. On the one hand, Johnny seems to want Charlie to take care of him. In this vein, he asks Charlie repeatedly to talk to his uncle who, because of his power, could dismiss or lighten Johnny's obligation to pay off his debts. However, Charlie is reluctant to involve his uncle because he knows that Giovanni does not like Johnny, and Charlie does not want to endanger his relationship with his uncle. On the other hand, Johnny dishonors and humiliates Charlie, who has repeatedly covered for and defended him. Johnny does not even show up for work at a job that Charlie helped him get. As a matter of fact, Johnny resents Charlie's taking care of him presumably because Charlie calls Johnny "stupid," a term that Charlie applies to Johnny when he scolds him for his juvenile behavior. Johnny also resents Charlie's relatively easy life, and he demands to know why *he* should work at a job when Charlie does not. Johnny seems to understand that Charlie needs to be liked by everyone, does not want to rock the boat, and always puts on a good face. Seemingly oblivious to the turmoil he is creating for his loyal friend, Charlie, and for his cousin, Teresa, both of whom care about him, Johnny swaggers into Tony's bar—the neighborhood hangout—seemingly without a care in the world, cocky as ever and showing off his new duds, fantasizing that he is a big man.

One of Johnny's creditors is Michael (Richard Romanus), a member of his friendship circle who is also a loan shark. Michael has extended the payback time for Johnny and decreased his debt from $3,000 to $2,000 because of Charlie's intersessions and his assurances to Michael that Johnny will pay back what he owes Michael. Nevertheless, when Johnny is confronted by Michael, who demands his money, Johnny insults him, calling him an "asshole" and a "jerk-off." Moreover, Johnny implies that Michael has been stupid in having lent him the money in the first place, and he threatens Michael with a gun (unloaded), thus chasing him out of the bar. Johnny's behavior causes Michael to feel humiliated in full view of his friends and associates, enrages Michael, and leads him to avenge this insult to his reputation and sense of power.

After Johnny's foolish encounter with Michael, Charlie fears that violence will befall Johnny Boy. He and Teresa usher Johnny into a car, and they drive off, hoping to hide Johnny from Michael. However, Michael and his gunman (played by Martin Scorsese) hunt down the trio in another car, and in retribution for the insult to Michael, the gunman shoots Johnny in the neck. Charlie is wounded as well, although less seriously. Johnny's juvenile behavior has utterly shattered the friendship network and sense of family that had existed between the men.

The character of Johnny Boy is exemplary of a troubled and potentially violent adolescent who fancies himself a big man and has a gun to bolster his image of himself as a powerful man. He is cocky and childishly grandiose, acting as if he can do whatever he wishes without suffering any consequences for his actions. With such a potentially explosive personality as Johnny's, any interference with his will could result in his becoming enraged and using his gun. Indeed, Johnny's gun enables him to fantasize that he is omnipotent, the weapon a substitute for and defense against any insecurities he might have about himself as a real and potent man. A personality such as Johnny Boy, who sets himself up to act as if he is superior to others and, because of this imagined superiority, feels that he does not have to abide by the same rules as other people, is apt to incite rage in others. Inevitably, in such a dangerous climate, revenge through acts of retribution are likely to occur, as shown in the film.

Charlie's loyalty to his friends indicates his capacity for relationships with male comrades. However, his continued protection of Johnny, which places him at risk for losing the support of his uncle, is indicative of another facet of his personality. Charlie fancies himself a peacemaker and wants to be seen as such by others. In protecting Johnny as he does, he demeans Johnny as being too stupid to take care of himself. In other words, the protection that Charlie extends to Johnny serves his ego, in effect, his helping Johnny enables Charlie to feel superior to him. This dynamic suggests that Charlie has his own insecurities about his manhood, and helping the seemingly childlike and hapless Johnny bolsters Charlie's self-esteem in terms of his being a "real" man.

Another aspect of Charlie's personality is evident in his relationship with Teresa. Like his counterpart, J. R., Charlie has a madonna-whore complex. Although he has sexual relations with Teresa on a regular basis, he refuses to acknowledge that he is in love with her because she is, in his words, a "cunt." Charlie's demeaning attitude toward Teresa and his obvious need to feel superior to her indicate that he is a phallic-narcissistic man. Interestingly, the opening scenes of the film appear to be home movies showing that Charlie and Teresa eventually marry and have a baby. These scenes, which include the celebration of their baby Christopher's baptism, suggest that Charlie overcomes his complex and attains a redemption of sorts.

There are a number of religious allusions in the film. In addition to keeping his uncle at bay, Charlie fears that some of his activities, including his sexual ones, are sinful and that they will condemn him to hell. He believes that he must do penance not in church, but in the streets, to avoid going to hell, and he periodically places the fingers of his hand in an open flame to toughen himself up to withstand the pain of the fire of hell. As the film progresses, Charlie wonders if his penance includes putting up with Johnny Boy.

As was the case with *Who's That Knocking at My Door?*, *Mean Streets* is semi-autobiographical. Scorsese has identified that in large measure he was Charlie.[2] Indeed, Scorsese dubbed his own voice in the film to represent Charlie's thoughts. Moreover, the activities of the young men in the film, as well as their racism and sexism, were familiar to the director who had lived and participated with the boys and men of Little Italy during his formative years. Scorsese has said that he put himself and his "old friends on the screen, to show how we lived."[3]

Scorsese's identifying himself with Charlie suggests that the phallic-narcissistic issues of the young men in the film—their insecurities about their potency and their defending against these insecurities by being "macho"—probably applied to Scorsese when he was a young man. Moreover, Scorsese could also identify with Charlie's conflict about sexuality and spirituality as well as his role as peacemaker. Charlie presents himself as a young man who has healthy ambition and pride. Undoubtedly, Scorsese was ambitious and prideful enough to want a successful career and to earn respect, applause, and recognition from the milieu and, eventually, from the world at large. For a time, at least, Scorsese probably struggled with his wish for success, wondering if the pursuit of real-world desires was consistent with the teachings of his religion. Scorsese's conflict about this issue is portrayed by Charlie in the film. The resolution that Scorsese evolved for Charlie and for himself was that real spirituality was to be found on the streets, not in church. In other words, a person can be spiritual in whatever place he finds himself.

Another autobiographical link applies to the character of Johnny Boy. As noted earlier, Scorsese had had experience within his extended family with a relative who did not pay his debts, and Scorsese explained that this was a very serious matter in their community.[4]

Jimmy Doyle

The character of Jimmy Doyle (Robert De Niro) in *New York, New York* (1977) represents the prototypic childlike narcissist. He is imperial, childishly grandiose, and demanding of constant admiration and attention. The story focuses on Jimmy, a creative saxophone player, and his love relationship with a talented singer, Francine Evans (Liza Minnelli). Their interactions serve to highlight Jimmy's tendencies for narcissistic display and demandingness.

From his first meeting with Francine in a nightclub on VJ Day in 1945, Jimmy appears as a cocky, aggressive, and competitive man who demeans women by spinning lies to them, referring to them as "broads," and acknowledging that he wants to "screw" them. He tries to pick up Francine, who is sitting alone at a table, but she refuses to give him her phone number. Nevertheless, he continues to sit at her table uninvited and dismisses her "no" as not having any meaning. Jimmy is determined to get his way—in this scene, getting "laid" is what he's after—regardless of the other person's wishes. Even after she leaves, he says to himself, "I'll get her." In addition to these personality aspects, Jimmy is a schemer and a petty crook, running up his hotel bill and using an assumed name so he can skip out without paying the bill.

This early encounter between Jimmy and Francine suggests that Jimmy's overly aggressive style with women is a defense that he utilizes, probably unconsciously, to defend against his vulnerabilities that threaten his potency as a man. Without a doubt, Jimmy is a phallic-narcissist.

Francine and Jimmy have distinctly different personalities. Their individual preferences for music are consonant with their respective styles. She is empathic, accommodating, and pleasing; he is selfish and self-centered, with little or no capacity for empathy and accommodation. She sings to swing as well as to show music and exudes romantic sensuality; he plays jazz that is shrill and brash, reminiscent of a child screaming for attention.

These differences in temperament and in music between Jimmy and Francine are evident in a scene which Jimmy auditions for a job in a club. Francine has accompanied Jimmy to the audition. Jimmy insists on playing only his style of music. Since his music does not suit the manager of the club, Jimmy is about to lose for the job. Francine, realizing what the problem is and willing to help, intervenes during the audition by singing to Jimmy's music. In accompanying Jimmy's sax with her voice, she softens the sound of the music. The manager gives Jimmy the job on the condition that he include Francine as his singer.

Jimmy is childishly grandiose, checking into the hotel where Francine is staying although he has no money. Again using an alias, he imperially demands that scotch be brought to his room, that the bellhop pay his cab fare, and that the amount of the cab be added to his hotel bill, knowing full well that he will never pay it. Understanding Jimmy's intentions, Francine, empathic and accommodating as always, gives him money and tells him to stay elsewhere so that she will avoid embarrassment at the hotel.

Soon thereafter Francine leaves the club as well as Jimmy to take a job with the traveling Frankie Harte band. She informs Jimmy about her leaving only after her departure and then by virtue of a note delivered to Jimmy by her agent. Jimmy follows chase and eventually finds her singing in a moun-

7. *Boys in Men's Clothing*   129

Talented singer Francine Evans (Liza Minnelli) with Jimmy Doyle (Robert De Niro), playing his saxaphone, from the musical, *New York, New York* (Photofest).

tain resort in North Carolina. He is furious with her for leaving him, which he perceives as an insult to his grandiosity, and says to her: "You don't say goodbye to me, I say goodbye to you." Moreover, in his arrogant manner, he commands her presence by his side as if she were a dog, "Come here, come here. I love you. I don't love you. I dig you. I like you a lot."

The language and style that Jimmy uses in talking to Francine are indicative of his imperial, pretentious style and show that it is difficult for Jimmy to acknowledge loving someone other than himself. When Francine tells him that he can audition for a job with Frankie Harte and join her in the band, he responds, grandiosely, that he won't audition for him, he will only play for him. It seems that Jimmy feels that auditioning is beneath him, an insult to his great talent.

In matters pertaining both to love and to music, Jimmy's sense of himself is organized by a childlike, grandiose fantasy of being the "top dog." This image of himself feeds Jimmy's low self-esteem and insecurities about his potency as a man in the world of music as well as in the world of loving relationships. However, Jimmy's fantasy about himself is so extreme and childish that it is disturbed easily. He requires constant affirmation to maintain his tenuous sense of self-worth.

Jimmy and Francine get married, but this seems to have been impulsive. After Jimmy reads a love poem that Francine had written to him, an ode to his grandiosity that mirrors his inflated sense of himself, he drags her off to a justice of the peace in the middle of the night to get married. When she demurs, he assures her that he loves her. Hesitantly, Francine agrees to the marriage proposal.

Eventually, Harte leaves the band, and Jimmy takes it over, calling it the Jimmy Doyle Band. In auditioning for club engagements, Jimmy runs into a familiar problem: his saxophone does not appeal, Francine's singing does. As the band tours the country, Francine gets more applause and attention than Jimmy does, but her name is smaller than his on the marquees. Always needing to be the top dog, Jimmy appears to be bored and disinterested when Francine is singing her solos. Moreover, he ignores newspaper articles that praise her singing. It is obvious that Francine is actually the star and that the band does little more than accompany her, but Jimmy cannot acknowledge that.

In one scene, during a rehearsal of one of Francine's numbers with the band, Jimmy demeans and humiliates the musicians who have made mistakes. Francine steps forward and suggests to Jimmy that he be more diplomatic to band members. Jimmy reacts to her suggestion with an imperious response: "Are you the band leader?" The obvious implication is that Jimmy is the all-knowing boss and that Francine has no right to offer suggestions to the imperial wizard that he imagines himself to be. Indeed, Francine's intersession is a threat to Jimmy's grandiose but tenuous fantasy of himself as the top dog.

A few minutes later, Francine and Jimmy are standing in front of the band, and Jimmy is using a count to kick it off. Francine makes the mistake of finishing the count. Jimmy stops the band and orders Francine to his side, saying in a commanding tone, "Francine, come here." When she reaches his side, he says: "You do not kick off the band. I kick off the band. Don't do it again, ever again," and then he spanks her on her behind and shoves her back to the opposite side of the floor where she had been standing. These actions, occurring in open display before the entire group of musicians, are degrading and humiliating to Francine. Jimmy's behavior in front of the band is consistent with his wish to be seen as the boss, the top dog. However, the musicians see him as a loser whose imperial style they disrespect. As is customary in their relationship, Francine endures Jimmy's abuse without comment.

Francine becomes pregnant while touring with the band. Against Jimmy's protestations, Francine decides to leave the band and go back to New York to wait for the birth, fearing for the baby's safety if she were to continue traveling. During her absence, Jimmy has an affair with the band's new girl singer,

Bernice (Mary Kay Place). Without Francine's singing and her personality, which buffeted his abrasive and insulting style, Jimmy fails to hold onto the band. One imagines that the musicians could no longer tolerate his haughty and pretentious style. Jimmy signs away the band to Paul Wilson (Barry Primers), the pianist. Later, when he is asked about the loss of the band, Jimmy lies and attributes it to his having had bad musicians. It is evident that Jimmy does not have the capacity to acknowledge his personal responsibility for mistakes and failures. Moreover, Jimmy has no awareness that he insults other talented musicians with his grandiose attitude.

A few months later, Jimmy joins Francine, now six months pregnant, in New York. He finds work playing his kind of jazz with black musicians at the Harlem Club; she makes recording demos. Jimmy, ever self-centered, is oblivious to Francine needing attention and support because of her pregnancy. As a matter of fact, he explicitly blames *her* for his losing the band.

An important scene that shows Jimmy's propensity for feeling threatened by someone else's success occurs when Paul opens with the band in New York, and he invites Jimmy and Francine to the club where they are performing. Jimmy is too humiliated to go, perceiving Paul's success as an indicator of his failure. At a less conscious level, Paul's success has shattered Jimmy's fantasy of being the top dog and a potent man.

Jimmy sends Francine inside the club alone while he parks the car. Some time later and after he has had a number of drinks, Jimmy makes an appearance and joins Francine, who is sitting with the producer of Decca records and his wife. Jimmy's feelings of hurt and humiliation spark his narcissistic rage. He is openly hostile and antagonistic to his wife and the others at his table, embarrassing Francine. Then he attacks Paul physically on the floor of the club. Jimmy is thrown out of the club unceremoniously. It is evident that Paul's success has triggered Jimmy's childish narcissistic display. In Jimmy's mind, the opening of what once had been his band is a public display of Jimmy's failure, something that Jimmy cannot tolerate. In other words, Jimmy feels that everyone—Paul, the musicians, Francine, as well as the audience— perceives him as a loser. His reaction to this imagined and grossly negative perception is a rage response.

Francine is offered a contract with Decca. In a scene at a table in the Harlem Club, Francine tells Jimmy about the contract, which is a real plum. The producer of the record company and Francine's agent are also present at the table. Showing her respect for him as well as her empathy for his feelings, Francine asks Jimmy for his advice before she signs the contract. Jimmy responds with characteristic disinterest in another person's success, essentially telling her to do as she pleases. He is also ungracious and noncongratulatory, cutting short the conversation and returning to the bandstand. It seems evident that he is envious of Francine's success and that her good fortune has deflated his ego. Minutes later, as he is playing a solo, Francine approaches the stage, believing that he had invited her to join him there, perhaps to sing. Abruptly, Jimmy stands and plays his sax louder and louder, in effect, chasing her off the stage as he gains everyone's attention with the sound of his sax. Feeling defeated by her success, Jimmy cannot share the limelight with his talented wife. Moreover, it is apparent that Jimmy uses his sax as a phallic substitute. By playing it louder and louder and gaining center stage, Jimmy defends against any hint that he has insecurities about his talent as a musician as well as his potency as a man.

Soon thereafter, and in a rage, Jimmy tells Francine that she, in her pregnant state, looks disgusting and that having the baby was her doing. When she says that she's scared, presumably about the impending childbirth, Jimmy screams at her, saying that she's got it easy, that he is scared, that he has nothing while she has everything. "It's always you, isn't it," Francine says, pointing directly to his self-centeredness. In this scene, Jimmy's vulnerabilities and insecurities are displayed openly. In light of her success, Jimmy's grandiose fantasy of himself has been shattered, and he is humiliated and ashamed. He feels like a loser in relation to her.

After the birth of their baby, Jimmy refuses to see his newborn son and abandons Francine and the baby. In leaving Francine, Jimmy may be retaliating for her once having left him, acting out his dictum that he leaves her, not the other way around. The ending scenes indicate that Jimmy and Francine, both ultimately successful, pursue their respective careers independently.

Jimmy's selfish behavior toward Francine, including his rejection of their newborn son, is as emotionally violent and brutal as that of other Scorsese characters who are physically abusive. Jimmy's refusal to see his child is indicative of his extraordinarily vulnerable and tenuous sense of self. Seeing his son, in effect, would have required his sharing the spotlight with his wife and baby. Jimmy cannot share himself with or extend attention to other human beings, particularly with a baby who, by his very nature, commands attention and is perceived by others as special. In other words, Jimmy feels competitive with his own baby.

The film illustrates that two creative individuals may have difficulties in evolving a successful marriage; Scorsese has indicated that he has experienced this kind of difficulty in his life.[5] Interestingly, Scorsese's long-term relationship was seemingly in trouble during the shooting of the film, and it ended soon after the film was completed.[6] In addition, Scorsese has stated that during his years of struggling to succeed as a film director, he was willing to "kill relationships" for the sake of work.[7]

However, there is much more involved in the relationship between Jimmy and Francine than problems that arise when two creative individuals who have separate careers try to evolve a married relationship or, for that matter, to resolve problems that arise when one partner is more committed to his or her career than to the relationship. As depicted, Jimmy is utterly selfish and self-centered, and he is emotionally abusive to his wife, demeaning and humiliating her on a consistent basis. As a prototypic phallic-narcissist, Jimmy must occupy center stage, receive all the applause, give the orders, and be obeyed without question. In this context, it is significant that when the pregnant Francine leaves the band and returns to New York, Jimmy has an affair with the band's new female singer. It is apparent that Jimmy is enraged with Francine for what he perceives as her abandoning him. Jimmy avenges this insult by having the affair. Moreover, in having sex with another woman, Jimmy expresses his phallic supremacy.

Jimmy is not able to sustain a mature marriage that requires cooperation and compromise between two people. From their first meeting, it is evident that Jimmy sees Francine as a possible conquest. He marries her only because she writes a poem that applauds him and affirms his grandiosity. He stays in the relationship as long as Francine accomodates him, is interested in his career, and mirrors his grandiosity. When she leaves the band because of her pregnancy, Jimmy perceives this as an act of repudiation of him. Moreover, she is obviously interested in the welfare of the baby, whom Jimmy perceives as a competitor for Francine's affection. From that time forward, Jimmy is no longer interested in maintaining a relationship with Francine. In light of Scorsese's comment that suggests that he has had problems in combining a successful career with a marriage, one can speculate that Jimmy's selfishness and self-centeredness were experiences with which Scorsese was familiar.

EDDIE FELSON AND VINCENT LAURIA

The Color of Money (1986) presents Eddie Felson (Paul Newman), twenty-five years older than his original appearance in *The Hustler* (1961). Eddie is a successful businessman, a distributor of bourbon whiskey. He has apparently retired from playing pool and has evolved into a suave older man, one who appreciates the finer things that whiskey-money and investments enable his materialistic appetite to attain: a Cadillac, expensive clothes, jewelry, and a beautiful and sophisticated partner, Janelle (Helen Shaver), with whom to vacation in the Bahamas.

Vincent Lauria (Tom Cruise) is the young and cocky pool shark who is reminiscent of the young Eddie Felson. Vincent travels about to a number of towns with his constant companion, Carmen (Mary Elizabeth Mastrantonio), a hustler herself, making a few bucks here and there.

Vincent is a fun-loving kid, a "natural flake," as Eddie describes him, who just likes to play games: 9-ball pool, video games, and "house" with his girlfriend. Carmen understands better than Vincent the value of making money and what it can buy, and she is intrigued by and relishes the comment Eddie makes to them: "Rich can be arranged."

Eddie recognizes Vincent's exceptional talent for pool and realizes that his flakiness is a natural come-on to other pool players. He decides to take

Vincent under his wing and teach him "excellence." Always the hustler, Eddie fancies himself as having a special area of expertise as a "student of human moves." According to his self-proclaimed expertise, excellence in pool means being able to divine human motivation and thus defeat opponents not on the basis of talent alone, but in terms of knowing what makes one's opponent "tick." He strives to teach Vincent the finer points of becoming a winner at hustling. Eddie uses Carmen's hunger for money and the threatened loss of her to entice Vincent to leave his job as a retail clerk at Child World—symbolic of his childlike innocence and narcissism—and go on the road to play pool and expand his skills as a hustler.

Eddie provides the bankroll for the three of them to travel for six weeks playing 9-ball in assorted towns. He wants to teach Vincent to hustle with psychological insight and excellence and thereby make big money, money that they will share 60/40, the larger share going to Eddie. The idea is for Vincent to lose or "take a dump" as they travel toward the big 9-ball tournament in Atlantic City. According to Eddie's thinking, if Vincent gets a reputation for being a loser, the gambling odds at the tournament will be set against him. When this occurs, Eddie and his friends will bet on Vincent and make big bucks. For Eddie, excellence in pool means not just knowing when to lose for the sake of a bigger win down the road but also just barely losing. A talented hustler knows how to control his stick so that his intentional miss is just a fraction of an inch off. Then it will appear that he did not take a dump but actually missed the shot just barely. Such hustling feeds Eddie's ego and greed for making money.

Vincent, although a genius at 9-ball, is cocky and arrogant, brandishing his pool stick, a phallic substitute, like a warrior would his sword. He is full-of-himself, a show-off who relishes his victories. He finds it hard to take a dump particularly when his opponents are show-offs themselves who rub it in if he misses a shot. In these instances, Vincent becomes enraged, sensing that he is perceived as a loser, and he ends up defeating his opponent instead of intentionally losing. Vincent continually resists Eddie's instructions for becoming a successful hustler until his mentor threatens to abandon the project. Eddie has a long talk with Vince, telling him how his own career was cut short and that watching Vincent has reinvigorated him. Eddie says that although he has plenty of money from his business, "money won is sweeter than money earned." Moreover, he advises Vincent that excellence in pool requires both brains and "balls" and that Vince has too much of one (that is, balls) and not enough of the other. The talk between the two men results in Vincent's idealizing Eddie as the only one who has ever taken a real interest in him, and he hugs his parental mentor in gratitude.

Watching Vincent play pool whets Eddie's appetite to play himself, and he picks up the pool stick again. Playing rekindles his love of and obsession with pool. Initially, Eddie is victimized by a hustler and is unable to stop himself from compulsively playing until he loses a lot of money to the trickster.

Eddie is narcissistically injured and humiliated as his fantasy of having expertise in divining human moves has been upturned. He is determined to improve his game as well as his psychological insight. He breaks off his arrangement with Vincent, although he gives Vincent money to continue his trip, in order to make his own way to Atlantic City. Vincent, who had looked up to Eddie as a father-figure, feels betrayed and utterly abandoned by Eddie and becomes enraged.

Eddie, like Travis in *Taxi Driver*, Jake in *Raging Bull*, and Max in *Cape Fear*, all of whom become warriors, goes into training to prepare himself for the tournament. He swims to get his body into shape, gets new glasses to improve his eyesight, and practices his pool shots single-mindedly for hours at a stretch. His new eyeglasses represent his ability to see more clearly that the green cloth of the pool tables is more important than the green of money.

When Eddie arrives in Atlantic City and enters the auditorium where the tournament is to be held, it is as if he is entering a cathedral, the pool tables representing church pews. Scorsese's choice of organ music in this scene heightens the sense that Eddie is affected by the majestic splendor of a cathedral-like space filled with pool tables in neat rows. In this context, Eddie appears to be a penitent sinner who has returned to his church.

Eddie wins in the early rounds of the tournament and then is matched against Vincent in the quarterfinals. Eddie defeats Vincent in a close contest, makes it to the semi-finals, and is overjoyed with his success. That evening, as Eddie is celebrating with Janelle, Vincent and Carmen come to Eddie's room, and Vincent gives Eddie an envelope with $8,000. Vincent, it seems, has learned Eddie's hustling lessons all too well and has turned the tables on his teacher. He tells Eddie that he had taken a dump in their match and had made a lot of money from a gambler who had bet on Vincent to win. He takes great pleasure in telling Eddie how he purposely missed some shots just barely, indicating true excellence as Eddie had taught him, and he emphasizes how truly beautiful his performance was. In other words, Vincent really rubs it in, injuring and humiliating Eddie. Sharing the money with Eddie is for Vincent the ultimate retaliation, an expression of his narcissistic rage for what he perceives as Eddie's betrayal and abandonment of him. Eddie's earlier success in the tournament means nothing, and he is utterly deflated.

The following morning, Eddie forfeits his semifinal match and confronts Vincent with a demand for his best game. The interaction between the two men indicates that Vincent is enraged with Eddie for having used him and claims that he will beat him in any match. The film ends with Eddie and Vincent about to begin a game and Eddie saying that if he doesn't beat him then, he will eventually, because as he puts it, "I'm back."

The story has ironic twists. Eddie, who spoke of excellence and, in the end, wants a pure game, corrupted Vincent while Vincent, who was excellent enough to win consistently and without any training from Eddie, was corrupted to take a dump. The hurt and rage that Vincent felt because of

Eddie's abandonment were so intense that retaliation against Eddie was sweeter than a win in the big tournament.

Eddie's motivation for tutoring Vincent was money, of course, not a desire for excellence per se. Greed and the thrill associated with gambling fueled Eddie's hustling, and he, apparently, converted Vincent to his way of thinking. In this way, true excellence became corrupted into clever manipulation of pool skills to trick others into losing money.

Both Eddie and Vincent are narcissistic. Vincent is cocky and arrogant, competitive, and full-of-himself. He expresses his imagined phallic superiority by using his pool stick to defeat other men. Eddie is a more mature personality, but he, too, imagines himself as a genius at divining other men's psychology.

The ending of the movie suggests that Eddie has been redeemed from his sinful and greedy ways. His going into training is indicative of his battle with himself to alter his values from a materialistic way of life to one that involves a pure love of the game. However, it seems that Vincent has fallen from grace into gambling and greed.

The film appears to express Scorsese's belief about the value of practicing one's vocation and being true to oneself, which is more important than the greedy pursuit of money and materialistic pleasures. This value position is consistent with that practiced by Scorsese with regard to his cinematic career.

Lionel Dobie

In "Life Lessons," Scorsese's contribution to *New York Stories* (1989), a fiftyish New York artist, Lionel Dobie (Nick Nolte), shares his extensive studio space with his young and pretty assistant, Paulette (Rosanna Arquette). Paulette strives to become a better artist, and, presumably, she has been learning life lessons from Dobie. However, she realizes that she has limited talent and decides to move out of the studio and return home.

When Paulette tells Lionel that she wants to move out, he convinces her to stay. He reminds her, grandiosely, that she is working for Lionel Dobie, for the "lion," as he puts it, and that because of her special relationship with him, she is learning about art, improving her painting, and gaining invaluable life lessons. "Plus a salary," he adds. He says to her, "This kills me, you leaving. It's a suicide." This statement of Lionel indicates that it is essential to him, rather than to her, that she remain, but he defends against acknowledging his need by indicating that leaving him will harm her.

Lionel is a man who is full-of-himself, consumed with his sense of self-importance, and one who obviously takes pleasure in being perceived by the artistic community as "the lion." Paulette agrees to stay after Lionel promises that she doesn't have to sleep with him anymore. Although assuring her that she is a free agent, he hovers over her and wants to know about her activities like an overbearing mother hen.

Lionel needs Paulette or some other nubile lover to provide him with the sexual and emotional tension that he needs to create his art. As he works on a canvas, his thoughts and sexual fantasies revolve around images of Paulette's body, and he gazes frequently at the window above his loft that opens to her bedroom. He uses her interest in another man to generate even more creative energy. Together with this emotional and sexual tension, he plays loud music and runs about the studio throwing basketballs into a hoop. Lionel uses all of these props to help him create the colors and forms that he places on his canvas.

Lionel is selfish and uses people to satisfy his own needs. His emotional and sexual involvement in relationships is intense, and it appears that this energy spurs his creativity. In his interactions with Paulette, Lionel shows that he is unempathic; he perceives the situation entirely from his vantage point. When, for example, he speaks to Paulette of the advantages to her of continuing to live with him, it is clear that these so-called advantages are in relation to his image of himself as a great artist, "the lion."

Eventually, when Paulette decides to leave Lionel because she feels like a human sacrifice, he meets another young would-be artist who admires him. As luck would have it, the young woman is having difficulty making ends meet. He offers her a great deal: priceless life lessons in assisting the great artist, her own room, and a salary. The young sycophant can hardly refuse.

In this film, Scorsese raises the creative process almost to a transcendental level, and he likens the world of art to a church. As Lionel states, "You make art because you have to. It's not about talent, it's about no choice but to do it." These words and the behavior of Lionel suggest that for some people, probably including Scorsese, creative work is more important than intimate relationships.

8

Self-Image, Rage, and Violence

The personalities and behaviors of the phallic-narcissistic characters that have been discussed in the previous three chapters provide a number of perspectives with which to appreciate the motivation for these characters: anger, rage, and paranoia as well as their potential for violence. This chapter provides a psychological understanding of the linkages between narcissistic disturbance, including phallic-narcissism, and a man's propensity for rage and violence. In addition to each character's personal feelings that are evoked within the context of his film story, a man's self-image and how he imagines the world sees him are important factors for the evocation of violence. A number of these characters are obsessed about control, seeming to fear that if they do not control others, they will be controlled. Moreover, the discussion shows how Scorsese applies the religious theme of redemption to these characters and how Scorsese's roots are linked to the issue of violence and his images of masculinity.

The rageful warriors, Travis Bickle in *Taxi Driver*, Jake LaMotta in *Raging Bull*, Max Cady in *Cape Fear*, and the batterer, Ben Eberhardt in *Alice Doesn't Live Here Anymore*, show themselves to be psychologically disturbed individuals whose narcissistic rage drives their brutal and violent behavior. The extent of their rage and the brutality of their violence are indicators that these men are highly vulnerable to unravel, psychologically, that is, to suffer self-fragmentation and become paranoid and homicidal when they feel rejected, controlled, or perceived as failures or impotent men in the world.

For these characters, their propensity for murderous rage emanates from their extreme low self-esteem, particularly with regard to their potency as men. Any perceived criticism or rejection or another's person's attempt to control them triggers in each man the feeling that he has been injured or wronged. The lower the man's self-esteem, the greater is his potential for feeling injured and humiliated, and he identifies the wrongdoer as the cause of his feeling distress. Once these feelings are triggered in each man's psyche, they overtake and consume his mind. He becomes single-mindedly preoccupied with accomplishing one task: obliteration of his perceived enemy. For each of these rageful warriors, expressing his rage through violence and, thus, evening the score, so to speak, indicates to him that he has restored his self-image of being a potent man. In the perception of these narcissistically-disturbed men, a "real" man does not tolerate (a) a woman's rejection that causes Travis Bickle to feel worthless and humiliates and exacerbates his distorted sense of the world as dirty; (b) other men lusting for Jake's wife; (c) the injustice and humiliation suffered by Cady that, in his mind, were caused by Sam Bowden; and (d) the attempt made by Ben's wife to interfere with and control Ben's sexual desires and his choice of a sexual partner.

The self-perception of these men is distorted by how they imagine they are seen by their milieu, either their immediate social network or the world at large. Travis Bickle imagines that he is seen as inadequate, particularly after he is rejected by Betsy in a public setting, that is, the campaign headquarters where she works. Once he is overtaken by narcissistic rage—a response to the humiliation he suffered—Travis readies himself to kill and thus get even with a world that he feels has rejected him and judged him as inadequate. After he has trained himself for his private war, Travis sees himself in the mirror as an armed warrior, ready to destroy all enemies. The mirror serves as a reflection of his fantasied, grandiose image of himself. Seeing himself as an armed warrior restores, temporarily at best, Travis's sense of himself as a potent man. The violence that he unleashes during his murder spree is the expression of a man who feels compelled to retaliate against imaginary enemies and, thus, retake control over a world that he perceives has been controlling him and turning him into a victim of its badness.

Jake LaMotta feels compelled to vindicate his sense of himself as worthless by beating his adversaries to a bloody pulp or, alternatively, by withstanding a horrible beating without falling to the mat. Jake cannot tolerate falling on the mat and being knocked out because, in his mind, doing so means not only losing a match, but, more importantly, losing his highly desired image of himself as a supremely potent man. In other words, if Jake gets knocked out, his fantasy of omnipotence or phallic supremacy would be shattered. Moreover, since the events in a boxing ring are on public display, Jake believes that if he suffers a knock-out, people will see him as an utter failure, an impotent man.

Jake's sense of himself as a strong and potent man is fragile with regard to his personal life as well as in the boxing ring, and he feels paranoid about his self-image with regard to his wife's behavior as well as that of his brother. Jake reacts to any imagined signs of threats to his manhood with a brutal retaliation. In *Raging Bull*, for example, his wife merely noticing the appearance of another man incites Jake to beat her. Jake turns against his brother because he believes (mistakenly) that Joey has had sex with Vickie, an act that Jake, in his paranoid state, considers a betrayal. In these instances, Jake's turning his narcissistic rage against the perceived perpetrator of the insult results in Jake's being able to restore his fantasy of himself as a supremely phallic man. This restoration is temporary however; it will last only until he next feels a blow to his vanity.

For Max Cady, who is utterly psychotic, the humiliations he suffers are entirely personal, and he feels strongly that they must be avenged. He relentlessly pursues his quarry—Sam Bowden, the man he considers as entirely responsible for the emotional pain he endured—with the single-minded goal of destroying him. Every act that Cady perpetrates against Bowden enables him to feel superior to Sam, in effect, as a more potent man.

Max and Jake use only their bodies as weapons of destruction; Travis uses guns as phallic substitutes to inflate his sense of potency. These men's violence is linked to their sexuality, which in all three cases, is perverted. Cady beats, rapes, and cannibalizes women; Jake batters his wife; Travis is sexually repressed; Ben uses his fists as well as a knife to control his wife as well as Alice into obeying him. The actions of these men show that their rage and pent-up sexual energy explode into violence. Jake, Ben, and Max Cady show their contempt for women, and they use sex to control and dominate women.

Travis Bickle grandiosely takes the law into his own hands and, in doing so, demonstrates that he is consumed by a megalomaniacal fantasy of being able to change the nature of reality—for example, the dirty streets or the fact that Iris is a prostitute—by means of violence. He imagines that after his killing spree, he will be perceived by his immediate community as a forceful and strong man, one of daring deeds and action. This wished-for perception inflates his sense of self and counters his feelings of paranoia, inadequacy, and impotency. The violence that he undertakes enables him to restore a positive self-image. Travis gets more accolades than he had ever imagined, and, in the end, the murderous Travis is hailed a hero by the media. The brutal acts of revenge that Cady commits indicate that he imagines that he is a god and that his acts are entirely in keeping with a godlike sense of justice and goodness. Moreover, he imagines that his actions constitute apt retaliation for Sam's betrayal of him. In Cady's psychotic mind, this leap of reason occurs as his personal sense of injury and loss become elevated to the status of sins against a godlike being.

Scorsese intertwines the violence in these films—*Taxi Driver*, *Raging Bull*, and *Cape Fear*—with spiritual allusions about sacrifice, purification, and salvation. Indeed, blood imagery is used as a potent force with regard to the religious meaning behind the violence. In this context, Scorsese is quoted as saying: "Blood is very important in the church. Blood is the life force, the essence, the sacrifice" and "I like the idea of spurting blood…. It's really like a purification."[1] One is reminded of the abundance of blood in Scorsese's student film, *The Big Shave*. In this short, made during the brutality of the Vietnam War, we can imagine that the young man, who opens up pools of blood while he is shaving, represents Scorsese's hoped-for purification of the "sins" that were committed in Vietnam.

Travis and Max, at least as these characters are drawn by Scorsese in their respective films, experience a regeneration (of sorts) through violence, and by the end of their stories, they enjoy an imagined redemption of their or others' sins. In *Taxi Driver*, Travis's redemption is rendered explicit by the fact that Travis is acknowledged as the saviour of Iris. In the case of Jake, the ending of the film suggests that he finally "sees" or has acquired some consciousness into his self-destructiveness, and he is given a new beginning as a man with some, albeit limited, insight.

Next consider to the violence of the gangster characters in *GoodFellas*, *Casino*, and *Gangs of New York*: Henry Hill, Jimmy Conway, Tommy De Vito; Sam Rothstein and Nicky Santoro; and Bill "the Butcher" Cutting, respectively. These men are loners (estranged from mainstream society) as well as members of a power elite. They feel that they must preserve their self-image as "real" men within their gangster family as well as within the outside world. These gangsters act out their sociopathic (Henry Hill and Sam Rothstein) or psychopathic (Jimmy Conway, Tommy DeVito, and Nicky Santoro) behavior so as to maintain their image of being omnipotent. It is difficult to label Cutting as either sociopathic or psychopathic because of the particularly barbaric, nineteenth-century milieu in which he lives.[2]

For each of the gangster characters who are placed in a relatively modern era, greed for money, power, or drugs is the driving force behind their violent behaviors. The greed of these disturbed and dangerous men becomes greater and greater, and they devolve into addicts who need more and more power. For example, we see that Tommy and Nicky are easily enraged and will kill at the drop of a hat and that Jimmy becomes progressively more murderous as the story progresses. These men's demand for more and more derives from a terrible sense of themselves as inadequate and empty. Their violent expressions of power give them an illusory feeling of superiority that covers over and thus defends against an awareness of their inner emptiness.

With regard to the women in the lives of the gangsters in *GoodFellas* and *Casino*, it is not unusual for them, although married, to have mistresses whom they see on a regular basis. It is in keeping with the greed and phallic narcissism of these characters to want it all and to display to the world that they have it all. As an example, Henry Hill not only has a mistress but he sets her up in an expensive apartment. His behavior suggests that he is exclaiming for all to see and hear: "Look at what a big man I am. I have enough sexual energy to keep two women attached to me." Sam Rothstein, although seemingly obsessed with Ginger, the beautiful hustler, actually wants her as his wife because he considers her an important acquisition, not unlike his money and jewelry. Once Sam and Ginger are married, he pays considerably more attention to his casino than he does to his wife.

Hill and Rothstein are humbled at the end of their respective stories. Hill betrays his former gangster family, and he enters a federal witness protection program. Rothstein returns to his work as a handicapper. Although these two former demigods have seemingly gained a semblance of redemption, all of the others are dead or in prison.

In the case of Bill "the Butcher" Cutting, although he is also greedy about his power and maintaining control of Five Points, he lives in an era that is more primitive in every respect than that of the other gangsters considered previously. As depicted in the film, a man living in Five Points during the middle of the nineteenth century almost must resort to violence to survive. Bill is most obsessed about his grandiose sense of superiority relative to the Irish immigrants, whom he considers grossly inferior. His self-righteous insistence of raising himself up while putting the Irish down is, ultimately, the cause of his fall from power and his death.

Rupert Pupkin in *The King of Comedy*, although less malevolent than the former characters, is another emotionally disturbed man who seeks success at any price. Pupkin feels that he is powerless, a "schnook," a "zero," and he fears that he is perceived in this way by others (for example, his secret love, Rita). His violent behavior derives from his seeking to defend against his extraordinary sense of shame that accompanies an image of himself as an utter failure and an impotent man.

Rupert's rage is triggered when Jerry rejects him and throws him out of his house. Rupert experiences the rejection as a betrayal. He feels humiliated and abandoned, and his former idealization of Jerry is obliterated. Rupert's shame is exacerbated because this painful rejection occurs in Rita's presence, and because of this, he feels that she sees him as a miserable failure. In reprisal, Rupert sets out to punish Jerry and to prove to Rita that his talent is real, that he is a great comedian, and that he can attain television stardom and great wealth. As the ending of the film indicates, Rupert attains great success, a redemption of sorts, because of the culture's propensity for idolizing celebrities.

Frank Pierce in *Bringing Out the Dead* strives to save lives, not destroy them. However, his self-image as a healer depends on his succeeding in saving people. When the people he administers to die, Frank's pride is affected. He feels shame because of what he perceives as his failure, and his self-image plummets. He also becomes enraged and devolves into violent behavior that is directed against himself, that is, drinking and using drugs. Saving people, which gives Frank a "high" from the adrenaline rush, has become an addiction. His sufferings and his realization that he can allow near-death people to expire enable him to transcend his self-destructive behavior. The ending of the film, which shows him cradled in the arms of Mary Burke in a pose that is reminiscent of the Pieta, indicates that he attains a symbolic redemption.

The violence in *Mean Streets* (and hints of the potential for it in *Who's That Knocking at My Door?*), which is focused most dramatically in terms of Johnny Boy and Michael, has a number of roots. Johnny and the other young men are embedded in a social milieu whose values define and constrain their behavior. Johnny is like a spoiled little boy who wants what all the other "big" guys have, including money for gambling, alcohol, and sex, without needing to work and earn the money. Johnny has no ambition, no interest in working at a regular job, and no powerful uncle such as Charlie has, who guarantees him the eventual management of a restaurant. Johnny cannot repay the debt that he foolishly incurs. Moreover, Johnny is easily enraged, particularly when he cannot get what he wants, this feeling deriving from a conscious sense of entitlement; unconsciously he feels utterly worthless as well as impotent, and he fears being seen as such by the other men in his community.

Charlie feels guilt about his sexual and less-than-legal activities, and he exposes himself to danger because of this guilt. He presumes that his penance is to care for Johnny Boy. In actual fact, Charlie "takes care" of Johnny to boost *his own* self-esteem and, thus, continue to feel superior to his foolish friend.

The lack of a sense of personal empowerment and no prospects for the future fuel Johnny's self-destructive behavior and violence. When Johnny Boy's rage explodes, he insults Michael in front of the other guys at the bar, which serves as his social milieu, his "family." Michael's self-image as a strong and powerful man, respected by the other men, is challenged. Michael feels humiliated, and he must retaliate *in order* to restore his reputation and his fantasied phallic supremacy within his social circle. In essence, both Johnny and Michael engage in violent behavior to preserve their respective self-images of being "real" men. As the reels of home movies show at the opening of *Mean Streets*, all of the "sinners," including Michael and Johnny Boy, recover from perceived and real injuries, suggesting that all of them attain redemption, at least insofar as Scorsese, who wrote the script, is concerned.

Jimmy Doyle in *New York, New York* is an infantile narcissist. His psychological violence, which is expressed primarily in terms of the emotional abuse of his wife, injures, demeans, and humiliates himself and others. Jimmy needs to feel superior to others to defend against the terrible insecurities and shame to which he is vulnerable. His much-desired self-image of being the "top dog" is fragile, and this fantasy topples when Jimmy perceives threats to his sense of superiority. His pretentiousness and emotional abuse of others occur in response to such threats. Without keeping up a facade that he is superior to everyone else, Jimmy feels he is nothing. In short, Jimmy lacks a sense of self, and he attempts, unconsciously, to compensate by posturing and displaying himself as well as by attacking and humiliating others. Jimmy does not have the psychological capacity for empathy; his self-centeredness is an indication that he lacks an adequate sense of self-worth. Indeed, the characterization of Jimmy shows a man with a terribly vulnerable psyche, whose narcissistic equilibrium is tenuous, particularly when he does not equal or surpass the success enjoyed by others. When he sees that Francine is more successful than he, for example, his self-worth collapses. He expresses this negative self-perception in a nutshell when he says to her, "You've got everything. I got nothing."

Eddie Felson and Vincent Lauria in *The Color of Money*, and Lionel Dobie in "Life Lessons" are not violent men, although they are aggressive and self-centered. For each of these characters, his sense of self is defined largely in terms of his respective talent or skill. His self-image depends on being successful and being seen as such by his "family," the artistic community in the case of Dobie, devotees of pool for Felson and Lauria. As depicted, Eddie puts aside his propensity for hustling and becomes a purist in playing pool; this a sign of his redemption, while Vincent falls from grace. Lionel Dobie, who uses people for the sake of creating his art, is self-centered and feels a sense of extraordinary self-importance.

As seen in chapters 5, 6, and 7, the personalities and behaviors of most of these characters are consistent with the characteristics of phallic-narcissistic men as defined and explained in Chapter 4. A number of these characters are also violent and sexist. Also explained in Chapter 4, phallic-narcissistic men tend to have misogynous attitudes about women; they fear sexual women, and they show contempt for them.

In the films whose focal male characters have been discussed in chapters 5 through 7, Scorsese seems to have been exploring particular faces of masculinity, men's attitudes toward women, and the variety of ways in which manhood may be expressed in the world.

Scorsese spent most of his childhood and his adolescence within the confines of Little Italy. He is now and probably was a keen observer of human nature from the time he was a child. Because of his frail health, he was forced to spend a good deal of his time looking out from his third-floor window that looked out to Elizabeth Street. From that vantage point, he was able to observe the people and their activities in the community below. From this perspective, although Scorsese was an insider, he also stood outside of the community, in effect, bearing witness to the goings-on in the community. Probably among his early impressions, both memories and fantasies, were violence, fear of violence, and people who were quite simply out of control. These impressions might have included boys who engaged in fighting and men who were gangsters and pushed other people around.

Even before Scorsese turned to the Catholic Church in his youth, something which he has said he did to attain some sense of security, he was an avid filmgoer. Since he and his father—with whom he had a special relationship particularly with regard to watching movies—loved westerns, the violence in these films probably affected the young Martin's internalized impressions as well.

As is consistent with normal development, as Scorsese began to approach adolescence, he must have been confronted with the issue of what it means to be a real man, one who has the respect of his community. In all likelihood, the prevalent model of manhood within Scorsese's Italian-American-Catholic community was one of macho masculinity, that is, masculinity that is equated with aggression and power. Scorsese's western heroes were probably macho as well. Undoubtedly, among the gangster element in or near his community Scorsese observed arrogant displays of superiority (that is, men's fantasies of phallic supremacy), aggression, and violence. The features of aggression and self-confidence probably also defined, in general, the more successful men in the community, men who might have served as role models for the boys. As a result of these experiences, Scorsese entered manhood with these internalized images of macho masculinity, power, and violence in his consciousness.

In his films that feature Italian-American men—J.R. in *Who's That Knocking at My Door?*, the characters in *Mean Streets*, Jake LaMotta in *Raging Bull*, and a number of the gangsters in *GoodFellas* and *Casino*—Scorsese presents macho, misogynous, and violent male characters, with whom he, seemingly, can empathize.

Scorsese might not have been comfortable with the notion that masculinity demanded aggressiveness and power. As noted in his biography, he suffered from asthma from the age of three, and because of his illness, he was not able to participate with other boys his age in competitive games and sports nor would he have engaged in fighting, at least willingly. Given that he lived in a tough neighborhood, he had to learn to absorb physical punishment inflicted by the more aggressive and mean-spirited boys.

In addition to the contributions of his ethnic roots, his street culture, as well as his ideas about masculinity, Scorsese was also affected by the teachings of the Catholic Church. On the one hand, he was exposed to the faces of masculinity presented by the priests he admired: asexual, compassionate, and probably less aggressive than the other men who were respected in Little Italy. On the other hand, in all liklihood, Catholic priests would have reinforced the misogynous attitudes about women that other men in that community held. These cultural attitudes about women were held with a sense of self-righteousness particularly because the Catholic church reinforced them and, thus, imbued these attitudes with the air of authority. Because of Scorsese's exposure to these misogynous attitudes, it is understandable that, in his early, personal films, Scorsese presented characters who had the madonna-whore complex. Indeed, as Scorsese has acknowledged, during his youth he did not think of women as real human beings.[3]

Without doubt, during his formative years, Scorsese was exposed to stereotypic notions about what it means to be a man. Drawing from Scorsese's films, some of these notions include the following:

A "real" man in Scorsese's cultural milieu does not get pushed around or treated like a fool (or schnook) without at least retaliating (shades of

Michael in *Mean Streets*, Jake in *Raging Bull*, Travis in *Taxi Driver*, Cady in *Cape Fear*, Tommy in *GoodFellas*, Nicky in *Casino*, and Pupkin in *The King of Comedy*).

A "real" man gives the appearance, at least, of respecting his family (as Henry Hill in *GoodFellas* is so advised to do by his elders in the mob), shows himself to be a good father (as does Sam Rothstein in *Casino*), and comports himself with purpose and measured action (as modeled by Uncle Giovanni in *Mean Streets*). Such a man pays his debts and does not fly off the handle as Johnny Boy (in *Mean Streets*) does or Tommy and Nicky do. We notice in the case of Tommy and Nicky that even the mob will not tolerate a man who loses control. In sum, a real man is in control of his feelings and passions, does not let others control him, and he exerts control whenever possible, particularly with regard to women. Moreover, a real man shows he can take punishment, as Jake LaMotta does; puts his "balls" on the line, as Eddie Felson and Jake LaMotta do; and is the ultimate authority in the home, as Jimmy Doyle, Henry Hill, and Jake strive to achieve.

Based on his personal experience and observation as well as his intelligence, Scorsese probably realized that aggressive and violent men are also narcissistically or emotionally disturbed, as so many of his male characters are, and that they are highly vulnerable to feeling threatened about their masculinity.

As seen through the actions of characters in these films, the insecurity about male potency and the demeaning and abusing of women go hand-in-hand. Indeed, misogynous attitudes appear to be essential for some of these male characters to feel potent, suggesting that strong women are threatening to the men's self-image of themselves as superior to women. In those films where women are not explicitly demeaned, they are, on the whole, in passive or submissive roles. This topic elaborated upon in Chapter 10, which discusses the female characters in Scorsese's films.

In depicting so many of his violent male characters as attaining redemption, Scorsese is expressing his belief that, given the limitations of their personalities and the conditioning of their culture, these men do the best they can in living on the "streets," as it were.

In the films examined that lack explicit violence, Scorsese shows other personality aspects that can be associated with masculinity. For example, in *New York, New York* and "Life Lessons," the dynamics of the stories imply that a man's ambition for professional success may be more important to him than a love relationship and a family (as was the case for Lionel Dobie and Jimmy Doyle). *In Bringing Out the Dead*, Scorsese suggests that a fully masculine man also can be compassionate and empathic.

The next chapter examines Scorsese's "good guys." These are men who possess a sense of sense of personal security, potency, and self-worth, and although they may be strong and self-assertive, they are capable of containing their rage and abstaining from violence.

9

The Good Guys

The "good guys" in Scorsese's movies are Bill Shelly in *Boxcar Bertha*, David in *Alice Doesn't Live Here Anymore*, Paul Hackett in *After Hours*, Jesus in *The Last Temptation of Christ*, Newland Archer in *The Age of Innocence*, the Dalai Lama in *Kundun*, and Priest Vallon and his son, Amsterdam, in *Gangs of New York*. The personalities of these men are decidedly different from those of the narcissistically disturbed characters examined previously. This contrast is useful in underscoring the selfishness, violence, and phallic narcissism of the characters that were discussed in chapters 5, 6, and 7. All of these good guys have the capacity to get beyond their individual needs and wishes and are able to consider the needs of others. They are also capable of empathy, and they treat women with respect. The character of Jesus is discussed briefly; additional elaboration of *The Last Temptation of Christ* is presented in Chapter 11.

BILL SHELLY

"Big" Bill Shelly (David Carradine) is the male lead in *Boxcar Bertha*, a 1972 Scorsese movie that is set in the rural south during the Depression. Shelly, who is Bertha's (Barbara Hershey) lover, is a union organizer of railroad men at a time when such activities were considered the work of anarchists and communists. He is arrested and imprisoned in a chain gang because of his union activities. He escapes from the chain gang because of Bertha's intervention. Once he attains freedom, Shelly and his cohorts, who include Bertha, Von Morton (Bernie Casey), and Rake Brown (Barry Primus), form a gang of train robbers. However, Shelly is a reluctant gangster and gun toter, giving his share of the stolen loot to the union. As depicted and as he states, he is a union man, not a criminal. In effect, Shelly steals from the rich and cruel railroad owner, Sartoris (John Carradine), to help the dispossessed and those striving for workers' rights. Although he wields a gun, Shelly neither injures nor kills anyone.

Bill is a man of good character, which is indicated by his brotherly attitude toward a black man, Von, as well as by the way he treats Bertha. He acknowledges his friendship for Von Bill is beaten by rednecks for befriending a "nigger." In his relationship with Bertha, he treats her with respect, protectiveness, and love. There is nothing in the film depiction that suggests that Shelly is a phallic-narcissist. Eventually, Shelly is captured by Sartoris's men and punished for his crimes against the railroad by first being beaten and then nailed to the side of a boxcar. This act is a symbolic crucifixion perpetrated on the martyr-like Shelly, rendering him representative of the biblical Christ-figure, who, like Shelly is compassionate and strives to help the poor.

DAVID

David (Kris Kristofferson) in *Alice Doesn't Live Here Anymore* (1974) seems to be a warm and generous man. He has a house and ranch and enjoys playing the guitar and singing. He is sexually attracted to Alice and spends time doing "guy things" with her son, Tommy. However, the viewer never knows why David's ex-wife left him, taking their children with her. It is also

David (Kris Kristofferson) and Alice (Ellen Burstyn) enjoying each other's company in a scene from *Alice Doesn't Live Here Anymore* (Photofest).

not known whether he sees his children and if not, why not. Indeed, it is troubling that he seems to have no feelings or concerns about his children. This information would be helpful in assessing his capacity for a relationship with Alice and Tommy. David's whacking Tommy "on the behind" in response to Tommy's outburst appears to be a measured response to the twelve-year old who knows no limits to his sometimes outrageous behavior. However, David's action in punishing Tommy enrages Alice, and she breaks off their relationship.

David is sufficiently mature, psychologically, to get past his pride and narcissistic vulnerability and come to the diner where Alice works to appeal to her to return to their relationship. Unlike many of Scorsese's male characters, David is unselfish and generous in offering to leave his ranch to take her to Monterey and, thus, help Alice to resume her singing career. As depicted, David is both sensitive and strong, and his personality and behavior suggest that he is a man who feels secure about himself. In short, David is a man who knows he is a man and does not have to prove it. Thus, although he is assertive and successful, David shows no sign of paranoia nor destructive aggression.

PAUL HACKETT

Paul Hackett (Griffin Dunne), a passive, buttoned-down word processor, is the focal character in *After Hours* (1985). He lives and works in an impersonal, unemotional, and vanilla world. The business suit he wears is beige; he has a nondescript desk among many others in a large Madison Avenue office. The building in which he works closes its massive metal gates at the end of the day as if it were disgorging the workers it had held hostage during the work day.

Paul is lonely and bored. We see him in his workplace gazing lovingly at a woman's hands as well as at a woman's cubicle that includes a picture of her son. Paul seems to be aching for a support system, family, wife, or girlfriend. After work he goes home to an empty apartment and a telephone answering machine devoid of messages. The living room of Paul's tidy apartment, all in beige and brown colors, lacks personal items; thus, it looks like a hotel room rather than a person's apartment. Paul flips through television channels, and, feeling desperate for companionship, he goes to a coffee shop late that evening with a book to read.

At the cafeteria, Paul meets Marcy (Rosanna Arquette), an attractive blonde who is dressed in white, and they have a conversation. Marcy gives him the telephone number of the loft in SoHo where she is staying with her friend Kiki, a sculptress. Marcy tells Paul that Kiki makes papier-mâché, cementlike figures including paperweights in the shape of bagels. Paul leaves the coffee shop, goes home, and decides to call the number. Marcy invites him over to the loft although it is 11:30 P.M. and he is about forty-five minutes away.

In SoHo, Paul encounters a number of bizarre women who first entice him and, later, threaten him. In addition, members of the SoHo community perceive him to be the burglar who has been robbing apartments in the area.

Paul is a victim of sexual frustration and loneliness. He seems to lack a sense of personal power that would enable him to say "no," to take charge of himself, and to control his destiny. Rather, as a more-or-less puppet, seemingly at the mercy of the whims of others, Paul becomes entangled in a web woven by other people, and he becomes confused and cannot find his way out.

The various characters in the story, some of whom are eccentric and others appear to be insane, as well as the seemingly random events that Paul experiences—including a suicide, burglaries, and a homicide—are interconnected and intertwined. Paul is an outsider in the SoHo milieu, while the various kooks he encounters are insiders. The lack of familiarity with people and place fosters some paranoia on Paul's part. However, a number of the people with whom he comes into contact in SoHo are more paranoid still probably because Paul is not from the neighborhood. Paul does not meet with much kindness during his time of distress.

Scorsese made *After Hours* directly after he had suffered a series of frustrations and setbacks in attempting to obtain financing for *The Last Temptation of Christ*, the film he had wanted to make for a number of years. The misadventures that Scorsese experienced while he tried to make *The Last Temptation* seem to have provided the personal passion, particularly about being an outsider, that Paul Hackett portrays in the film. Paul's lack of a sense of belonging when looking into or entering a strange new place and his suspiciousness toward the unfamiliar can be likened to those experiences of Scorsese. The "place" could be considered Hollywood, the adult Scorsese's new neighborhood, or any strange milieu that the young Scorsese entered or tried to enter around his old neighborhood. Perhaps like Paul, Scorsese felt uncomfortable with the unfamiliar, fearing that he would not be accepted in the new milieu by the insiders.

The film, with its bizarre twists and turns, is a commentary about seeking acceptance in a place where one is an outsider. Rather than gaining acceptance, however, Paul's reputation is besmirched, and he is run out of the neighborhood. Paul's experiences, particularly with regard to the lack of acceptance, capture what may have been Scorsese's experiences in Hollywood when he tried to get the financing he needed to make the controversial film, *The Last Temptation of Christ*. After his frustrating experiences in Hollywood, like Paul, Scorsese may have felt that his reputation had been injured as, undoubtedly, his feelings were.

After being chased through SoHo by a mob of vigilantes and fearing for his life, Paul is rudely deposited at his workplace the following morning. Given his then-recent experience in Hollywood, Scorsese could relate to Paul's circular experience in SoHo, that is, that Paul ended up where he began and with nothing to show for his efforts. After years of effort trying to make

The Last Temptation of Christ, Scorsese ended up essentially where he had begun and entirely empty-handed.

In *After Hours*, Scorsese has given us another view of New York streets during the hours of the night. Like Travis Bickle in *Taxi Driver* and Frank Pierce in *Bringing Out the Dead*, Paul is lonely and alone, lacking a human support system. Each of these three men feels powerless. Travis takes matters into his own hands and goes on a shooting spree; Frank hallucinates seeing ghosts; Paul is displaced from a placid life to one of utter chaos and probably suffers some degree of mental breakdown or fragmentation. Nevertheless, Paul never resorts to violence to retaliate against those who have attacked or betrayed him. His behavior gives no indication of his being selfish or self-centered. Indeed, he tries to be understanding and empathic to all those he encounters during his odyssey. Paul relates to the women he encounters as if he perceived them as equals.

JESUS

The character of Jesus (Willem Dafoe) in *The Last Temptation of Christ* is a carpenter from Nazareth who makes crosses for the Romans with which they crucify Jews who oppose their rule. As such, Jesus is a betrayer of his people. Jesus is depicted as confused, conflicted, and subject to headaches and hallucinations. He is, moreover, lonely and sexually repressed. He makes crosses, he says, in order to fight God, and he hopes that by doing so, God will hate him. The tormented and fearful character of Jesus is a reluctant spiritual leader and representation of divinity, asking repeatedly if it is God or the devil that is speaking to him (via the voices he hears in his head).

Jesus sits outside Magdalene's brothel as men come and go all day, but he does not participate. Mary Magdalene (Barbara Hershey) accuses him of being like the other men with sexual desires, but refusing to admit it. Taking into consideration his tormenting thoughts as well as his sexual abstinence, Jesus is reminiscent of Travis Bickle in *Taxi Driver*. Jesus, as regards his humanity, is also a sinner. He accuses himself of being a liar and a hypocrite as well as a prideful and greedy man. In this context, this character is similar to a number of Scorsese's narcissistically disturbed men. However, unlike many of these other characters, Jesus does not retaliate or resort to violence.

At one stage of his ministry, as encouraged to do so by Judas (Harvey Keitel), Jesus considers leading an army. This role would have rendered him a warrior whose goal was the betterment of his people rather than a self-serving end. However, Jesus rejects the role of warrior and accepts the divine plan that is revealed to him that includes his crucifixion and death.

Although tempted (in fantasy) down from the cross to marry and have a family, ultimately, Jesus returns to the cross to fulfill his divine mission and, thus, gain salvation for the sins of humankind. As such, the human side of the character of Jesus is shown to be both courageous and selfless.

In Scorsese's value system, Jesus represents the prototype of the ordinary human sinner who struggles successfully with temptations of the flesh. Indeed, with regard to the faces of masculinity in Scorsese's movies, the character representing the human Jesus stands as a model of noble manhood. Confronted by challenges and temptations, Jesus acknowledges his failings and shortcomings and, ultimately, takes on the mantle of divinity without succumbing to pride. In the film, he is presented as a man to admire, emulate, and idolize.

NEWLAND ARCHER

Newland Archer (Daniel Day-Lewis) is the major male character in Scorsese's 1993 costume drama, *The Age of Innocence*. The story is set in fashionable New York society during the 1870s.

Newland is a self-controlled and self-contained young man who is engaged to marry May Welland (Winona Ryder). The match is considered a good one as it brings together two prestigious families. Newland lives in a high-society culture, that is governed by strict rules of conduct and appearance. A man of fine taste, dignity, and comportment, Newland feels that he is superior to other men in his milieu but, nevertheless, is compelled to conform to the group's rules about form and family.

The heart of the story revolves around Newland's infatuation with and sexual yearnings for the Countess Ellen Olenska (Michelle Pfeiffer), a cousin of May Welland. Ellen has recently moved to New York from Europe, having left her husband, the Count. The Wellands have supported their cousin in spite of the fact that in their society a woman who separates from her husband is the subject of gossip. Ellen wants to divorce her husband, but Newland, in his role as legal counselor, is called upon by his firm to advise Ellen not to do so lest her husband's allegations about her indiscretions surface. He tells her that the inevitable scandal would hurt her and the family.

After a number of encounters with Ellen, Newland realizes that he is sexually attracted to her, and, feeling anxious about these feelings, he tries to push up the date of his marriage to May. May suspects that Newland has feelings for her cousin, but she conceals whatever hurt she feels by wearing her ever-present smile.

Even after the marriage, however, Newland's fantasies and feelings for Ellen continue, and he begins to waver with regard to his customary conformity to the discipline of his social circle. Indeed, he seems to be willing to sacrifice his good name and his relationship with his wife for the sake of the satisfaction of his sexual desires. He wants Ellen as his mistress, but Ellen resists his advances both because she cannot betray the family that has sup-

Newland Archer (Daniel Day-Lewis) sharing a tender moment with Ellen Olenska (Michelle Pfeiffer) in *The Age of Innocence.* **(Photofest)**

ported her and because if she and Newland were to have a sexual liaison, she fears that they would lose respect for one another.

Ellen returns to Europe, but not to her husband. Mrs. Mingott (Miriam Margolyes), a wealthy and elderly relative (actually, May's grandmother) provides Ellen with an income so that she can live in Europe and maintain her independence. Ellen's leaving prompts Newland to tell May about his feelings for Ellen. Newland does not know that May told Ellen that she is pregnant or that this news caused Ellen to decide that she must leave for Europe. Once Newland is told about the pregnancy, he knows that there is no hope for a relationship with Ellen. He accepts his destiny and remains a faithful husband, fulfilling his obligations to his wife and children for the rest of his life. His romantic fantasies of the Countess Olenska remain preserved within his mind as memories.

Like so many others of Scorsese's heroes, Newland is bridled by a limited perspective of himself because of the constraints imposed by his social milieu, trained by experience to restrain from emotional expression. Ellen provides Newland with openness, stimulation, and emotional honesty while May promises him a life that will continue to be dull and false. Nevertheless, Newland endures the pain of unconsummated love for the sake of family cohesion and maintenance of his position within his social milieu.

Newland shares with Travis Bickle in *Taxi Driver* the yearning for a woman he cannot have; both characters are rejected by their respective love objects. However, where Travis goes on a shooting spree, Newland contains his feelings, accepts the situation as it is, and goes on with his life. He plans no retaliation and engages in no violence. In light of the difference in behavior between Travis and Newland, one can appreciate the greater maturity and psychological health of Newland Archer.

THE DALAI LAMA

The Dalai Lama (as an adult, played by Tenzin Thuthob Tsarong) in *Kundun* is depicted both as a child and as an adult. As a young child living with his parents and two older brothers, he is imperial, believing that he is a king and usurping his father's place at the dinner table. While still a child but having been chosen as the 14th Dalai Lama, he seems to feel pleasure when his parents and siblings bow to him.

When he grows up and accepts his special role in Tibet, the Dalai Lama realizes the extent of his self-sacrifice of home and family for the sake of his people. After China invades Tibet, he chooses to leave his country to safeguard the Buddhist religion and the honor of Tibet. In short, the adult man demonstrates that he is capable of selfless love and sacrifice as well as compassion. It goes without saying that the Dalai Lama does not engage in violence.

PRIEST AND AMSTERDAM VALLON

Gangs of New York essentially opens with a battle that takes place in 1846 and pits Priest Vallon (Liam Neeson) fighting against Bill "the Butcher" Cutting (Daniel Day-Lewis). The battle is between warriors, and it has religious overtones.

Priest looks and acts as if he were a religious figure. He wears a ministerial collar, prays with his young son, Amsterdam (Leonardo DiCaprio), to "St. Michael, the Archangel who cast out Satan from Paradise," and carries a metal cross in his hand as he proceeds to the battlefield. In the context of the story, Bill Cutting represents Satan. As depicted on the screen, Priest's mission, to help his people rather than himself, is an honorable one. In going into a violent battle, his goal is to help the Irish Catholics free themselves from the yoke of bigotry and oppression imposed by Bill Cutting and his gang of Protestant Nativists. Priest is felled in the battle and dies; his son is taken away to a reform prison. Bill Cutting assumes complete control of the Five Points area.

Later in the film, Amsterdam, now grown into manhood, returns to the Five Points. He is committed to avenging his father's death. Amsterdam explains the meaning behind the name of his father's former gang, the Dead Rabbits, as referring to the fact that so many of their tribe have died and are still willing to die. An image of the crucified Christ appears on the screen. Thus, it appears that Priest Vallon represents a Christlike figure, who is willing to die for the sake of his people whom he loves. As stated in Chapter 2, in leading his people through the catacomb-like tunnel that leads up to Paradise Square Priest Vallon, is also reminiscent of Moses who leads his people out of a country where they are demeaned and enslaved and into the Promised Land.

At first, Amsterdam wants to kill Bill Cutting only because of his personal feelings of revenge. Indeed, he feels honorbound to avenge the death of his father. However, these feelings are driven by his pride and his selfish pursuit of personal honor. When Amsterdam makes his first attempt to kill Cutting, he is savagely rebuffed and publicly humiliated. Later and upon reflection, Amsterdam realizes that his father's fundamental goal was to help his people. He learns that he must do as his father had done. He expands his vision beyond his selfish pursuits and begins uniting his people to work for the common goal. He gains political power for the Irish and eventually leads them into a battle against Cutting and the Nativists.

In the context of his time and place, Amsterdam has no choice but to engage in the violence that was rampant in the Five Points if he is to survive. His eventual battle against the "Satan" of the Five Points is undertaken to help the Irish immigrants rather than for himself alone.

The "good guys" discussed in this chapter either are not violent, or if do engage in violence, their actions are motivated by the wish to help people rather than by wishes for self-gratification. Their personalities are more-or-less mature, in a psychological sense; they feel security about who they are. They are able to tolerate sexual frustration and, in general, contain their aggression and anger. They are not abusive toward women. Indeed, they are respectful and loving toward women, and they try to understand them. Moreover, they show respect for black people (Shelly) and gays (Paul Hackett). If there is violence, as is true for Shelly and the Vallons, it is directed toward unselfish goals.

With the character of the Dalai Lama and that of Jesus Scorsese shows that extraordinary men have compassion for humanity and that this generosity may preempt their human desires for an intimate relationship and a family. Another value expressed in these characterizations of "good guys" is that although a man may experience betrayal and frustration (as do Paul Hackett and Newland Archer), maintaining control and composure is important in terms of being a "real" man. Newland Archer's loyalty to his wife and children is presented as an ideal to be admired.[1]

10

Women and Relationships

Consistent with Scorsese's declaration that he makes movies of the world of men, the focal characters of his films are most often (heterosexual) men while female characters play secondary and supporting roles.[1] With the exception of Alice Graham Hyatt in *Alice Doesn't Live Here Anymore* (1974), Bertha "Box-car" Thompson in *Boxcar Bertha* (1972), Countess Ellen Olenska in *The Age of Innocence* (1993), and Francine Evans in *New York, New York* (1977), the women in Scorsese's films are companions, sometimes mere appendages, to the men around whom the stories revolve. Moreover, the characterizations of female companions tend to be less finely drawn than those of the men with whom they are involved, their psychological makeup, less complex and less clear than that of the male characters. On the whole, in their relationships with the more dominant male characters, the women are subordinate or submissive, often having no life of their own except in relationship to their husbands or boyfriends. A number of women in Scorsese's films are depicted as seducers, betrayers, whores, or madonna figures. Rarely do Scorsese's female characters engage in violence, and only a few show any aggressiveness. From a functional perspective, the female characters provide for conflict within the respective stories, or they serve as projective screens.

Since the female characters are in relationships with men, the quality of these relationships enable us to appreciate how the men view the women. This information, in turn, adds to an understanding of the personalities of the male characters as well as of Scorsese's perspectives about masculinity and femininity.

In addition to the roles played by actresses that are discussed in the following sections, Martin Scorsese's mother, Catherine, played small parts in a number of her son's films, usually in the role of someone's mother.

Focal Characters

BERTHA THOMPSON

Bertha "Boxcar" Thompson (Barbara Hershey) is an aggressive and strong young woman. She has been on her own since the untimely death of her father in a plane crash that occurs at the opening of the film. As a victim of the Great Depression, Bertha has no money and no job, and she rides boxcars in the rural South.

Bertha meets and falls in love with Bill Shelly (David Carradine). A courageous risk-taker, Bertha succeeds in helping Bill escape from a chain gang. She enjoys sexual freedom and does what is necessary to survive, including becoming a thief and a prostitute. She joins the three men, Shelly, Von, and Rake, in forming a gang of train robbers. During these robberies, Bertha wields a gun and appears to enjoy the excitement and risk that the robberies entail as well as the money and jewelry they steal. At film's end, Bertha watches in anguish and grief as her lover, Bill, is crucified to the side of a boxcar. In this portrayal, she seems to be in the role of Mary Magdalene to Shelly's Christ.

ALICE GRAHAM HYATT

Alice Graham Hyatt (Ellen Burstyn) is a thirty-five-year-old housewife and mother. She is as lonely a female character as Scorsese has presented on film. When we first see the adult Alice, she is married to Donald (Billy Green Bush), a truck driver, and she has an eleven-year-old precocious son, Tommy (Alfred Lutter). As depicted, she is the prototypical American housewife of the early 1970s. She is the caretaker, cook, and housekeeper in the family while Donald is the breadwinner. Alice feels stifled in the role of housewife. Later in the story, Alice relates that she had hoped for a career in show business when she was single and living in Monterey. Indeed, she had begun a career of sorts, evolving an entertainment act with her brother. After she married Donald, however, he insisted that she abandon her singing career and that they live in his hometown in New Mexico. As she describes it, her response to Donald's demand was, "Yes, master," and she tells us that his imperial attitude was consistent with her idea of how a man should be, that is, strong and dominating. Alice obeyed her husband, abandoned her career, and became a housewife.

Alice is a people-pleaser and, in all likelihood, she strives to please others so that she will be liked or loved. Whenever she is angry and asserts herself, she ends up apologizing for her feelings. She subordinates her wishes and desires for the sake of a hoped-for caring response from her emotionally distant and threatening husband. She tries to please Donald, for example, by cooking him his favorite foods. Although, as Alice relates, she is afraid of Donald, she takes comfort in his seeming to care for her. Actually, This is a fantasy.

After Donald is killed in an accident, Alice finds herself on her own as a single mother, struggling to make a living for herself and Tommy. Donald has left her very little money, and Alice uses most of it for his funeral. Apparently, Donald did not take care of his family after all. That Alice uses the small amount of money she has to pay for Donald's funeral indicates she has more concern for pleasing Donald, so to speak, and for the public display of his funeral than she has in securing her financial viability and that of her son.

Alice and Tommy leave New Mexico with a goal of reaching Monterey, where she hopes to resume her singing career. In Phoenix, Arizona, she gets a job singing in a bar, and she meets Ben Eberhardt (Harvey Keitel), a twenty-seven-year-old with whom she has a brief sexual relationship. However, soon thereafter, she learns that Ben is married and that he abuses his wife. When Ben assaults his wife with a knife in Alice's presence and threatens Alice as well, Alice and Tommy leave Phoenix hurriedly.

Mother and son stop next at Tucson, where Alice gets a job as a waitress in a diner. Here she meets David (Kris Kristofferson), an attractive and divorced man who is a rancher. David shows interest in Tommy and spends time with him, and he and Alice begin a relationship. However, the fledgling relationship appears to come to an end when Alice and David have a fight about Tommy. Alice does not set limits on her son, and when the twelve-year-old and David quarrel about music, Tommy has a hysterical outburst, and David strikes the boy on his behind. Alice is very angry with David, and she leaves his ranch, each accusing the other of not knowing how to raise kids. (David had children during his first marriage, but when his wife left him, she took them with her. The film provides no information about the difficulties that David had in the marriage.)

Soon after the breakup, Alice acknowledges to her waitress-friend, Flo (Diane Ladd), that she loves David but that she also wants to sing. She also admits that she does not know how to live without a man. David returns to the diner and pleads with Alice to resume their relationship. He says that he wants to try to understand her. When Alice tells him that she wants to be a singer, David says that he is willing to leave his ranch and take her to Monterey. Although David assures her of his support if she wants to pursue a singing career, the movie ends with Alice and son agreeing that they will stay in Tucson because, as she rationalizes, she can be a singer anywhere.

What Alice apparently wants most is a home and family, believing that these will assure her happiness. Indeed, she admits that she does not know how to live without a man. David promises her a home and financial security so she will not need to continue working as a waitress. A singing career for Alice is a fantasy; it is obvious that her talent is mediocre.

Although we can sympathize with the plight of a single mother, the film shows that Alice lacks good parenting skills. She has almost no boundaries between herself and her son. As is typical for a people-pleaser, Alice satisfies Tommy's every whim, and she does not discipline him, although she repeatedly threatens to do so. As another example of her people-pleasing, Alice spends all the money she had been saving to finance her move to Monterey to buy Tommy a cowboy outfit for his birthday. The interactions between Alice and Tommy show that Alice is as dominated by her son as she was by Donald.

More disturbingly, Alice relates to Tommy as if he were her adult companion rather than her pubescent son. She uses provocative language with him, shaves her legs in his presence, and talks about some of her sexual experiences with him. In both Phoenix and Tucson, she leaves Tommy alone, unaware of what he does with his time while she is away at work. In one scene when she arrives back at their motel feeling tired and frustrated, Tommy comforts his mother, rubbing her forehead and speaking words of encouragement as she lies across his lap on a sofa. Alice seems to be oblivious to this inappropriate reversal of roles, taking comfort from her son who has adopted the role of the adult male who is the caretaker in their relationship.

Compounding Alice's sexually stimulating behavior toward her son, which suggests that she has incestuous feelings for him, in Phoenix the emotionally incestuous mother-son relationship is enacted more explicitly. When Alice first meets Ben, who claims to be twenty-seven, she describes him as a "teenager," suggesting that she perceives Ben as a contemporary of her son. Nevertheless, she goes to bed with Ben. Remarkably, a scene of Alice and Ben lying in bed together, presumably after they have had sex, cuts to a scene of Alice in bed with Tommy. The boy is asleep, and Alice cuddles close to him, covering his ears with her hands so he will not hear the loud noises emanating from another room.[2] It is possible that this mother-son interaction is intended to show that Alice feels guilty because in leaving Tommy and meeting up with Ben, Alice feels that she had abandoned Tommy. Nevertheless, the sudden shift between scenes also suggests that Alice feels guilty of her unconscious, incestuous feelings for Tommy, which have come to the fore because of her sexual feelings for Ben.

The physical closeness between Alice and her pubertal son in a bed is at least provocative, and this closeness can be viewed as sexually stimulating to Tommy. Indeed, on the basis of the various interactions between mother and son in the story, Tommy shows that he has been stimulated by his mother. In this context, during a later scene on David's ranch, Tommy milks a cow and refers to the cow's "tits" being the "size of cucumbers."

In Tucson, the lonely and bored Tommy begins to spend time with the rebellious and streetwise Audrey (Jodie Foster). Audrey is older and turns Tommy onto petty theft and drinking. Interestingly, in a scene when Alice has set limits on Tommy, it is evident that he feels abandoned by his "first love" and acts out his anger toward his mother by going to Audrey's home and getting drunk. These portrayals suggest that Audrey represents Tommy's mother-substitute.

Alice's behavior toward Tommy may also be described as suffocating. This is alluded to in the film in the closing scene when Alice hugs Tommy and calls him "my boy." Tommy responds by telling his mother that he cannot breathe.

Memory and fantasy intermingle in the film, and, thematically, the story suggests the lost ideals and dreams of childhood, with "Monterey" representing home as well as happiness.[3] The theme of childhood dreams probably connects autobiographically with Scorsese. Like Alice, the young Scorsese was a fledgling artist and probably dreamed of becoming a star. He, like Alice, may have felt trapped and constrained by his family and social milieu.

The religious symbolism that is almost inevitable in a Scorsese film appears most evidently when Flo shows that she is wearing a cross around her neck that is made from safety pins. She describes the cross as the thing that holds her together.

ELLEN OLENSKA

The Countless Ellen Olenska (Michelle Pfeiffer) is the strongest and most independent of the female characters in Scorsese's films. The director remained faithful to the characterization of Ellen created by Edith Wharton in her novel, *The Age of Innocence.*

It is important to note that Ellen has left her husband, Count Olenski, she is childless, and she lives alone. Among the class of women in New York high society during the 1870s in which the story is set, it was rare for a woman to leave her husband and choose to live alone. For that matter, such an independent woman is a rarity among the Scorsese heroines that appear in the director's earlier films.

Ellen is beautiful and intelligent, possessing a rare combination of emotional openness and dignity. She has left her husband in Europe because of unspecified infidelities, and she arrives in New York to live among her family. In leaving her home and husband, Ellen has made a bold move and assumed that people would accept her regardless of the circumstances surrounding her marriage. She is mistaken in this assessment and discovers that she is the subject of gossip. Nevertheless, Ellen never wavers in presenting herself with dignity and grace.

Ellen follows Newland Archer's (Daniel Day-Lewis) advice that she not pursue her wish for a divorce because he believes that allegations of indiscretions would surface if she did so. These rumors and allegations would expose Ellen and the family to scandal Although Ellen feels sexually attracted to Newland Archer, she remains loyal to his wife's good name (her cousin, May Welland (Winona Ryder)) and to her family, the Mingotts. In her relationship with Newland, Ellen remains reality-bound, while he engages in fantasy. After she learns from May that she is pregnant, Ellen returns to Europe so that temptations will not lead her and Newland to abandon their values and their respect for one another. Ellen's decision to leave New York is an indication of her values and ethical outlook. However, it should be noted that Ellen is able to live an independent life in Europe only because she has the financial means to do so provided by her wealthy great-aunt.

The end of the film occurs some twenty years later in France, where Ellen has been living. Newland, a widower for several years, comes to France with his son, who urges his father to visit the Countess. Although Newland gets as far as the courtyard of her home, he sees her signal from the window that indicates that Ellen does not want to rekindle their relationship. His memories of their relationship will remain as memories.

ABUSED WIVES

The following two female characters are survivors of physical or emotional abuse perpetrated by their respective husbands: Francine Evans in *New York, New York* (1977) and Vickie LaMotta in *Raging Bull* (1980). Alice, discussed previously, is also a survivor twice-over. She responds to her domineering husband by becoming docile. Later, in reaction to Ben's threatened brutality, she is more self-assertive in deciding to leave the area.

Francine Evans (Liza Minnelli), although a talented musical star in her own right, stands out as a woman who subordinates her emotional and professional needs for the sake of those of her husband. Moreover, for the greater part of the film, she endures tremendous emotional abuse from her husband, Jimmy Doyle (Robert De Niro), whose personality was described earlier as childlike and narcissistically disturbed.

Again and again, Jimmy wears down Francine with his demanding nature. He rarely hears her "no" and her point of view. Indeed, he utterly disregards them. Once she and Jimmy are married, she is particularly attentive to his needs while she subordinates her own. Although she is the more popular musical star, she tolerates his orders, his humiliation of her, and his demands that his name be larger than hers on advertising posters.

Francine does not assert herself definitely until she becomes pregnant. In deciding to curtail her traveling with the band and to stay in New York to wait for the birth of their baby, she places her needs ahead of those of Jimmy. Perhaps she is able to do so at this time because she feels she is not being selfish in taking care of herself for the sake of the baby's health and safety.

Although badly mistreated by Jimmy, Francine continues to be empathic about his sensitivities and insecurities, seemingly understanding his narcissistic needs. During their last argument, she says knowingly, "It's all about you." In spite of untold emotional abuse, Francine does not leave Jimmy but, rather, he abandons her immediately after their baby is born. She proceeds to become successful in an independent career. In sum, the character of Francine Evans can be described most aptly as a woman who puts aside her needs and interests for the sake of pleasing an abusive husband and, thus, maintaining a relationship with him.

VICKIE LAMOTTA

The beautiful Vickie LaMotta (Cathy Moriarty), an Italian-American as is her husband, becomes involved with Jake LaMotta when she is fifteen years old. Since her husband has a fiery temper and an iron fist, and he is often paranoid and out-of control, Vickie must be careful about what she says in his presence lest she incur his wrath. She cannot go out without being watched and questioned, and she gets slapped around by Jake on a consistent basis. Through most of the film Vickie remains behind the shadows of being Jake's wife and a silent victim of his abuse. After several years of marriage (and abuse) and their move to Miami, Vickie leaves Jake when it has become obvious that he has had affairs with other women.

Early in the film, Vickie is pictured with light shining on her flowing blonde hair. In this scene, she seems to be angelic as well as virginal, and it can be assumed that Jake sees her as such. However, after they are married, Jake begins to wonder if he can trust her, and he asks his brother, Joey, to keep his eyes on her. This paranoia of Jake suggests that he suspects that his wife is a whore. In other words, the whore-madonna complex, presumably in Jake's mind, is implicit, rather than explicit, in this film.

Companions or Partners

The roles of a number of female characters in Scorsese's films are as companions or partners to their male counterparts.

CARMEN AND JANELLE

Carmen (Mary Elizabeth Mastrantonio) in *The Color of Money* (1986) is Vincent Lauria's (Tom Cruise) companion and lover. As depicted, she is a more greedy and capable hustler than he is. Vincent seems to need her in order to do his best work in the world of pool playing. Janelle (Helen Shaver) is the attractive companion of Eddie Felson (Paul Newman); no dynamics or dialogue are presented that would help describe her personality.

Paulette

Paulette (Rosanna Arquette) in "Life Lessons" (1989), is Lionel Dobie's (Nick Nolte) young, live-in assistant and a fledgling artist, perhaps mediocre at best. However, she realizes that she will not develop herself as an artist in her own right as long as she remains in the shadow of the "lion." Indeed, she comes to understand that she will be viewed only as his mistress as long as she lives with him. Feeling used by Lionel, Paulette finally leaves the relationship.

Leigh

Leigh (Jessica Lange), is wife of Sam Bowden (Nick Nolte) and mother of her precocious daughter Danny (Juliette Lewis), in *Cape Fear* (1991), Leigh is depicted as a woman of the 1990s. In contrast to several other female characters in Scorsese's films who are married to or are partners of Italian-American men, Leigh has no ethnic, class, or religious constraints dictating her behavior.

Although financially supported in comfortable style by her attorney-husband, Leigh has begun or is beginning a travel business of her own. Portraying her with this independent career, Scorsese gives Leigh's personality more breadth than would otherwise have been the case. Leigh is not preoccupied solely with her daughter's or her husband's interests, and she does not subordinate her needs to suit those of her husband.

As depicted, Sam and Leigh have been in marital counseling because Sam had had an affair with another woman. This liaison has left Leigh feeling suspicious and bitter, but she is able to be sexual with her husband. She is also cynical about Sam's sometimes less-than-ethical behavior. Her outside interests notwithstanding, Leigh seems to be an attentive and caring mother. Particularly dramatic in this context is her willingness to sacrifice herself to a

Sam Bowden (Nick Nolte) and his wife, Leigh (Jessica Lange), sharing their fear about the danger posed by their stalker, Max Cady, in *Cape Fear* (Photofest).

humiliating rape by Max Cady (Robert De Niro) to save her daughter from a similar fate.

Karen Hill

Karen Hill (Lorraine Bracco) in *GoodFellas* (1990) is a strong-willed woman, asserting herself and expressing her anger when Henry Hill (Ray Liotta) first stands her up for a date. Later, however, she is impressed by Henry's access to money and his connections. She feels important because he has the power to get a ringside table at nightclubs without needing to have made reservations, and she is excited when she handles a gun for the first time. Karen marries Henry and allows herself to fall prey to the seductiveness of power, seemingly in denial about the immorality of his gangster activities.

The self-assertiveness apparent early in their relationship re-emerges when Karen learns that her husband has a mistress and that he is supporting her financially in an apartment of her own. Indeed, Karen's rage explodes when she discovers the infidelity. However, she is not willing to give up Henry or to share him. She goes to the apartment building where his girlfriend lives, pushes the doorbells of the various apartments, and screams to the tenants that the woman in question is a whore. Karen threatens Henry with a gun, and she uses her position to urge the powerful, married men in the family to force Henry back into the familial relationship with her and their children. As the story evolves, it is evident that Karen has sociopathic tendencies. She abuses cocaine herself and becomes Henry's partner in drug trafficking.

Jenny Everdeane

Jenny Everdeane (Cameron Diaz) in *Gangs of New York* (2002) is another stong-willed and high-spirited woman. Since childhood, Jenny has used her wiles and her abilities to survive in the treacherous slum known as Five Points. She is an accomplished pickpocket and thief.

As she describes to Amsterdam Vallon (Leonardo DiCaprio), she had sex with Bill Cutting (Daniel Day-Lewis) when she was young, but only when she asked him to do so. She became pregnant but, as she relates, the baby was "cut out" of her.

Jenny becomes Amsterdam's lover and nurses him back to health after he is wounded by Bill. Although she tries to leave Five Points before the final bloodbath, the gunfire and mayhem caused by the Union troops prevent her from doing so. In the end, she is reunited with Amsterdam.

The character of Jenny has been described as "more of a structural necessity—the linchpin of male jealousy—than a fully imagined person."[4] The limitation of Diaz's role points to the film's almost complete lack of women except as prostitutes, some of whom serve as playthings for Bill Cutting and his cohorts. However, given the time and place of the film, Jenny is shown to be especially intelligent, strong, courageous, and capable. She is also independent and willing to leave Amsterdam and the Five Points to have a better life.

Manipulators

Two of the more manipulative and deceitful female characters in Scorsese's films are Ginger Rothstein in *Casino* (1995), and May Welland in *The Age of Innocence* (1993).

GINGER ROTHSTEIN

Although beautiful and seemingly intelligent, Ginger McKenna Rothstein (Sharon Stone) is a hustler in Las Vegas casinos. In addition, she is the emotional property of her pimp and has been since she was fourteen years old. She is depicted as greedy and materialistic, swept away, as it were, by Sam's (Robert De Niro) offering her money, clothes, and jewelry to convince her to marry him. Although Ginger becomes the mother of a daughter, she is never seen in a motherly role. Indeed, after her marriage to Sam, she seems to deteriorate psychologically, and one night Ginger leaves her child tied to her bed so she can go out to a club unimpeded by the need to take care of the child. In the context of the story, Ginger is treacherous and manipulative, betraying her husband who had trusted her completely. The theme of betrayal is set forth at the opening of the film, showing Sam walking from his home to his car. As he takes the walk, a voice-over (De Niro) declares:

> When you love someone, you've got to give them the key to everything that's yours. Otherwise, what's the point? And, for a while, that's the kind of love I had.

Then, as Sam enters the car, it blows up, and a figure is shot flying into the sky. These words in the screenplay were written by screenwriter Nicholas Pileggi and Scorsese. The implication is clear: Sam's love was betrayed by the treacherous Ginger.

At best, Ginger is a dependent personality whose sense of self is linked to that of the men in her life who can offer her safety and affection of sorts and with whom she has sex. The core dimension of Ginger's personality is indicated by her propensity for alcohol and drug abuse. Perhaps she is as addicted to sex and money as she is to these chemical substances. Eventually, Ginger falls apart completely. She leaves Sam and, later, dies because she was given a dose of "hot" drugs.

May Welland

May Welland (Winona Ryder) is the fiancé and, later, the wife of Newland Archer (Daniel Day-Lewis). She is portrayed as a sweet, innocent, and dull woman, particularly in comparison to the worldly and sensual Ellen Olenska. After her marriage to Newland, May is strikingly controlling and snobbish. Although at first it appears that she is unaware of her husband's attraction to Ellen, as the drama unfolds, it is evident that she knew about their flirtation and Newland's love for Ellen all along.

May's capacity for deceit and trickery becomes apparent during the scene in which Newland, who is feeling depressed because of Ellen's scheduled departure for Europe, tells May that he needs a break and wants to travel. At this stage of the story, Newland hopes to join Ellen in Europe. May, who knows what is on his mind, responds that he cannot go without her and, further, that she cannot go because she is expecting a child. She relates to Newland that she had told Ellen about her condition earlier. Newland then realizes that Ellen's decision to leave New York was influenced by her learning about May's pregnancy. However, since May had said that she had become certain about her pregnancy only that day and that she had last spoken to Ellen two weeks earlier, Newland wonders how May could have told Ellen the news. May responds that she told Ellen that she was pregnant at their earlier meeting, although May was not certain about the pregnancy at the time. Newland, looking unbelievingly at May, now understands that May had intentionally lied to Ellen so as to separate the lovers. Newland realizes that he has no choice but to accept the life that May has ordained and planned for him.

Virgin-Madonnas or Whores

Several female characters in Scorsese's films represent virgin–madonnas or whores. In some films, they are depicted explicitly as one or the other. In other films, the women represent the madonna-whore complex in the minds of the male characters. These figures are the Girl in *Who's That Knocking at My Door?* (1969), Teresa in *Mean Streets* (1973), Betsy and Iris in *Taxi Driver* (1976), Mary Magdalene in *The Last Temptation of Christ* (1988), and Mary Burke in *Bringing Out the Dead* (1999). In addition to the so-called madonnas and whores discussed in the following sections, Ginger Rothstein in *Casino* and Bertha Thompson in *Boxcar Bertha* are depicted as engaging in prostitution.

The Girl

As a companion and love-object to J.R. (Harvey Keitel) in *Who's That Knocking at My Door?*, The Girl (Zina Bethune) foreshadows Teresa in *Mean Streets*, who is lover and companion to Charlie. Both of these women have lost their virginity, the Girl because of a date rape, and Teresa because of her relationship with Charlie. Both of the male partners in these films suffer from the madonna-whore complex.

The Girl, an attractive white Anglo-Saxon Protestant, is not presented as a finely defined personality. She lives in her own apartment, suggesting that she has attained a degree of independence from her family. In some scenes her long blonde hair glistens, suggesting the halo of an angel or virgin. The lack of a name suggests that she exists in the story only to the extent that she is in a relationship to J.R., in effect, his love object, and that any other "girl" would serve the same purpose. Certainly, the lack of a specific name to a character suggests that the character lacks individual identity. It is important to note that Scorsese did not give names to the female characters in his student films, *What's a Girl Like You Doing in a Place Like This?* (1963) and *It's Not Just You, Murray!* (1964). Rather, he alluded to them in terms of their functional roles in their relationship to the male characters in the films, for example, "analyst," "wife," and "mother."

Since J.R. is "between jobs," as he puts it, and obviously short of money, he takes the Girl on cheap dates: to a movie, the roof of a building to watch pigeons, his mother's house. The Girl appears willing to accommodate herself to J.R.'s wishes, including going with him to a macho film. In her relationship with J.R., the Girl is less constrained by religious taboos (she is not Catholic) and is more comfortable with sex than he is. Before he knows about her having been raped, J.R. believes that she is a virgin, and he is unwilling to have sex with her unless they are married.

After the Girl tells him about the rape, she becomes, in his mind, a whore. Although J.R. insults her, blaming her for the rape that she suffered, she lets him into her apartment early one morning. At first, she seems willing to forget and forgive the insult since he apologizes for having called her a whore. However, when J.R. says that he forgives her for having been raped and not being a virgin, the Girl asserts herself and tells him to leave.

In sum, the Girl is accommodating to J.R. for the sake of a potential relationship and marriage with him. The change that occurs in J.R.'s mind, from his perception of her as a virgin to that of a whore, is indicative of his unconscious tendency for splitting. J.R. splits his mental perceptions of and feelings about women into the dichotomous extremes of madonna and whore.

Teresa

The character of Teresa (Amy Robinson), lover to Charlie (Harvey Keitel) and cousin of Johnny Boy (Robert DeNiro), is an Italian-American and an epileptic. Giovanni, Charlie's uncle and gangster boss (Cesare Danova), presumes that her illness means that she has a mental problem. Although Teresa speaks about getting her own apartment, she continues to live at home.

She is openly sexual with Charlie and tells him that she is in love with him. Remarkably, she remains in the relationship with him although he calls her a "cunt" and says that he cannot reciprocate her love. Scenes of home movies at the opening of the film show that, eventually, Teresa marries Charlie and has a son with him. Teresa subordinates her identity, her potential for independence and growth, for the sake of a potential marriage to a macho man.

Mean Streets also shows that sexist attitudes go hand-in-hand with racist and anti–Semitic ones. Charlie avoids a possible date with beautiful black woman, who is a go-go dancer in the club frequented by the guys, because she is black. Another example, a woman at the bar is described by one of the guys in terms of her being Jewish. The man says that Jewish girls like her "go out with a different guy every night."

Betsy

Betsy (Cybill Shepherd) in *Taxi Driver*, blonde, clean-looking, wholesome, and originally dressed in white, is Travis's (Robert De Niro) angel, a madonna-like figure. Appearing aloof and vain, the film story reveals little about Betsy except that she works in politics, likes the music of Kris Kristofferson, and refuses to sit through a porno film. It is not clear why she agrees to go on a date with Travis in the first place. Perhaps she is lonely, or it may be that his flattery appeals to her vanity. Although originally Betsy is perceived by Travis as clean and angelic, after she rejects Travis, she becomes, in his disturbed mind, dirty and evil, the devil incarnate. After the dramatic climax of the film and Travis is hailed as a hero, Betsy appears to feel regret that she had rejected him.

Iris

Iris (Jodie Foster) is essential in providing the raison d'étre for the dramatic conclusion of *Taxi Driver*. She is a twelve-year-old prostitute, who is controlled by her pimp, Matthew (Harvey Keitel). She left home because she felt that her parents did not care about her. She is extraordinarily streetwise, trained and capable of providing a wide variety of sexual pleasures to men, and she is a drug addict. Although Iris is not presented as a well-defined personality, it is obvious that she is hungry for affection. Matthew offers her the promise of love with his sweet words about his needing her and how much he treasures the gratification she gives him, something, he tells her, he is willing to share with other men. After the bloodbath that occurs in her room and the death of Matthew, Iris returns home to her parents.

Mary Magdalene

Mary Magdalene (Barbara Hershey) is the major female figure in *The Last Temptation of Christ*.[5] Mary, the mother of Jesus, and the sisters Mary and Martha play smaller roles. Early on in the story, Mary Magdalene is a temptress and prostitute. As described in the film, she and Jesus (William Dafoe) knew each other as children, and although they had loved each other, he had eschewed having a sexual relationship with her. The dialogue between them when Jesus visits Magdalene at her brothel suggests that his neglect of her contributed to her becoming a prostitute. Jesus asks her for forgiveness. Later in the story, Jesus saves her from being killed by stoning. His capacity for love and forgiveness reforms her and converts her into a madonna-like follower. She is present at the Last Supper.

In the fantasy sequence of the film, Jesus leaves the cross and marries Magdalene, who appears as a virginal bride. They have sex, and Magdalene becomes pregnant. However, Mary Madgalene dies, and Jesus is distraught about his loss. The devil, in the guise of a sweet girl/angel (Juliette Caron), advises Jesus that he can marry another Mary, the sister of Lazarus. Later, the girl/angel/devil advises Jesus that he can have sex with her sister, Martha, as well. Justifying this swapping of women as sexual objects, the girl/angel/devil says to Jesus: "They're all the same women, different faces." Jesus proceeds to have children with both of the sisters.

The comment, "They're all the same women, different faces," points to the notion that these women, in their role as semen-acceptors and carriers of children (or baby-makers), are interchangeable. This attitude about women, albeit expressed by the devil, is consistent with that of the patriarchal culture of the time during which the movie is set as well as that of the modern church with which Scorsese identified during his childhood and adolescence. The idea of women being interchangeable is related to the notion that women have no individual identity. As stated, in *Who's That Knocking at My Door?* and in two of Scorsese's student shorts, all of which were written by Scorsese, the female characters have no name.

Mary Burke

Mary Burke (Patricia Arquette) is the daughter of the man whose cardiac arrest brings Frank Pierce (Nicolas Cage) on the scene. Her presence in the film seems to have a twofold purpose. First, she is someone Frank can relate to and try to comfort by helping her father stay alive. Second, although she is not one of the near-dying and drug abuse victims that Frank encounters in Hell's Kitchen, she is a recovering addict and, as such, a person Frank can save (unlike Rose whom he lost and about whom he hallucinates). Although Mary succumbs to drugs during the deathwatch of her father, Frank rescues her from the crash pad where drugs are dispensed. Mary is also a projective screen for Frank's hallucinations of Rose. In the end, when Frank tells her that her father has died, Mary and Frank lie together in a Pieta-like pose. In this pose, Mary represents a madonna figure, embracing her "son," who has just been freed from his symbolic cross.

Bizarre Characters

Scorsese's films also contain some strange or bizarre female characters. Among them are Masha in *The King of Comedy* (1982) and several women in *After Hours* (1985).

Masha

Masha (Sandra Bernhard) is a rather silly woman, an autograph hound and coconspirator with Rupert Pupkin who is obsessed with Jerry Langford (Jerry Lewis) much as Rupert is. Unlike Rupert, however, she is not ambitious about attaining personal celebrity. Rather than hoping to attain stardom, she wants to make personal contact with Jerry so she can make love to him. She also differs from Rupert in that she has money and a fine apartment. It is interesting that Masha plays the stereotypical female who is more interested in a personal relationship with a man (Jerry) than aggressively pursuing a career-oriented and ambitious path as Rupert does.

Masha, like Rupert, loses her hold on reality and slips into insanity, participating with Rupert in kidnapping Jerry. While Jerry is a captive in her apartment, she produces an almost-completed sweater that she has been knitting for the television star and, with apparent seriousness, places it over Jerry's body to see how it fits. When she is eventually alone with Jerry, who is taped to a chair, she, in a delusional state, talks to the star about her love for him and imagines that he will reciprocate the feeling. While she undresses in anticipation of their having sex, Jerry takes the opportunity to escape.

Females in *After Hours*

After Hours features a number of bizarre and insane women characters who entice, betray, frighten, and hound Paul Hackett, (Griffin Dunne). The first of these is Marcy (Rosanna Arquette), whom Paul encounters in a cafeteria late at night. She is blonde and dressed in white. Marcy invites him to the apartment where she is staying with Kiki (Linda Fiorentino), a sculptress.

Kiki invites Paul to share in her papier-mâché work, entices him with her body, and then falls asleep as he is giving her a massage. After Marcy returns to the apartment, she stops to take a shower before the implicit plan to have sex with Paul. Marcy behaves strangely about her visit to a drugstore and arouses Paul's suspicions about a prescription for a burn-cream as well as by having a book on the subject of human burn victims. She offers him a "joint," which he believes is bad, and after Paul leaves her without explanation, she commits suicide.

Julie (Teri Garr), the waitress in the bar Paul escapes to after discovering that he has no way to get back home, offers to take care of him and invites him to her apartment. There Paul sees mousetraps placed on the floor around her bed so that, according to her, she can catch a guy who gets out of line. Nevertheless, it appears that she wants to entice Paul into sex. She draws a sketch of Paul, but after he leaves her, she uses the sketch to create "wanted" posters. She makes copies of these posters and distributes them around the neighborhood. It seems that she does so in retaliation for what she perceives as Paul's abandonment of her.

Gail (Catherine O'Hara), the driver of a "Mister Softee" ice-cream truck, offers to bandage Paul's arm after she injures him. Cruelly, she interferes with his trying to telephone one of his friends for help. She discovers a piece of news print stuck on his arm that describes a burglar, and after seeing one of the "wanted" sketches of Paul, she comes to believe that he is the burglar who has been terrorizing the neighborhood. She alerts a vigilante mob, and, using her truck, she and the mob search for and chase Paul around the streets of SoHo.

June (Verna Bloom) befriends the frightened and exhausted Paul in a near-empty club, comforts him, and protects him from the mob by turning him into a plaster-of-Paris and papier-mâché sculpture. When the danger has passed, however, she refuses to release him from his virtual imprisonment, even rendering him speechless by taping over the opening for his mouth.

All of the women who entice and then betray Paul—Marcy, Julie, Gail, and June—are attractive blondes who seem pleasant and nonthreatening, but all of them ultimately engage in bizarre and treacherous behavior.

Summary

The majority of the female characters in Scorsese's films represent women who subordinate their needs and their identities for the sake of maintaining relationships with men. Even the bizarre and delusional Masha in *The King of Comedy*, who joins with Rupert in kidnapping Jerry Langford, is interested only in having a sexual relationship with Jerry, while Rupert is ambitious to have career success. A number of these female characters tolerate emotional or physical abuse by their boyfriends or husbands, and yet they remain with them. The exceptions to these stereotypical and sexist portrayals of female characters, depicting women who value relationships at the cost of their individual identities and psychological growth, are Ellen Olenska in *The Age of Innocence,* Leigh Bowden in *Cape Fear,* and Jenny Everdeane in *Gangs of New York.*

Consistent with the attitudes of the macho men, who feature prominently in Scorsese's films, the majority of the female characters are depicted as sexual objects, mothers-in-waiting, temptresses and betrayers, as well as virgins or whores. Women who are depicted as seductive and manipulative include Ginger Rothstein in *Casino* and May Welland in *The Age of Innocence*. Even Alice in *Alice Doesn't Live Here Anymore* is sexually stimulating and emotionally incestuous in her relationship with her twelve-year-old son.

In the great majority of Scorsese's films, women are portrayed as passive and accommodating, on the one hand, and dangerous and destructive, on the other hand. The idea of women being dangerous is captured in the depiction of the devil, who tempts Jesus down from the cross in *The Last Temptation of Christ*, as a sweet-looking, girl/angel. As stated in Chapter 11, in the original novel upon which the film is based, the devil who tempts Jesus in this scenario is a man. In choosing to change this representation of the devil-incarnate to a girl, Scorsese leaves the impression that he believed (at the time he made the film) that even women who look angelic may be dangerous.

Only a few of the female characters in Scorsese's films are aggressive or violent. Boxcar Bertha wields a gun and she engages in sociopathic behavior. As depicted, however, she is driven to do so because she is poverty-stricken, a victim of the Depression, as well as by her attachment to and wish to help her lover, Bill Shelly. Karen Hill (*GoodFellas*) and Ginger Rothstein (*Casino*), both of whom are married to gangsters, engage in drug abuse, and Karen joins her husband in drug trafficking. Karen, like her husband, is addicted to the high associated with money and power. Ginger, the emotional and sexual property of her pimp since she was fourteen, was an addict before her marriage to Sam but, as depicted, she deteriorates further after her marriage. Jenny Everdeane is an accomplished thief.

The madonna-whore dichotomy, a vestige of the influence of the Catholic Church on Scorsese and other men in his social milieu, is encapsulated in one person in *Who's That Knocking at My Door?* (The Girl) and in *The Last Temptation of Christ* (Mary Magdalene), and split into two characters in *Taxi Driver* (Betsy and Iris). A more implicit madonna-whore figure is Vickie LaMotta (*Raging Bull*), who exists as such in the mind of her phallic-narcissistic husband, Jake. In the closing scenes of *Bringing Out the Dead*, Mary Burke assumes a pose of the Virgin Mary cradling her dead son.

The ways in which women are portrayed in Scorsese's films reflect the ways that the narcissistic male characters view women. Given Scorsese's careful attention to placing his characters in specific times and places, in a number of his films the female characters are portrayed as they actually would have behaved and would have been regarded in accordance with the circumstances represented in the films. Nevertheless, the view of women that the films reveal is that their primary role is of being in relationship with men and, in general, subordinate to the men. Moreover, women are depicted as neither ambitious nor assertive about their needs. These viewpoints about women seem to reflect the cultural milieu in which Scorsese was raised, that is, his roots. As cited earlier, the director has acknowledged that in that milieu women "didn't seem like real human beings."[6] This comment suggests that Scorsese's early attitudes about women, which were formed in the cultural milieu of Little Italy, were misogynous. As noted earlier, these early influences about femininity seem to have contributed to Scorsese's seeming inability to attach specific names to female characters in his earliest films and to the ways in which he has portrayed women in his films in general.

11

The Last Temptation of Christ as Template

This chapter is devoted to an exposition of *The Last Temptation of Christ* (*TLTC*), a film that has had special meaning for Scorsese to whom religion remains a primary interest. Made during the late 1980s and released in 1988, the film contains patterns and images that express Scorsese's values and beliefs, which derive from his roots. These appear in Scorsese's earlier films as well as in those he made subsequently. *TLTC* is a hologram of sorts, containing a number of themes that are found in most of Scorsese's feature films, and it represents Scorsese's ultimate religious statement. It has been described by Scorsese as focusing on the humanity of Jesus Christ without denying his divinity.

Scorsese is comfortable with the idea that Jesus was, in part, an ordinary man who had to cope with the same kind of temptations that confront men who live contemporary lives in the real world. Although in the film, Jesus (William Dafoe) at first succumbs to temptations of the flesh, he eventually realizes his divine nature and accepts his spiritual mission that involves his suffering and dying on the cross. According to Christian belief, because of Christ's sacrifice and the shedding of his blood, man is redeemed. The theme of redemption or rebirth after purification by blood occurs in a number of Scorsese films including *Mean Streets, Taxi Driver, Raging Bull,* and *Gangs of New York.*

A Christ-like character who sacrifices his life so that others might improve their lives is Bill Shelly (*Boxcar Bertha*). Shelly's work consists of helping to organize the poor and oppressed so they may be able to gain their rights. He gives his life in the pursuit of his mission, and dies by being crucified on the side of a boxcar. In a related sense, the character of Amsterdam Vallon (*Gangs of New York*) resembles a Christ-like figure when he accepts his father's mantle of leadership and prepares to risk his life for the sake of helping his people fight oppression.

In *TLTC*, Jesus is portrayed as a reluctant spiritual leader at the beginning of his ministry. As he walks alone across the desert, Jesus wonders whose footsteps he believes he hears behind him, as if someone is following him. This wondering amounts to a question that forms in the mind of Jesus: What does God or Satan want of me? This query, posed to himself, has been with Scorsese throughout his adult life and career. Contextually, Scorsese raised this question by virtue of the title he chose for his first commercial release in 1969, *Who's That Knocking at My Door?*

Scorsese has struggled personally for most of his adult life with the issue of how to live a spiritual life in the material world with its temptations that attract the flesh and in light of the vulnerabilities of men to fall prey to pride, vanity, and greed (in other words, to aspects of infantile narcissism). Once an altar boy and an aspiring priest within the Catholic religion, Scorsese internalized the values and images associated with the life and passion of Jesus Christ. Apparently he came to see Jesus as a man who had struggled with the same temptations that all men have. Eventually, Scorsese transferred his religious passion to a secular passion for making movies that would express his experiences, his beliefs, and his conflicts, films that Scorsese hoped would have meaning.

The story of Jesus in *TLTC* is one of conflict between divinity and humanity, between body and soul. From the beginning of his cinematic career, Scorsese raised the issue of how one lives a good life, one of love and compassion, while contending with the challenges posed by the culture of the streets.

In Scorsese's early film, *Mean Streets*, he depicted in a realistic fashion the actual streets and the day-to-day activities of people who live in Little Italy with which he was familiar. He also portrayed the internal struggles of the men of that milieu, including himself, with sexuality, religiosity, and sin.

The character of Charlie in *Mean Streets* as well as J.R. in the earlier *Who's That Knocking at My Door?* are stand-ins for Scorsese, and their struggles with sex, pride, greed, and ambition amount to Scorsese's challenge of trying to integrate the realm of the spiritual with the material. In *Mean Streets*, Scorsese, in the guise of Charlie, declares that it is more courageous to strive to live a good life on the streets than to do so in church.

This dictum of Scorsese, first expressed in *Mean Streets*, is encapsulated in *TLTC*. When Jesus tells Mary Magdalene (Barbara Hershey) that he is going to the desert, she accuses him of going there to escape from *real life* because he is scared. Indeed, Jesus says of himself that he does not steal or kill, not because he does not want to, but because he is afraid. These feelings of insecurity and self-doubt of Jesus are reminiscent of those of Charlie, who is mindful of the illicit sex and criminality in which he engages. Charlie struggles with guilt, and he fears eternal damnation, as undoubtedly Scorsese did as well.

11. The Last Temptation of Christ *as Template*

As depicted in *TLTC*, Jesus is sexually repressed; he does not engage in sex with Mary Magdalene in her brothel although he has ample opportunity as well as her invitation to do so. Jesus's abstaining from sexual activities that are readily available to him is reminiscent of the behavior of Travis Bickle (*Taxi Driver*) when he is in the sex parlor with Iris. The linkage between sexuality and religiosity that is apparent in *TLTC* is also present in other Scorsese films. In the brothel scene in *Taxi Driver*, for example, Iris has a panoply of lit candles as if her parlor were a church. This scene is recreated in the later *The King of Comedy* during Masha's attempted seduction of Jerry Langford. In *Cape Fear*, Max Cady is both a religious fanatic and a sexual pervert, using sex as a weapon with which to harm women as well as a symbol of his fantasied phallic supremacy.

Mary Magdalene (Barbara Hershey) in *The Last Temptation of Christ* (Photofest).

In *TLTC*, Jesus explicitly identifies his sinfulness as fear and pride. He describes himself as a liar as well as a hypocrite, and he characterizes his shunning women as something that makes him feel proud about himself. As Jesus struggles internally with feeling like a sinner, a young and seemingly holy man says to him, "The more devils there are inside of us, the more of a chance we have to repent." This value, which presumably is consonant with Scorsese's beliefs, allows the director to depict the dangerous and murderous Travis—obviously a man with a great many devils inside of him—as attaining redemption.

Similarly, Scorsese presents the self-destructive, bedeviled Jake LaMotta (*Raging Bull*), who lacks even a modicum of control over his impulses, as the personification of the blind man who, according to scripture, was given the gift of sight by Jesus. At the end of *Raging Bull*, the character of Jake begins to "see" and, thereby, gains some insight into his destructive behavior. Moreover, Scorsese implies that Jake's suffering is similar or analogous to that of Jesus. In *Raging Bull*, Scorsese depicts or otherwise cites fourteen of Jake LaMotta's actual boxing matches; Jesus passed through "fourteen stations of the cross" on the road to his death on the cross.

With regard to Bickle and LaMotta in particular, Scorsese seems able to look beyond the violence that these characters perpetrate on other people, and rather than condemn them for their brutality, he presents them as long-suffering sinners who deserve redemption.

In this context and as stated previously, Scorsese has a finely developed sense that who a person (usually a man) is, how he sees the world, and how he reacts to events that confront him are affected by that man's sense of his place in the world, or, in other words, by his roots and his perception of his involvement in that culture. Indeed, Scorsese, cautions us about judging another person (as he does with the biblical inscription shown on the screen at the end of *Raging Bull*) and, in effect, asks, "How do you know what you would do if you were in that person's shoes?"[1]

Redemption is a common theme in Scorsese's films and he has applied this theme to his own life. As LaMotta had engaged in self-destructive acts before his ultimate redemption (at least as depicted in the film, *Raging Bull*), so Scorsese felt that he himself had done with drugs and other stressors to his body during the mid– to late–1970s. Scorsese came to realize his self-inflicted destruction, abandoned the behavior, and recommitted himself to taking care of himself and making films.

The theme of sinners attaining redemption also occurs in *Mean Streets*. In the concluding scenes of this film, Johnny Boy self-destructs and seemingly takes Charlie and Teresa along with him. However, as the home movies at the opening of the film suggest, all three recover from their wounds and go on to celebrate the baptism of Charlie and Teresa's baby, Christopher, an obvious symbol of redemption and rebirth.

In *Cape Fear*, the psychotic Max Cady believes that he is the avenger and the redeemer, in effect, a psychotic and bedeviled Christ-like figure. On his back is a large tattoo of a cross, reminiscent of the cross on the back of a Catholic priest's vestments. Cady seeks to cause Sam Bowden, who betrayed him, grievous suffering and, as a result, gain salvation while he, Cady, sacrifices himself. This theme, which links sacrifice, betrayal, and redemption, is expressed explicitly by Jesus in *TLTC*. In this context, Jesus says to Judas that he, Jesus, must be sacrificed as a lamb is slaughtered, declaring that his sacrifice, his death, will bring about the redemption of sin. In other words, his death is the door to salvation. In *Cape Fear*, Cady declares, as he is dying, that his death will enable Sam's salvation. The latter film also depicts both fire and water (or flood) as instruments of death and retribution. In *TLTC*, Jesus promises that in replacing the old law with the new, there will be a flood and a fire. In *Cape Fear*, the water of the river plays a symbolic role as an instrument of both purification and destruction.

In *Gangs of New York*, "fire" from the guns and cannons of the Union army kills the rioters and leaves the area and the people in it covered with ash. The message inherent in these scenes and those that follow, showing the modern skyline of Manhattan, is that from the ashes of the old, representing death and destruction, the new arises.

11. The Last Temptation of Christ *as Template*

In *TLTC*, Scorsese deals explicitly with the sin of pride, or an aspect of infantile narcissism, something with which a number of his characters and Scorsese, himself, contend.

When Jesus is in the desert, attempting to discern what God wants of him, the serpent (or devil) challenges him with the statement: "What arrogance to think that you can save the world." Scorsese applies this theme in both *Taxi Driver* and *Bringing Out the Dead*. In the former film, Travis comes to believe, by virtue of the voices in his head, that he can cleanse the world of its dirt through of the bloodbath that he brings about in the brothel single-handedly.

The character of Frank Pierce in *Bringing Out the Dead* can be described as succumbing to the sin of pride, believing that he, like God, has the power to bring back to life those people who are near death. Other comparisons can be made between the images in *TLTC* and those in *Bringing Out the Dead*. In the former, there are scenes of people who are bedeviled emerging from holes dug in the earth in which they live. Jesus commands the devil to leave these people. These bedeviled, near-dead people are akin to the dregs of society who, metaphorically, live in the sewers of the streets that Frank traverses with his ambulance (as does Travis with his taxi cab). Frank imagines that he can save these "sewer rats" as Jesus did the bedeviled ones in *TLTC*.

Another portrayal in *TLTC* is reminiscent of a scene in *Bringing Out the Dead*. In the former, Jesus raises Lazarus from the dead, an important miracle that demonstrated to the people that Jesus has a divine nature. The film includes a scene that depicts the mourners for Lazarus who, as they cover their faces, look remarkably similar to Frank Pierce's "ghosts" who are haunting him. The body of Lazarus, wrapped in a shroud, had been placed in a hole dug out from a hill; a heavy stone covers the opening. The stone is rolled away and Jesus enters the space, grasps the hand of Lazarus with his, and brings Lazarus out alive. This image of Jesus literally "bringing out the dead" is, obviously, the thematic underpinning of the movie with this title that was made subsequent to *TLTC*.

In addition to pride, Scorsese depicts Jesus in *TLTC* as struggling with greed. Again while in the desert, the devil, in the guise of a lion, appears to Jesus. He says: "I'm your heart, your heart is greedy, it wants to conquer the world—dreams of power." The representation of power using a male lion brings to mind the character of Lionel Dobie in "Life Lessons," who refers to himself as "the lion," an allusion, no doubt, to Dobie's greed for recognition and acclaim.

The theme of men seeking unlimited power, a feature of the narcissistic demigods, appears in the characterizations of men in a number of Scorsese's films. In *GoodFellas*, *Casino*, and *Gangs of New York*, Scorsese's gangsters—Henry Hill, Jimmy Conway, Tommy DeVito, Sam Rothstein, Nicky Santoro, and Bill "the Butcher" Cutting—are most exemplary of men obsessed by greed and fantasies of unlimited power or phallic supremacy.

In a somewhat different but related context, Rupert Pupkin wants to be the *king* of the world of comedy and Jimmy Doyle (*New York, New York*), the *top dog* in the world of jazz. Eddie Felson in *The Color of Money* also contends with greed. He faces his "final temptation" and decides to play pure pool rather than use hustling tactics for the sake of making more money.

There are additional similarities between *TLTC* and other Scorsese films. For example, in a scene in *TLTC* that occurs late in his ministry, Jesus's mother, Mary, approaches a group that is surrounding Jesus, and she attempts to speak to her son. However, Jesus behaves as if he does not know her, saying, "I don't have a family.... My father is in heaven." These statements suggest that at this stage of his ministry, Jesus is convinced of his divinity, and as a result, his sense of connection to his "father in heaven" has transcended more earthly ties to human love, mother, and family. Similarly, in *Kundun*, the young Dalai Lama leaves home and family for the sake of a higher calling to serve his religion and his people.

This idea of a man's higher calling transcending ordinary pursuits is expressed in *Gangs of New York* with regard to Priest's and Amsterdam's striving to unite their people. The theme, in a more real world or materialistic sense, is also represented in the film, *New York, New York*. In the latter, Jimmy Doyle feels that his achieving fame with his music, which, in effect, represents his ministry in the world, is more important to him than a life with his wife and child. In a related sense, in "Life Lessons," Lionel Dobie's yearning for artistic creativity seemingly transcends his wish for a committed love relationship.

In all of these instances, Scorsese likens the struggles of his male characters with those of Jesus. These analogies between the life of Jesus that is depicted in *TLTC* and that of Scorsese's male characters in other films, enable the director and his audience to appreciate the fervor of ordinary men's struggle in the real world.

Perhaps understandably, given the setting (time and place) as well as the director's predilections, in *TLTC*, women are depicted in ways that are similar to their roles in a number of other Scorsese films, including temptress-whore and mother-virgin. The major female character in the film, Mary Magdalene (Barbara Hershey), is a temptress and prostitute who is reformed by virtue of Jesus's love and capacity for forgiveness. This depiction brings to mind the relationship between Iris and Travis Bickle in *Taxi Driver*, which includes Travis trying to reform the young prostitute. In *Who's That Knocking at My Door?*, J.R. "forgives" the Girl for not being a virgin, as if he were Jesus forgiving Magdalene. This is quite a grandiose identification by the self-serving J.R.

The madonna-whore split that is personified by Magdalene in *TLTC* is depicted in *Taxi Driver* in terms of the Betsy-Iris duo, and it is present as a complex in the minds of J.R. in *Who's That Knocking at My Door?* and Charlie in *Mean Streets*. The association between mother and virgin or goodness is implied in *Who's That Knocking at My Door?* by virtue of the juxtaposition between scenes of the maternal figure (played by Scorsese's mother, Catherine Scorsese) with shots of the statue of the Virgin and Child that is displayed prominently in the kitchen. A number of the pictured scenes of "the Girl" in this film are remarkably similar to that of the face of the statue of the Virgin.

Another depiction in *TLTC* that suggests a misogynous attitude about women derives from the casting of the character of the devil who tempts Jesus down from the cross. The devil is represented by an angelic-looking girl rather than by a man, as in the novel upon which the film is based.[2] This casting in the film represents woman as the stereotypic temptress-devil.

The important and controversial fantasy-dream sequence in *TLTC* involves Jesus being married to and impregnating Mary Magdalene. When Magdalene dies and Jesus becomes distraught because of his loss, the devil, in the guise of the girl/angel, advises Jesus to marry Mary, the sister of Lazarus. Later, the devil/angel, tells Jesus that he can also sleep with Mary's sister, Martha. Indeed, the girl/angel/devil says to Jesus: "They're all the same woman, different faces." As discussed in Chapter 10, the idea that women are interchangeable or lacking individuality is consistent with what appears to have been Scorsese's view of women when he wrote *Who's That Knocking at My Door?* as well as *It's Not Just You, Murray*. In the latter, written when Scorsese was still a student at N.Y.U., he gave the female characters no name, referring to them solely in terms of their functional roles in the life of the male character, for example, "wife," "analyst," and "mother." Scorsese's apparent difficulty in perceiving women as individuals is consonant with what he has acknowledged about himself in this regard, namely, that women were not perceived as real human beings in the social milieu in which he was raised.[3]

It is evident in *TLTC* that Jesus is more comfortable with men, particularly his close companion and confidant, Judas, as well as his disciples and apostles, than he is with women. In light of Jesus's apparent discomfort with women, one wonders if he feels insecure about his masculinity. Interestingly, there is a homoerotic subtext to the relationship between Jesus and Judas. Judas calls Jesus, "Adonai," and he kisses Jesus on the mouth. In turn, Jesus asks Judas to stay with him, and he sleeps cradled in his arms. These portrayals of close bonding among men and its converse, the relative discomfort of men with regard to women, are reminiscent of depictions in *Who's That Knocking at My Door?* and *Mean Streets* as well as of the Jake-Joey relationship in *Raging Bull*. Since these three films are drawn from Scorsese's personal experiences among Italian-American men in his milieu, we can assume that the director is giving expression to what he observed about the attitudes of these men with regard to their relationships with women, on the one hand, and those with men, on the other hand. In addition, we can speculate that these men's misogynous attitudes toward women may have sprung from and served as a defense against these men's insecurities about their potency as well as their fears about having homosexual feelings.

In *TLTC*, Magdalene and Jesus knew each other when they were children. As implied in the dialogue, Magdalene's becoming a prostitute is linked to Jesus having ignored her amorous feelings for him. This theme is also expressed in *Cape Fear*. In the latter film, Lori is hurt and angry because Sam has told her that he will not pursue a sexual relationship with her. Seemingly in retribution for her feeling abandoned by Sam, Lori becomes provocative and tries to entice Cady into having sex with her. Of course, it is Cady who is manipulating Lori and not the other way around. Indeed, Cady has a plan for getting Lori alone with him so that he can beat and rape her.

The idea that women will resort to promiscuity or prostitution because men do not pay attention to them, present thematically in *TLTC* and *Cape Fear*, suggests that women are affectively immature. Such dynamics are self-serving for the men who create them, and they elevate men to a grandiose and powerful position relative to women.

The special place of family in the director's scheme of life is underscored in *TLTC*. Scorsese has explained that Jesus marries Magdalene and "makes love to her for the purpose of having children," that is, for having a family.[4] This rationale that presumably explains Jesus's attraction to Magdalene stereotypes women as babymakers. In other words, the idea that Scorsese seems to be expressing in this statement is that women are sexually

Willem Dafoe as Jesus in *The Last Temptation of Christ* (Photofest).

tempting only insofar as they can be impregnated by men and bear them children.

In one scene in *TLTC* when Jesus is beginning his ministry, he asks the people who are near him to form a circle, and he describes them as a family. In describing his followers as a family, Jesus, a religious leader, intertwines church and family. This linking of church and family is implicit or explicit in several Scorsese films. For example, fantasies about family togetherness provide the glue that binds the gangsters to each other in *GoodFellas*, gangsterism being their church or religion. In *Casino*, a linkage between family and church is implied since making money is the "religion" practiced by Sam and his family of gangsters in the Tangiers, their "paradise on earth." Similarly, playing pool is the church and provides for family-like togetherness in *The Color of Money*; television is the church in *The King of Comedy*; insular Little Italy is the church in *Mean Streets* and in *Who's That Knocking at My Door?* In *Gangs of New York*, the linkage between church and family is explicit. The various Irish tribes, each, in effect, a family, are joined together by virtue of their common Catholic religion.

Food plays a central role in maintaining family cohesion, particularly within the Italian American family with which Scorsese is familiar. At the Last Supper depicted in *TLTC*, which Jesus shares with his disciples, that is, his family, Jesus lifts up bread and asks his followers to each take a piece of it and eat it. They do so, Jesus declares, in remembrance of him because bread is his body. This spiritual communion, via the ingestion of human food, unites the family and allows each member to share in God's divinity. In other words, food is considered to provide both physical and spiritual nourishment.

Food is depicted as symbolic communion in *Who's That Knocking at My Door?* This movie opens with a scene of a maternal figure (Catherine Scorsese), making bread dough, stuffing it with what appears to be a meat mixture, and baking it. Later, under the watchful eye of a statue of the Virgin Mary and Child present in the kitchen, the maternal figure removes the baked calzone from the oven, cuts it into slices, and serves these to the five children seated around the kitchen table. The implication is clear: The making and sharing of food is a communal and spiritual act that unites the family in the same way that Jesus uses food to unite his followers in *TLTC*.

In a similar vein, in *Gangs of New York*, just before Priest Vallon arrives at the battle scene, he is given a piece of bread (or a Eucharistic wafer) by his followers. He shares this bread with his young son, Amsterdam. This sharing of communion joins father and son in their quest to gain justice for their people and imbues their quest with religious significance.

In a more secular sense, the character of Alice in *Alice Doesn't Live Here Anymore* has fantasies about having a happy family, and she uses food to try to please her husband and, thereby, help to cement her family. In *The Age of Innocence*, numerous and elaborate food courses, the ritualistic use of specific place settings, and sharing of meals help to define the family and their place in their cultural milieu.

The issue of what it means to be a man is considered in *The Last Temptation of Christ*. Early on in the story, Magdalene challenges Jesus's manhood by saying, "You never had the courage to be a man. If you weren't hanging onto your mother, you were hanging onto me. Now you're hanging onto God." With these words, Magdalene confronts Jesus's insecurities about his masculinity in terms of his abstaining from sex, his bonding with his mother, and his fearfulness.

Magdalene's statement suggests that lack of sexual intercourse, indeed, being fearful about having sex with a woman, translates into diminished manhood. In the film, a linkage is made between a man abstaining from sexual intercourse and his going crazy, as if semen has some special power to affect sanity. When Jesus returns to his home town of Nazareth and presents his message to the people there, they reject him and think that he is crazy. They say of Jesus, "This is what happens when a man doesn't get married. Semen backs up to his brain." The implication is that a man's pent-up sexual energy can explode into other forms, including violence, an idea that is depicted in other films.

In *Raging Bull*, for example, Jake LaMotta ices down his aroused penis and refuses to have sex with his wife before a boxing match presumably because he believes that he needs his semen to have power in the ring with which to attack his opponent. As another example, the sexually repressed and crazed Travis Bickle does not become violent until after the porno show during which he associates a hardened penis with a gun and brute force.

In *TLTC*, after his forty days in the desert, Jesus says to his disciples, "I'm inviting you to a war." He then extracts his heart from his chest and says, "I believed in love [reminiscent of Travis's initial feelings toward Betsy in *Taxi Driver*], now I believe in the ax" [Travis's feelings after he feels rejected by Betsy]. Jesus's "invitation to a war" phrase invites comparison with the attitudes of Max Cady, Travis Bickle, and Jake LaMotta, none of whom have healthy sexual relationships, and all of whom prepare for their respective wars by training their bodies to become fighting machines. However, unlike the "rageful warriors," Jesus does not become aggressive and go to war but, rather, accepts his divinely conceived mission that includes his crucifixion.

Kundun, Scorsese's other explicitly religious film, made ten years after *TLTC*, is linked to the Christ film by virtue of what might be termed the "drama of the gifted child." While in the desert in *TLTC*, the devil appears to Jesus as a tongue of fire and says, "When you were a little boy you cried, 'Make me a God.'" In *Kundun*, the little boy who eventually is deemed to be the reincarnation of the Buddha, is imperial and thinks of himself as a king long before he is discovered and revered as such.

There is no doubt that *TLTC* ranks as Scorsese's most self-defining film. Scorsese was given a copy of the book, written by Nikos Kazantzakis, by Barbara Hershey when they were filming *Boxcar Bertha*. He was attracted to the story because it emphasized the human side of Jesus, including his frailties and vulnerabilities. Scorsese wanted to turn it into a motion picture because this story of Jesus is consistent with the director's personal values, both secular and religious.

Certainly, the major theme of the film is consonant with Scorsese's belief that it is a challenge for a man to lead a good life on the streets, as it were, with the temptations inherent in the real world including issues related to pride, greed, and lust (drugs, sex, striving for power, and success), and yet attain redemption. The metaphorical knock at one's door, or heart, symbolizes man's yearning for God, this yearning often competing with the temptations of the flesh.

Insofar as women are concerned, *TLTC* shows an emphasis on their stereotypic roles as temptresses, whores, virgins, and blessed mothers.[5] The film also suggests the idea that as sexual beings, women lack individuality. As discussed earlier, these views of women are reflective of Scorsese's experience in Little Italy including the attitudes of the patriarchal church of that culture as well as his observations from watching films of the 1940s and 1950s. Scorsese's profound wish to make *The Last Temptation of Christ* informs us that his core belief about men's quest and challenge for living a good or spiritual life colors all of his work. Moreover, the images, symbolism, and values in the film, particularly as they appear in so many other Scorsese films, are obviously important to him, and they define, in large measure, his world view.

12

Conclusion

The films of Martin Scorsese have given us an extraordinary and extensive picture of a number of worlds where heterosexual men predominate and within which male perceptions are seen as central. His films also give us a portrait of himself, his experiences, and his values as well as his attitudes about masculinity and femininity. This concluding chapter discusses what Scorsese's films tell us about him, the world of men with its concomitant traits of power and ambition, the place of women in Scorsese's schema, and his spiritual query of how a man can live a life of love and compassion in the real world. The worlds of men as seen in Scorsese's characterizations and in his films link directly to his roots.

Scorsese has an exquisite sense of how his own roots have influenced who he is as a person and as a film maker. He applies his sense of the importance of roots in formulating his characters and his film stories. He knows from his own background that men who live constrained and limited lives, as he once did, and see no way out can become enraged and violent (Travis Bickle in *Taxi Driver*, Jake LaMotta in *Raging Bull*, Johnny Boy in *Mean Streets*) as well as self-destructive (LaMotta again and Frank Pierce in *Bringing Out the Dead*). Moreover, he knows all too well that a stifling religiosity can lead men to having racist and misogynous attitudes as well as conflicts about sex and spirituality as he did or, for that matter, to having questions about the spiritual value of material world pursuits (J.R. in *Who's That Knocking at My Door?* and Charlie in *Mean Streets*).

Scorsese also knows that a man who grows up in such a confining milieu can have a consuming ambition to go beyond its limits and strive to achieve success (Rupert Pupkin in *The King of Comedy*) as he did or to continue to feel frustrated and lack ambition (J.R. and Johnny Boy). Moreover, as was once true for Scorsese, his films show that an ambitious and creative man can be so driven for success that he ignores relationships (Jimmy Doyle in

New York, New York) or uses people to achieve his creative goals (Lionel Dobie in "Life Lessons").

Scorsese has known how a man who is embedded in a social milieu can feel and act if he feels he belongs as well as how to play the game to secure that sense of belonging (Charlie in *Mean Streets* and Newland Archer in *The Age of Innocence*). In the converse, Scorsese also knows from his life experience how it feels to be an outsider (Paul Hackett in *After Hours*) and strive to get inside and become a part of something he admires and wants for himself (Henry Hill in *GoodFellas and* Masha and Rupert Pupkin in *The King of Comedy*).

Having grown up within a working-class home and family and having achieved international fame in his adult life, Scorsese has known very different social circumstances. With his characters of Newland Archer in *The Age of Innocence* and Amsterdam Vallon in *Gangs of New York*, in particular, Scorsese shows how two men who live in New York during the same approximate era, but in decidedly different social circumstances, can have remarkably different life experiences and views about life and death.

Scorsese once struggled with the issue of what it means to be a real man, that is, with the issue of masculinity, as his characters in his early films do (J.R. in *Who's That Knocking At My Door?*, Charlie in *Mean Streets*, and Johnny Boy in *Mean Streets*). Having experienced firsthand a milieu in which some men had special power, that is, the gangsters, Scorsese is aware of the place of power and control in the lives of men as well as the attraction of people to the gangster life (as Henry Hill did in *GoodFellas*.)[1] Scorsese learned early on that it was important to have control over his life, and this may have stemmed from his fear of being controlled.

Although not a violent man himself, Scorsese has presented a number of brutal characters in his movies. He experienced violence in his old neighborhood, and perhaps, at least early in his career, such fictional depictions gave him an opportunity to express his rage and frustrations as well as his fantasies of how macho and powerful men behave.

From his own experience, Scorsese knows the importance of mentorship—as he had with his father, a particular priest, and, later, Haig Manoogian at N.Y.U.—with regard to a young man having ambition and being able to realize it in the world (Henry Hill in *GoodFellas* and Vincent Lauria in *The Color of Money*). He has also known the experience of feeling betrayed, as he apparently once did with regard to a priest whom he admired. Indeed, the theme of betrayal and abandonment appears in a number of his film characterizations (Max Cady by Sam Bowden in *Cape Fear,* Pupkin by Jerry Langford in *The King of Comedy*, Vincent by Eddie Felson in *The Color of Money*). Scorsese has acknowledged that he has experienced the feeling of rejection with regard to romantic relationships as the characters of Travis and Newland Archer feel in their respective films, *Taxi Driver* and *The Age of Innocence*.[2]

Scorsese acquired spiritual values and an interest in religion early in his life. He has expressed these values implicitly in a number of his films, for example, via the theme of redemption (*Mean Streets, Taxi Driver, Raging Bull*) and the destructiveness of greed (*It's Not Just You, Murray!, GoodFellas, Casino*). More explicit expressions occur in the models of compassion presented by Frank Pierce in *Bringing Out the Dead*, Jesus in *The Last Temptation of Christ*, and the Dalai Lama in *Kundun* as well as by virtue of those male characters who are willing to sacrifice themselves for the good of their people (Bill Shelly in *Boxcar Bertha*, Priest and Amsterdam Vallon in *Gangs of New York*).

As discussed in earlier chapters, Scorsese's early models of manhood or masculinity derived from his ethnic roots, his church, the street culture of Little Italy, and what he saw in the movies. These various aspects of Scorsese's roots also contributed to his perceptions and attitudes about women. It is a reasonable assumption that sexist and misogynous attitudes were prominent in that cultural and religious milieu among both men and women. As stated earlier, Scorsese has acknowledged that women "didn't seem like real human beings." In light of this self-revelation, it is understandable that early in his career, Scorsese was unable to give women characters actual names, and he tended to see women as sexual objects or in functional terms exclusively. On the basis of his film characterizations, it is apparent that during most of his cinematic career, Scorsese has tended to make films in which the role of women in the affairs of the world is minimized. As pointed out in Chapter 10, in some of his films Scorsese has seemed to be insensitive to how particular characterizations might be offensive to women. However, he has shown in some of his more recent films that he has become more comfortable with characterizations of strong women who have complex personalities (Leigh Bowden in *Cape Fear*, Ginger Rothstein in *Casino*, Ellen Olenska in *The Age of Innocence* and Jenny Everdeane in *Gangs of New York*).

Paul Schrader's comment that when he first met Scorsese in 1972, Scorsese told him that there were two films that he especially wanted to make— *The Last Temptation of Christ* and *Gangs of New York*, identifies these two films as seminal in the Scorsese opus.[3] Each of these two films contains a number of the themes found in Scorsese's other movies, and both of them connect with his roots. The former expresses Scorsese's belief that men must find redemption on the streets, rather than in church, as Scorsese has tried to do. The character of Jesus in the film serves as the prototype of a man who tries to come to terms with who he is and struggles with fear and insecurities, ambition, and pride. These experiences of the character of Jesus are consonant with those of Scorsese.

The more recent film, *Gangs*, focuses directly on a street culture and shows how this culture affects the people who live there. Included in *Gangs* as well are Scorsese's familiar insider-outsider dichotomy and experiences of violence, both drawn from Scorsese's early history, and father-son relationships. As discussed earlier, this film is revelatory about the young Scorsese's relationship with his father.

Scorsese's films show most cogently the theme of people, or characters, in relation to place or roots. Scorsese presents his perceptions of the nature of people as honestly as any director working in films today.

Filmography

This filmography contains feature films and shorts directed by Martin Scorsese. It does not include his documentaries except those included in the discussion of Chapter 3.

What's a Nice Girl Like You Doing in a Place Like This? (1963)
Produced by the New York University Department of Television, Motion Pictures, and Radio Presentations, Summer Motion Picture Workshop
Screenplay by Martin Scorsese

It's Not Just You, Murray! (1964)
Produced by the New York University Department of Television, Motion Pictures, and Radio Presentations
Screenplay by Martin Scorsese and Mardik Martin

The Big Shave (1967)
Home Vision Cinema
Produced by Martin Scorsese
Screenplay by Martin Scorsese

Who's That Knocking at My Door? (1969)
Trimod Films Production, Warner Brothers
Produced by Joseph Weill, Betsi Manoogian, and Haig Manoogian
Screenplay by Martin Scorsese

Boxcar Bertha (1972)
American International Pictures
Produced by Roger Corman
Screenplay by Joyce H. Corrington and John William Corrington based on *Sister of the Road* by Boxcar Bertha Thompson

Mean Streets (1973)
Warner Brothers
Produced by E. Lee Perry and Jonathan T. Taplin
Screenplay by Martin Scorsese and Mardik Martin

Alice Doesn't Live Here Anymore (1974)
Warner Brothers
Produced by David Susskind and Audrey Maas
Screenplay by Robert Getchell

Italianamerican (1974) **documentary**
Home Vision Cinema, National Communications Foundation
Produced by Saul Rubin and Elaine Attias

Taxi Driver (1976)
Columbia Pictures
Produced by Michael Phillips and Julia Phillips
Screenplay by Paul Schrader

New York, New York (1977)
United Artists
Produced by Irwin Winkler and Robert Chartoff
Screenplay by Mardik Martin, Earl Mac Rauch

The Last Waltz (1978) **documentary**
PM Productions for United
Produced by Robbie Robertson

Raging Bull (1980)
United Artists
Produced by Robert Chartoff and Irwin Winkler
Screenplay by Paul Schrader and Mardik Martin (based on the book by Jake LaMotta)

The King of Comedy (1982)
20th Century–Fox
Produced by Arnon Milchan
Screenplay by Paul Zimmerman

After Hours (1985)
Warner Brothers; Double Play/The Geffen Company
Produced by Amy Robinson, Griffin Dunne, and Robert F. Colesberry
Screenplay by Joseph Minion

"Mirror, Mirror," in *Amazing Stories*, **Book Four (1985)**
Amblin Television and Universal City Studios
Conceived and developed by Steven Spielberg (executive producer), Joshua Brand, and John Falsey

Produced by David E. Vogel
Screenplay by Joseph Minion

The Color of Money (1986)
Touchstone, Buena Vista
Produced by Irving Axelrad and Barbara De Fina
Screenplay by Richard Price from the novel by Walter Tevis

The Last Temptation of Christ (1988)
Universal Pictures and Cineplex Odeon Films
Produced by Harry Ufland and Barbara De Fina
Screenplay by Paul Schrader from the novel by Nikos Kazantzakis

"Life Lessons" in *New York Stories* (1989)
Touchstone Pictures
Produced by Barbara De Fina and Robert Greenhut
Screenplay by Richard Price

GoodFellas (1990)
Warner Brothers
Produced by Barbara De Fina and Irwin Winkler
Screenplay by Nicholas Pileggi and Martin Scorsese

Cape Fear (1991)
Universal Pictures, Amblin Entertainment, Cappa Films, and TriBeCa Productions
Produced by Barbara De Fina
Screenplay by Wesley Strick from the original screenplay by James R. Webb

The Age of Innocence (1993)
Columbia Pictures, Cappa/De Fina
Produced by Barbara De Fina
Screenplay by Jay Cocks and Martin Scorsese (from the novel by Edith Wharton)

Casino (1995)
Universal Pictures and Syalis D. A., Legende Enterprises, and De Fina/Cappa
Produced by Barbara De Fina
Screenplay by Nicholas Pileggi and Martin Scorsese from the novel by Nicholas Pileggi

A Century of Cinema: A Personal Journey with Martin Scorsese through American Movies (1995) **documentary**
Buena Vista Video (three cassettes); Miramax Films
Produced by Florence Dauman
Written by Martin Scorsese and Michael Henry Wilson (co-directors)

Kundun (1997)
Touchstone Pictures, Cappa/DeFina
Produced by Barbara De Fina and Laura Fattori
Screenplay by Melissa Mathison

Bringing Out the Dead (1999)
Paramount Pictures and Touchstone Pictures
Produced by Scott Rubin and Cappa/De Fina
Screenplay by Joe Connelly from his book

Il Mio Viaggio in Italia (My Journey to Italy) (2001) **documentary**
A Mediatrade Presentation/Cappa
Produced by Barbara De Fina, Giuliana Del Punta, Bruno Restuccia
Screenplay by Sysu Checchi D'Amico, Raffaele Donato, Kent Jones, and Martin Scorsese

Gangs of New York (2002)
Cappa/Miramax Pictures
Produced by Albert Grimaldi and Harvey Weinstein
Screenplay by Steven Zaillian, Kenneth Lonergan, Jay Cocks, and Martin Scorsese from the book by Herbert Asbury

Other Films

The Directors (2001)
"The Films of Martin Scorsese"
A Production of Media Entertainment, Inc.
Produced in cooperation with The American Film Institute
Written, Directed, and Produced by Robert J. Emery

Cape Fear (1960)
Universal International Pictures
Directed by J. Lee Thompson
Produced by Sy Bartlett
Screenplay by James R. Webb

The Hustler (1961)
20th Century–Fox
Produced and Directed by Robert Rossen
Screenplay by Sidney Carroll and Robert Rossen (from novel by Walter S. Tevis)

Notes

Preface

1. Alex Williams ("Passion Play," *New York*, December 16, 2002, p. 29) reports that Paul Schrader, a screenwriter who has worked on four of Scorsese's movies, said that when he met Scorsese in 1972, Scorsese told him that there were two films that he wanted to make: *The Last Temptation of Christ* and *Gangs of New York*.

Introduction

1. All of Scorsese's major works as a film director are detailed and reviewed in Chapter 3.
2. "Body and Blood: An Interview with Martin Scorsese" by Richard Corliss. In *Film Comment*, 24(5), 1988, p. 42.
3. Dade Hayes, "Birth of a Nation," *Variety*, December 9–15, 2002, p. A-2.
4. Scorsese made this remark to Katie Couric on a *Dateline NBC* segment titled, "Good Fella," that was televised on December 17, 2002.
5. The real people who appear in Scorsese's documentaries are omitted entirely from the analyses of the fictional film characters. Moreover, the analysis of the characters of Jesus in *The Last Temptation of Christ* and that of the Dalai Lama in *Kundun*, is done in the context of the characterizations presented on the screen rather than referring in any way to the historical/biblical Jesus or the actual Dalai Lama.
6. See Robert Kolker, *A Cinema of Loneliness*, third edition, (New York. Oxford University Press), for his discussion of the theory of auteurism which he considers largely outdated.
7. Ibid, p. 222. Kolker does not apply this definition of a director as auteur specifically to Scorsese as is done in this book.
8. Kim Masters, "Harvey, Marty, and a Jar Full of Ears," *Esquire*, July 2002, pp. 38, 40–41, 108–109.
9. "Martin Scorsese" interview by David Rensin in *Playboy* 38 (4), April 1991, p. 57.
10. "Martin Scorsese's Gamble," interview by Guy Flatley, *New York Times*, February 8, 1976, reprinted in *Martin Scorsese Interviews,* ed. by Peter Brunette (Jackson: University Press of Mississippi, 1999), p. 57.

Chapter 1

1. *Scorsese on Scorsese*, ed. by David Thompson and Ian Christie (London: Faber and Faber, 1987); *The Scorsese Picture: The Art and Life of Martin Scorsese* by David Ehrenstein (New York: A Birch Lane Press Book [Carol Publishing], 1992).
2. "The Films of Martin Scorsese," *The Directors* (video), Robert J. Emery in cooperation with the American Film Institute.
3. "Interview with Martin Scorsese," January 13, 2002, the *New York Times on the Web*.
4. Ehrenstein, p. 33.
5. "Interview with Martin Scorsese" in *Once a Catholic: Prominent Catholics and Ex-Catholics Discuss the Influence of the Church on Their Lives and Work*, Peter Occhiogrosso (Boston: Houghton Mifflin, 1987), p. 90.
6. "Interview with Martin Scorsese" by A. DeCurtis and A. Watson, *Rolling Stone*, November 1, 1990, issue 590, pp. 60–61.
7. "Martin Scorsese," interview by David Rensin, *Playboy*, 38(4), April 1991, p. 67.
8. Comments made by Scorsese with regard to *Bringing Out the Dead* (1999) contained in the Special Edition video of the film.
9. Occhiogrosso, p. 91.
10. *Ibid.*
11. *Ibid.*
12. "Martin Scorsese's Cinema of Obsessions," interview by Amy Taubin, *Village Voice*, September 18, 1990, reprinted in *Martin Scorsese Interviews*, ed. by Peter Brunette (Jackson: University Press of Mississippi, 1999), p. 139.
13. Mary Pat Kelly, *Martin Scorsese: A Journey.* (New York: Thunder's Mouth Press, 1996), pp. 26–27.
14. Rensin p. 65.
15. "Martin Scorsese's Gamble," interview by Guy Flatley, *New York Times*, February 8, 1976, reprinted in *Brunette*, p. 57.
16. *Scorsese on Scorsese*, p. 145.
17. *Ibid.*
18. Kelly, p. 34.
19. In a so-called macho culture, there are stereotypical perceptions of masculinity and femininity. Masculinity represents strength, aggression, power, and superiority; femininity represents weakness, passivity, submissiveness, and inferiority. In such a culture, a boy quite naturally could become misogynous, rejecting and demeaning femininity, as part of his process of identifying with images of masculinity and becoming a man.
20. Occhiogrosso, p. 94.
21. Ibid, pp. 97–98.
22. Ibid, p. 99.
23. "Dialogue on Film: Martin Scorsese," The American Film Institute, 1975; reprinted in *Brunette*, p. 35.
24. "What the Streets Mean," interview by Anthony DeCurtis, 1991, in *South Atlantic Quarterly*, Spring 1992; reprinted in *Brunette*, pp. 178–179.
25. "The Films of Martin Scorsese," *The Directors* (video), Robert J. Emery in cooperation with the American Film Institute.
26. Occhiogrosso, p. 93.
27. Ibid, p. 96.
28. "Woman Talk," interview of Martin Scorsese by Marjorie Rosen, *Film Comment*, 34 (3), May–June 1998, p. 29.
29. Scorsese mentions this film in *A Century of Cinema: A Personal Journey of Martin Scorsese through American Movies* (1995).
30. "Martin Scorsese's Mortal Sins," interview by Marcelle Clements, *Esquire*, 120(5), November 1993, p. 101.
31. Occhiogrosso, p. 92.
32. *Scorsese on Scorsese.*
33. "Slouching Toward Hollywood," interview by Peter Biskind, *Premiere*, November, 1991; reprinted in Brunette, p. 191.

34. *Scorsese on Scorsese.*
35. Internet Movie Database, Worldwide Web.
36. "Scorsese's Past Colors His New Film," interview by Michiko Kakutani, *New York Times*, February 13, 1980, reprinted in *Brunette*, p. 101.

Chapter 2

1. Kim Masters, "Harvey, Marty, and a Jar Full of Ears," *Esquire*, July 2002, pp. 38, 40–41; 108–109. See also, Dade Hayes, "Birth of a Nation," *Variety*, December 9–15, 2002, pp. A-1–A-4; A-10.; Laura Holson, "2 Hollywood Titans Brawl Over Gang Epic," *New York Times*, April 7, 2002, p.1, p. 20.
2. "Interview with Martin Scorsese" by Kevin Baker, *American Heritage*, November/December, 2001, p. 54.
3. Interview of Martin Scorsese by Janet Maslin, January 13, 2002, *New York Times on the Web*.
4. Alex Williams, "Passion Play," *New York*, December 16, 2002, p. 30.
5. *American Heritage*, November/December, 2001, p. 53.
6. Hayes, p. A-2.
7. Williams, p. 31.
8. *Gangs* depicts a triangular or oedipal relationship involving Amsterdam, Jenny, and Bill. Such a relationship, *if* it existed in Scorsese's unconscious when he was a boy, is not as important to Scorsese's personality as is the real relationship he had with his father.

Chapter 3

1. In addition to the films cited in this chapter, Scorsese has made commercials for Giorgio Armani and several documentaries, but these are not included. For the documentaries, see J. Sangster, *Scorsese*, London: Virgin Film, 2002. All of the works included were viewed in VHS format with the following exceptions: *My Voyage to Italy* and *Gangs of New York* were seen in movie theaters.
2. Sangster.
3. *Sister of the Road*, the autobiography of Box-Car Bertha (Thompson) as told to Dr. Ben L. Reitnab (New York: Gold Label Books, Inc.) 1937.
4. Sangster.
5. "The Films of Martin Scorsese," *The Directors* (video), Robert J. Emery in cooperation with the American Film Institute, 2001.
6. *Ibid.*
7. Interviews of Martin Scorsese, "You've Got to Love Something Enough to Kill It: The Art of Non-Compromise," Chris Hodenfield, *American Film*, March 1989, reprinted in *Martin Scorsese Interviews*, ed. by Peter Brunette (Jackson: University of Mississippi Press, pp. 128–137), 1999; "What the Streets Mean," Anthony DeCurtis 1991, *South Atlantic Quarterly*, Spring 1992, reprinted, in Brunette, pp. 158–185,
8. *Scorsese on Scorsese*, p. 72.
9. See Sangster, who includes detailed information about the music Scorsese has used in his films.
10. Mark Jacobson, "Band Unbound." *New York*, April 15, 2002, p. 29.
11. *The Directors* (video), 2001.
12. Interview of Martin Scorsesse, "Sorsese's Past Colors His New Film," by Michiko Kakutani, *New York Times*, February 13, 1983. Reprinted in Brunette, pp. 100–105.
13. *The Directors*.
14. In the screenplay of *After Hours* by Joseph Minion (dated June 6, 1984, 4th draft), the ending shows Paul looking out from the back window of the van through his paper-mache suit. Then the van heads north on the empty street and eventually disappears from sight, p. 99.
15. *The Directors*.

16. *Ibid.*
17. Ed Gonzales, "Il Mio Viagio in Italia," *Slant Magazine*, worldwide web, p. 1, 2001.
18. Steven Holden, "Scorsese Pays Tribute to Italian Culture," *New York Times*, October 12, 2001, page E15.

Chapter 4

1. See C. Lasch, *The Culture of Narcissism* (New York: W.W. Norton, 1991 [1979]) and M.T. Miliora, *Narcissism, the Family, and Madness: A Self-Psychological Study of Eugene O'Neill and His Plays* (New York: Peter Long, 2000), for elaboration on these ideas.
2. See J. Laplanche and J.B. Pontalis, *The Language of Psychoanalysis* (London: Karnac Books and The Institute of Psycho-Analysis, 1988), for an in-depth discussion of the meaning of the phallus. See E. S. Person "Male Sexuality and Power" in R.A. Glick and S.P. Roose, eds., *Rage, Power, and Sexuality* (New Haven and London, 1993), pp. 29–35 for a discussion of male sexuality and power.
3. Reich, p. 201
4. *Ibid.*, p. 203.
5. *Ibid.*
6. Person, 29–35.
7. R. Edgcumbe and M. Burgner, "The Phallic Narcissistic Phase," *Psychoanalytic Studies of the Child*, 1975, (30), p. 170.
8. See Edgcumbe and Burgner for more information about developmental problems in the case of phallic-narcissistic individuals.
9. See S.F. Bauer, L. Balter, and W. Hunt, "The Detective Film as Myth: *The Maltese Falcon* and Sem Spade, "*American Imago*, 1978, 35 (3), pp. 275–296, for a discussion of this tendency and examples from fiction.

Chapter 5

1. *Schrader on Schrader*, ed. by Kevin Jackson (London: Faber and Faber, 1990) p. 126.
2. "Martin Scorsese's Gamble," interview by Guy Flatley, New York Times, February 8, 1976, reprinted in ed. P. Brunette, *Martin Scorsese Interviews* (Jackson: University Press of Mississippi, 1999), p. 56. See also "Martin Scorsese Tells All: Blood and Guts Turn Me On!" interview by Richard Goldstein and Mark Jacobson, *Village Voice*, April 5, 1976, reprinted in Brunette, pp. 63–64. See also "What the Streets Mean," interview by Anthony DeCurtis, *South Atlantic Quarterly*, Spring 1992, reprinted in Brunette, pp. 158–185.
3. DeCurtis.
4. "Raging Bull," interview by Michael Henry, *Positif*, April 1981, reprinted in Brunette, p. 88. See also M.P. Kelly, *Martin Scorsese: A Journey* (New York: Thunder's Mouth Press, 1996), p. 177, for more details about Scorsese's personal problems during the late 1970s.
5. "Interview of Martin Scorsese" by James Lipton, *Inside the Actors Studio*, televised on Bravo, December 15, 2002.
6. "Martin Scorsese Interview" by David Ansen, Interview Enterprises (New York), January 1989, pp. 49–51.
7. See Flatleg; Goldstein and Jacobson; and DeCurtis.

Chapter 6

1. Scorsese's Past Colors His New Film," interview by Michiko Kakutani, *New York Times*, February 13, 1983, reprinted in *Martin Scorsese Interviews*, ed. by Peter Brunette (Jackson: University Press of Mississippi, 1999), pp. 100–105.
2. *Bringing Out the Dead*, Special Edition Video.

Chapter 7

1. "Woman Talk," interview by Marjorie Rosen, *Film Comment*, 34(3), May–June 1998, p. 29.
2. "Dialogue on Film: Martin Scorsese," interview, The American Film Institute/1975; reprinted in *Martin Scorsese Interviews*, ed. Peter Brunette (Jackson: University Press of Mississippi, 1999), p. 35.
3. *Scorsese on Scorsese*, edited by David Thompson and Ian Christie (London: Faber and Faber, 1987), p. 48.
4. "The Films of Martin Scorsese," *The Directors* (video), Robert J. Emery in cooperation with the American Film Institute.
5. *Scorsese on Scorsese*, p. 72.
6. "Slouching toward Hollywood," interview by Peter Biskind, *Premiere*, November 1991; reprinted in Brunette, p. 190.
7. "Scorsese's Past Colors His New Film," interview by Michiko Kakutani, *New York Times*, February 13, 1983, reprinted in Brunette, pp. 100–105.

Chapter 8

1. "Body and Blood: An Interview with Martin Scorsese," interview by Richard Corliss, *Film Comment*, 24 (5), September–October 1988, p. 41. See also *Martin Scorsese*, Les Keyser (New York: Twayne Publishers, 1992), p. 182, and "Martin Scorsese Tells All: Blood and Guts Turn Me On!" interview by Richard Goldstein and Mark Jacobson, *Village Voice*, April 5, 1976, reprinted in *Martin Scorsese Interviews*, ed. by Peter Brunette (Jackson: University Press of Mississippi, 1999), p. 68.
2. Sociopaths have no regard for the laws of society; psychopaths have no regard for other human beings.
3. "Woman Talk," interview by Marjorie Rosen, *Film Comment*, 34(3), May–June 1998, p. 29.

Chapter 9

1. In an interview Scorsese gave in 1994, Scorsese described Archer Newland as follows: "Basically he is what they call in America a stand-up guy—a man of principles who would not abandon his wife and children." See Ian Christie, "The Scorsese Interview," *Sight and Sound*, 1994, 4(2), pp. 10–15.

Chapter 10

1. "Martin Scorsese" interview by Davis Rensin in *Playboy*, 38(4), April 1991, p. 57.
2. This scene of Alice cuddling with her son is not in the screenplay written by Robert Getchell (Hollywood: Script City, 1974). Perhaps the scene emerged during the filming and was meant to represent Alice's loving feelings for her son. However, the scene also suggests that Alice's behavior toward her son is provocative and titillating and that she uses Tommy as a substitute for a husband and lover.
3. See *The Scorsese Connection* by Lesley Stern (Bloomington: Indiana University Press, 1995) p. 117, 123.
4. A.O. Scott, "To Feel a City Seethe as Modernity Is 'Born,'" movie review, *Gangs of New York, New York Times*, worldwide web, December 21, 2002.
5. See chapter 11 for more elaboration about this character.
6. "Women Talk," interview of Martin Scorsese by Marjorie Rosen, *Film Comment*, 34(3), May–June 1998, p. 29.

Chapter 11

1. Interview of Scorsese by James Lipton, *Inside the Actors Studio*, Bravo, televised on December 15, 2002.
2. *The Last Temptation of Christ* by Nikos Kazantzakis (New York: Simon & Schuster, 1960).
3. "Women Talk," interview of Martin Scorsese by Marjorie Rosen, *Film Comment*, 34(3), May–June 1998, p. 29.
4. *Scorsese on Scorsese*, ed. by David Thompson and Ian Christie (London: Faber and Faber, 1987), pp. 124–126.
5. These roles derive from biblical references and teachings, including those associated with the Catholic Church.

Chapter 12

1. "The Films of Martin Scorsese," *The Directors* (video), Robert J. Emery (in cooperation with the American Film Institute), 2001.
2. Guy Flatley, "Martin Scorsese's Gamble," *New York Times*, February 8, 1976, reprinted in *Martin Scorsese Interviews*, ed. by P. Brunette (Jackson: University Press of Mississippi, 1999), pp. 48–58.
3. Alex Williams, "Passion Play," *New York*, December 16, 2002, p. 29.

Bibliography

The American Film Institute (1975), "Dialogue on Film: Martin Scorsese," reprinted in *Martin Scorsese Interviews*, P. Brunette (Ed.). Jackson: University Press of Mississippi, 1999, pp. 9–47.
Ansen, D. (1989), "Martin Scorsese Interview," *Interview Enterprises,* January, pp. 49–51.
Asbury, H. (1927), *The Gangs of New York: An Informal History of the Underworld.* New York: Thunder's Mouth Press, 1998.
Baker, K. (2001), "Interview with Martin Scorsese," *American Heritage*, November/December, pp. 50–55.
Bauer, S.F., Balter, L., and Hunt, W. (1978), "The Detective Film as Myth: *The Maltese Falcon* and Sam Spade," *American Imago*, 35(3), 275–296.
Biskind, P. (1991), "Slouching Toward Hollywood," *Premiere*, November 1991, reprinted in *Martin Scorsese Interviews*, P. Brunette, (Ed.). Jackson: University Press of Mississippi, 1999, pp. 186–199.
Box-Car Bertha (Thompson) (as told to Dr. Ben L. Reitman) (1937), *Sister of the Road,* New York: Gold Label Books, Inc.
Brunette, P. (Ed.). (1999), *Martin Scorsese Interviews*. Jackson: University Press of Mississippi.
Christie, I. (1994), "The Scorsese Interview," *Sight and Sound*, 4 (2), pp. 10–15.
Clements, M. (1993), "Martin Scorsese's Mortal Sins," *Esquire*, 120(5), pp. 98–103.
Connelly, J. (1998), *Bringing Out the Dead*. New York: Random House.
Corliss, R. (1988), "Body and Blood: An Interview with Martin Scorsese," *Film Comment*, 24(5), pp. 36–42.
Dateline NBC, (2002) television broadcast, "Good Fella" segment, December 17.
DeCurtis, A. (1991), "What the Streets Mean," *South Atlantic Quarterly*, Spring 1992, reprinted in *Martin Scorsese Interviews*, P. Brunette, (Ed.). Jackson: University Press of Mississippi, 1999, pp. 158–185.
DeCurtis, A., and Watson, A. (1990), "Interview with Martin Scorsese," *Rolling Stone*, issue 590, pp. 58–65.
Edgcumbe, R., and Burgner, M. (1975), "The Phallic-Narcissistic Phase," *Psychoanalytic Studies of the Child*, 30, pp. 161–180.
Ehrenstein, D. (1992), *The Scorsese Picture: The Art and Life of Martin Scorsese*. New York: Birch Lane.

Flatley, G. (1976), "Martin Scorsese's Gamble," *New York Times*, February 8 reprinted in *Martin Scorsese Interviews*, P. Brunette (Ed.). Jackson: University Press of Mississippi, 1999, pp. 48–58.

Getchell, R. (1974), screenplay, *Alice Doesn't Live Here Anymore*. Script City, Hollywood, CA.

Goldstein, R., and Jacobson (1976), "Martin Scorsese Tells All: Blood and Guts Turn Me On!" *Village Voice*, April 5, reprinted in *Martin Scorsese Interviews*, P. Brunette (Ed.). Jackson: University Press of Mississippi, 1999, pp. 59–70

Gonzales, E. (2001), "Il Mio Viaggio in Italia," *Slant Magazine*, p. 1, worldwide web.

Hayes, D. (2002), "Birth of a Nation," *Variety*, December 9–15, pp. A-1–A-4; A-10.

Henry, H. (1981), "Raging Bull," *Positif*, April, reprinted in *Martin Scorsese Interviews*, P. Brunette (Ed.). Jackson: University Press of Mississippi, 1999, pp. 84–99.

Hodenfield, C. (1989), "You've Got to Love Something Enough to Kill It: The Art of Non-Compromise," *American Film*, March, reprinted in *Martin Scorsese Interviews*, P. Brunette (Ed.). Jackson: University Press of Mississippi, 1999, pp. 128–137.

Holden, S. (2001), "Scorsese Pays Tribute to Italian Culture," *New York Times*, October 12, p. E15.

Holson, L. (2002), "2 Hollywood Titans Brawl Over a Gang Epic," *New York Times*, April 7, p.1, p. 20.

Internet Movie Database (IMDB), Worldwide Web.

Jacobson, M. (2002), "Band Unbound," *New York*, April 15, p. 29.

Kakutani, M. (1983), "Scorsese's Past Colors His New Film," *New York Times*, February 13, reprinted in *Martin Scorsese Interviews*, P. Brunette (Ed.). Jackson: University Press of Mississippi, 1999, pp. 100–105.

Kazantzakis, N. (1960[1988]), *The Last Temptation of Christ* (trans., P.A. Bien). New York: Simon and Schuster.

Kelly, M.P. (1996), *Martin Scorsese: A Journey*. New York: Thunder's Mouth Press.

Keyser, L. (1992), *Martin Scorsese*. New York: Twayne Publishers.

Kolker, R. (2002), *A Cinema of Loneliness*, third ed. New York: Oxford University Press.

LaMotta, J. (1970), *Raging Bull*. Englewood Cliffs, N.J.: Prentice-Hall.

LaPlanche, J., and Pontalis, J.B. (1988), *The Language of Psychoanalysis*. London: Karnac Books and The Institute of Psycho-Analysis.

Lasch, C. (1991 [1979]), *The Culture of Narcissism*. New York: W.W. Norton.

Lipton, J. (2002), "Interview of Martin Scorsese," *Inside the Actors Studio*, Bravo, broadcast December 15.

Maslin, J. (2002), "Interview of Martin Scorsese," January 13, *New York Times on the Web*.

Masters, K. (2002), "Harvey, Marty, and a Jar Full of Ears," *Esquire*, July, pp. 38, 40–41; 108–109.

Miliora, M. T. (2000), *Narcissism, the Family, and Madness: A Self-Psychological Study of Eugene O'Neill and His Plays*. New York: Peter Lang.

Minion, J. (1984), screenplay, *After Hours*, (4th draft) June 6.

Occhiogrosso, P. (1987), "Martin Scorsese: In the Streets," in *Once a Catholic: Prominent Catholics and Ex-Catholics Discuss the Influence of the Church on Their Lives and Work*. Boston: Houghton Mifflin, pp. 88–101.

Person, E.S. (1993), "Male Sexuality and Power," in R.A. Glick and S.P. Roose (Eds.), *Rage, Power, and Sexuality*. New Haven and London: Yale University Press, pp. 29–44.

Pileggi, N. (1985), *Wiseguy: Life in a Mafia Family*. New York: Simon and Schuster.

_____. (1995), *Casino*. New York: Simon and Schuster.

Reich, W. (1933), *Character Analysis*. London: Vision.

Rensin, D. (1991), "Martin Scorsese," *Playboy* 38 (4), pp. 57–74, 161.
Rosen, M. (1998), "Woman Talk," interview of Martin Scorsese *Film Comment*, 34(3), May–June, p. 29.
Sangster, J. (2002), *Scorsese*. London: Virgin Books.
Schrader, P. (1990), *Schrader on Schrader*, Kevin Jackson (Ed.). London: Faber and Faber.
Scorsese, M. (1987), *Scorsese on Scorsese*, David Thompson and Ian Christie (Eds.). London: Faber and Faber.
_____. (1991), *Martin Scorsese Interviews*, P. Brunette (Ed.). Jackson: University Press of Mississippi, 1999.
_____. (2001), Comments in *The Directors* (video), Robert J. Emery in cooperation with the American Film Institute.
Scott, A. O. (2002), "To Feel a City Seethe as Modernity Is 'Born'" movie review, *Gangs of New York*, *New York Times*, worldwide web, December 21.
Stern, L. (1995), *The Scorsese Connection*. Bloomington: Indiana University Press.
Taubin, A. (1990), "Martin Scorsese's Cinema of Obsessions," *Village Voice*, September 18, reprinted in *Martin Scorsese Interviews*, P. Brunette (Ed.). Jackson: University Press of Mississippi, 1999, pp. 138–145.
Tevis, W. (1984), *The Color of Money*. New York: Warner Books.
Wharton, E. (1999), *The Age of Innocence*. New York: The Modern Library.
Williams, A. (2002), "Passion Play," *New York*, December 16, 2002, pp. 29–34.

Index

Abbott, Diahnne 47
Academy Awards, nominations 47, 54, 55, 57, 62, 67
Adonis, Frank 46
After Hours 20, 48–52, 149, 151–153, 173, 190
The Age of Innocence 9, 20, 61, 62, 149, 154, 159, 168, 174, 185, 190, 191
The Age of Innocence (novel by Wharton) 61, 163
"Alice Hyatt" (*Alice Doesn't Live Here Anymore*) 18, 40–42, 70, 95, 150, 151, 159–163, 175, 185
Alice Doesn't Live Here Anymore 16, 19, 40–42, 72, 95, 139, 149–151, 159, 175, 185
Allen, Woody 55, 112
American Film Institute 7
"Archer, Newland" (*The Age of Innocence*) 8, 9, 61–62, 149, 154–157, 163, 164, 169, 198
Argo, Victor 54
Arquette, Patricia 79, 94, 118, 172
Arquette, Rosanna 48, 55, 136, 151, 166, 173
Asbury, Herbert 22, 66
Ashton-Griffiths, Roger 66
Auld, Georgie 44
auteur, auteurism, theory of 7

Baker, Joe Don 57
Balsam, Martin 57
The Band 45
Been, Michael 54
Bergman, Ingrid 66
Bermuth, Peter 35
Bernhard, Sandra 47, 112, 173
Bethune, Zina 35, 122, 169
"Betsy" (*Taxi Driver*) 42, 43, 76–79, 140, 169, 171
"Bickle, Travis" (*Taxi Driver*) 8, 18, 27, 42–43, 73, 75–84, 116, 119, 135, 140, 153, 156, 182, 189
The Big Shave 17, 33, 35, 142
Bloom, John 62
Bloom, Verna 48, 54, 174
"Bowden, Danielle (Danny)" (*Cape Fear*) 57–60, 89, 92–95, 166
"Bowden, Leigh" (*Cape Fear*) 7–60, 89, 92–95, 166
"Bowden, Sam" (*Cape Fear*) 57–60, 89, 92–95, 166, 190
Bowie, David 54
Boxcar Bertha 19, 27, 36, 37, 149, 177, 187, 191
"Box-car" Bertha (Thompson) 36, 159, 160, 175
Boyle, Peter 42
Bracco, Lorraine 57, 97, 167
Braveman, Sarah 33

Brennan, Larraine Marie 19
Bringing Out the Dead 64, 143, 147, 153, 169, 170, 180, 181, 189, 191
Broadbent, Jim 25, 66, 108
Brooks, Peter 42
"Brown, Rake" (*Boxcar Bertha*) 36
"Burke, Mary" (*Bringing Out the Dead*) 64, 65, 143, 169, 172, 175
Burstyn, Ellen 40, 42, 160
Bush, Billy Green 40, 160

"Cady, Max" (*Cape Fear*) 57–60, 72, 73, 75, 89–95, 136, 140, 166, 167, 180–186, 190
Cage, Nicolas 64, 117, 172
Cameron, Julia 19
Cannes Film Festival 44, 52
Cape Fear (1961) 57, 59
Cape Fear (1991) 20, 34, 57–61, 72, 73, 89–93, 135, 166, 174, 180, 184, 190, 181
Cappa (production company) 7
Capra, Frank 63
"Carmen" (*The Color of Money*) 53, 54, 133–135, 165
Caron, Juliette 54, 172
Carradine, David 36, 149
Carradine, John 36, 149

Casey, Bernie 36, 149
Casino 9, 20, 35, 62, 63, 70, 103, 107, 142, 168, 169, 185, 195
Cassavetes, John 37, 63
Catholic Church 10, 13, 16, 18, 21–24, 121, 122, 145, 146
Cavett, Dick 52
A Century of Cinema: A Personal Journey with Martin Scorsese through American Movies 15, 20, 91
Chaplin, Geraldine 61
"Charlie" (*Mean Streets*) 17, 19, 28, 37, 38, 121, 124–128, 169, 178, 180, 182, 190
Chong, Thomas 48
Christian fundamentalists 51
Clayton, Eric 45
Cocks, Jay 62
Colasanto, Nicholas 46
The Color of Money 9, 20, 53, 54, 71, 121, 133–136, 145, 165, 182, 185, 190
Connelly, Joe 93
Conway, "Jimmy" (*Goodfellas*) 56, 70, 97, 101, 102, 142, 181
Coppola, Francis Ford 55, 63
Corman, Roger 19, 36
Cruise, Tom 20, 53, 133, 164
"Cutting, Bill" (*Gangs of New York*) 5, 23–26, 30, 66, 70, 73, 106–110, 142, 143, 156, 157, 167, 181

Dafoe, Willem 54, 153, 177
The Dalai Lama (*Kundun*) 63, 64, 149, 156, 157, 182, 191
Danko, Rick 45
Danova, Cesare 38, 124
"David" (*Alice Doesn't Live Here Anymore*) 40–42, 149–151, 161, 162
Day-Lewis, Daniel 23, 61, 66, 154, 156, 163, 167, 169
The Dead Rabbits 36, 39, 40, 67, 108, 157
DeFazio, Sam 39

DeFina, Barbara 19, 195, 196
Demigods 97–120
DeNiro, Robert 37–39, 42, 46–48, 56, 57, 60, 62, 76, 84, 89, 97, 103, 110, 124–127, 164, 167, 168, 171
DeSica, Vittorio 66
"DeVito, Tommy" (*Goodfellas*) 56–70, 97, 99–102, 142, 181
"Diamond, Lester" (*Casino*) 103, 104
Diamond, Neil 45
Diaz, Cameron 24, 66, 109, 167
DiCaprio, Leonardo 23, 66, 108, 156, 157
DiLeo, Frank 56
Dobie, Lionel ("Life Lessons") 55, 121, 136, 137, 145, 147, 166, 180–182, 190
Douglas, Illeana 57
"Doyle, Jimmy" (*New York, New York*) 20, 44, 45, 70, 73, 121, 127–133, 144, 147, 164, 165
Dunne, Griffin 48, 52, 151, 173
Dylan, Bob 45

"Eberhardt, Ben" (*Alice Doesn't Live Here Anymore*) 40, 41, 72, 76, 96, 96, 139, 161, 162
Elizabeth Street (N.Y.C.) 12, 21, 145
"Evans, Francine" (*New York, New York*) 128–133, 145, 159, 164, 165
"Everdeane, Jenny" (*Gangs of New York*) 24–26, 66, 109, 167, 168, 174, 191

fantasy 4, 85, 87, 91, 100, 105, 108, 109, 111–114, 116, 120, 121, 129, 130, 132, 135, 145, 163, 178
Faye, Alice 40
Fellini, Fredico 66
"Felson, Eddie" (*The Color of Money*) 9, 53–54, 121, 133–136, 144, 145, 165, 182, 190
Film preservation and restoration 20

Fiorentino, Linda 48, 173
The Five Points (N.Y.C.) 26, 27, 66, 107, 108, 156, 167, 168
Flax, Lori Anne 46, 87
"Flo" (*Alice Doesn't Live Here Anymore*) 40, 161, 162
Ford, John 63
Foster, Jodie 40, 42, 162, 171
Fox, Billy 85

"Gail" (*After Hours*) 48, 174
Gallo, Mario 46
Gangs of New York 2, 6, 20–31, 70, 106, 149, 169, 174, 177, 180–182, 190, 191
The Gangs of New York (book by Asbury) 22
Garr, Teri 174
Getchall, Robert 194
"The Girl" (*Who's That Knocking at My Door?*) 35, 36, 122, 123, 169, 170, 175
Gleason, Brendan 25, 66
Gleason, Jackie 53
Golden Globe, awards and nominations 7, 42, 45, 47, 52, 54, 55, 57, 61, 62, 67
GoodFellas 19, 20, 28, 35, 56, 57, 70, 97–106, 142, 167, 175, 181, 185, 190, 191
Goodman, John 64
Greco, Paul 54
Gregory, Andre 40
The Grifters 20
Guilty by Suspicion 20

"Hackett, Paul" (*After Hours*) 5, 48–52, 149, 151–153, 157, 173, 174, 190
Harris, Leonard 42
Hawks, Howard 63
Heard, John 48
Helm, Levon 45
Hershey, Barbara 36, 37, 54, 149, 153, 171, 181
"Hill, Henry" (*GoodFellas*) 19, 28, 56, 70, 97–102, 113, 142, 167, 181, 190
"Hill, Karen" (*GoodFellas*) 56, 99–101, 167, 175

Hollywood 48, 52, 152
Hollywood Film Festival 7
homosexuality, fear of 88
Hudson, Garth 45
Hurt, Mary Beth 61
The Hustler 53, 133

"Iris" (*Taxi Driver*) 42, 43, 82, 169, 171 179
Italianamerican 11, 12, 21, 40
It's Not Just You, Murray! 17, 33–35, 102, 170, 191

"Janelle" (*The Color of Money*) 53, 133, 165
"Jesus" (*The Last Temptation of Christ*) 54, 55, 149, 153, 154, 157, 172, 177–187
"Johnny Boy" (*Mean Streets*) 8, 28, 37, 38, 121–127, 144, 170, 180, 189, 190
Johnson, Cullen O. 64
"J.R." (*Who's That Knocking at My Door?*) 8, 35, 36, 70, 73, 121–124, 169–171, 182, 189, 190
"Julie" (*After Hours*) 48, 174
"June" (*After Hours*) 48, 174

Kazantzakis, Nikos 37, 55, 186
Keitel, Harvey 35, 37–40, 42, 54, 95, 121–124, 153, 161, 169–171
"Kersek" (*Cape Fear*) 37, 92
"Kiki" (*After Hours*) 48, 51, 151, 173
King, Alan 62
The King of Comedy 18, 19, 28, 71, 110–116, 179, 185, 189, 190
Kristofferson, Kris 40, 149, 161, 171
Kundun 20, 63, 64, 148, 182, 186, 191
Kuras, Lennard 35

Ladd, Diane 40, 42, 161
"LaMotta, Jake" (*Raging Bull*) 9, 46, 47, 72, 75, 86–89, 135, 140, 165, 179, 186, 189

"LaMotta, Joey" (*Raging Bull*) 46, 86, 87
"LaMotta, Vickie" (*Raging Bull*) 46, 87, 164, 165, 175
Lang, Fritz 63
Lange, Jessica 57, 89, 166
"Langford, Jerry" (*The King of Comedy*) 28, 47, 48, 111–115, 173, 179, 190
The Last Temptation of Christ 3, 17, 20, 22, 23, 28, 37, 52, 54, 55, 95, 149, 152, 153, 169, 171, 175, 177–187, 191
The Last Temptation of Christ (novel by Kazantzakis) 37, 55
The Last Waltz 45
"Lauria, Vincent" (*The Color of Money*) 53–54, 71, 121, 133–136, 145, 165, 190
Laurie, Piper 76
Lewis, Jerry 47, 111, 173
Lewis, Juliette 57, 61, 90, 166
"Life Lessons" (*New York Stories*) 55, 121, 136, 145, 147, 166, 181
Liotta, Ray 56, 97, 166
Little Italy (N.Y.C.) 5, 7, 36, 38, 102, 117, 121, 122, 124, 145, 176, 182, 191
"Lori (Davis)" (*Cape Fear*) 72, 91
Louis, Joe 129
Lucas, George 63
Lutter, Alfred 40, 160

macho sexuality 198n19
Mad Dog and Glory 28
madonna-whore complex 24, 36, 43, 73, 124, 126, 169, 175, 182
Magnani, Anna 66
Mahon, Kevin 46
"Manmouth, Jordan" ("Mirror, Mirror") 52, 53
Manoogian, Haig 17, 190
Manuel, Richard 45
"Marcy" (*After Hours*) 48–51, 151, 173
Margolyes, Miriam 61, 155
Martin, Andrea 34
Martin, Mardik 15

Martin, Richard Cheech 48
"Mary Magdalene" (*The Last Temptation of Christ*) 37, 54, 55, 153, 160, 169, 171, 172, 175, 178, 179, 182, 183, 186
masculinity 15–18, 143, 145–147, 159, 183, 198n19
"Masha" (*The King of Comedy*) 28, 47, 48, 112–116, 173, 179, 190
Mastrantonio, Mary Elizabeth 53, 133, 165
Mean Streets 14, 15, 17, 19–21, 27, 36–39, 73, 121, 124, 127, 143, 169, 177, 178, 180, 189, 191
megalomania 100, 101, 108
"Mel" (*Alice Doesn't Live Here Anymore*) 40
Memmoli, George 38, 44
"Michael" (*Mean Streets*) 38, 125, 144
Michaelis, Zeph 33
Miller, Barry 66
Minnelli, Liza 44, 111, 115, 128, 164
"Minnesota Fats" (*The Hustler*) 53
Il Mio Viaggio in Italia (*My Voyage to Italy*) 6, 16, 20, 22
Miramax 7, 21
"Mirror, Mirror" 34, 52, 53
Mitchell, Joni 45
Mitchum, Robert 57, 60
Moriarty, Cathy 46, 87, 165
Morris, Helen S. 19
Muddy Waters 45
music 9, 45, 135
My Voyage to Italy see *Il Mio Viaggio in Italia*

narcissism 69–74, 75, 92, 103, 105, 110, 131, 136, 137, 140, 142, 178
narcissistic rage 70, 73, 79, 86, 90, 96, 97, 116, 139, 140, 144
Neeson, Liam 23, 66, 108, 156
Newman, Paul 20, 53, 54, 133, 165
New York, New York 19, 20, 44–45, 70, 121, 127, 144, 147, 159, 164, 190

New York Stories see "Life Lessons"
New York University 17, 33, 190
Nolte, Nick 55, 57, 89, 136, 166

Oedipal period of development 74
O'Hara, Catherine 48, 174
"Olenska, Ellen, Countess" (*The Age of Innocence*) 61, 154, 155, 159, 163, 164, 169, 174, 191
O'Neal, Patrick 55
outsider (theme) 14, 28, 48, 76, 145, 152

Palme d'Or 44
"Paulette" ("Life Lessons," *New York Stories*) 55, 136, 137, 166
Peck, Gregory 57
Penn, Arthur 63
Person, Ethel S. 72
A Personal Journey with Martin Scorsese through American Movies see *Century of Cinema*
Pesci, Joe 46, 47, 50, 57, 62, 86, 97, 103
Pfeiffer, Michelle 61, 62, 154, 163
phallic narcissism 70–75, 81, 87, 90, 95, 96, 99, 107, 113, 121, 123, 124, 126, 133, 139, 145, 150; phallic-narcissistic stage of development 73
phallic supremacy 92, 99, 101, 102, 104, 109, 133, 136, 140, 181
phallus 69, 72, 80, 90
"Pierce, Frank" (*Bringing Out the Dead*) 18, 64, 65, 117–120, 143, 153, 172, 181–189, 191
Pileggi, Nicholas 56, 57, 62, 168
Place, Mary Kay 44, 131
Primus, Barry 36, 44, 149
Prince, Steven 42, 44
Prophet, Melissa 62
Proval, David 37
"Pupkin, Rubert" (*The King of Comedy*) 9, 18, 20, 47, 48, 71, 110–117, 173, 181, 189, 190

Raging Bull 18, 19, 28, 46, 47, 84–88, 135, 164, 177, 179, 183, 184, 186, 189, 191
Ray, Nicholas 63
rebirth, redemption 65, 84, 88, 93, 95, 127, 136, 142
The Red Shoes 18
Reich, Wilhelm 71–73
Reilly, John C. 66
religious symbolism, themes 51–52, 84, 88, 90, 94, 95, 120, 123, 127, 141, 150, 156, 157, 163, 172, 177–187
Rhames, Ving 64
Rickles, Don 62
Robbins, Tim 52
Robertson, Robbie 45
Robinson, Amy 37, 38, 170, 171
Robinson, Sugar Ray 46, 85, 86
Romanus, Richard 38, 125
Rossellini, Isabella 19
Rossellini, Roberto 65, 66
"Rothstein, Ginger" (*Casino*) 62, 63, 103–106, 168, 169, 175, 191
"Rothstein, Sam" (*Casino*) 62, 63, 70, 103–106, 142, 168, 181
Rubin, Ira 34
Ryder, Winona 61, 62, 154, 164, 169

St. Patrick's Old Cathedral 13, 14
Saldano, Theresa 46
"Santoro, Nicky" (*Casino*) 9, 62, 63, 70, 103, 104, 106, 142, 181
Scala, Michael 35
Schoonmaker, Thelma 67
Schrader, Paul 18, 22, 191, 197n1
Scorsese, Catherine (mother) 11, 34, 40, 159, 183, 185
Scorsese, Charles (father) 11, 40, 192
Scorsese, Frank (brother) 11, 14
Scorsese, Martin: appearance in his films 35, 42, 47, 126; early life 11–19; films *see* filmography; individual listings

Scott, George, C. 53
Search and Destroy 20
Shaver, Helen 52, 53, 135, 165
"Shelly, Bill" (*Boxcar Bertha*) 27, 36, 37, 149, 150, 157, 160, 175, 177, 191
Shepherd, Cybill 42, 78, 171
Shill, Steve 54
Sirk, Douglas 63
Sivero, Frank 56
Sizemore, Tom 64
SoHo (N.Y.C.) 48–52, 151, 152
Sorvino, Paul 56, 98
Spielberg, Steven 52
"Sport" ("Matthew") (*Taxi Driver*) 42, 83, 171
Stander, Lionel 44
Stanton, Harry Dean 54
Stark, Mimi 33
Starr, Mike 99
Starr, Ringo 45
Stone, Sharon 62, 103, 168

Taxi Driver 8, 18–20, 27, 34, 42–44, 73, 76, 81, 135, 153, 169, 171, 175, 177, 170, 186, 190, 191
Tayback, Vic 40
"Teresa" (*Mean Streets*) 37–38, 124–126, 167–171
Thomas, Henry 23, 96, 109
Thompson, Bertha *see* "Box-car Bertha"
Thompson, Fred Dalton 37
"Tom" (*After Hours*) 71, 72
"Tommy" (Hyatt) (*Alice Doesn't Live Here Anymore*) 40–42, 150, 151, 160–163
"Tony" (*Mean Streets*) 37, 38
Tsarong, Tenzin Thuyhob 63, 156
"Tweed, William" (*Gangs of New York*) 24, 66, 108, 109

"Vallon, Amsterdam" (*Gangs of New York*) 5, 7, 23–30, 66, 67, 108–110, 149, 156, 157, 167, 177, 182, 190, 191

"Vallon, Priest" (*Gangs of New York*) 8, 9, 23, 27, 29, 66, 108–110, 149, 156, 182, 185, 191
Vidor, King 63
Vincent, Frank 46, 56, 62
violence 27, 75, 76, 80, 84, 86, 96, 116, 139, 144, 145, 147, 190, 192

Waterston, Sam 52
Wayne, John 15, 122
Weinstein, Harvey 7, 121
"Welland, May" (*The Age of Innocence*) 61, 62, 154, 155, 164, 168, 169
Welles, Orson 63
Wharton, Edith 61
What's a Nice Girl Like You Doing in a Place Like This? 17, 33, 34, 53
Who's That Knocking at My Door? 12, 15, 17, 19, 21, 35, 36, 70, 121–127, 169, 172, 175, 177, 182, 183, 185, 189, 190
Wilder, Billy 63
William K. Everson History of Film Award 66

Wilson, Michael Henry 63
Wilson, Stuart 61
women, attitudes regarding 17, 121, 124, 145, 146, 172, 175, 176, 183, 184, 187, 191
Woods, James 62, 103
Woodstock 17
Woodward, Joanne 61
World Trade Center (N.Y.C.) 27, 28

You Can Count on Me 20
Young, Neil 45

www.ingramcontent.com/pod-product-compliance
Lightning Source LLC
Chambersburg PA
CBHW081555300426
44116CB00015B/2893